Northern Constellations
New Readings
in
Nordic Cinema

Other books from Norvik Press

Anglo-Scandinavian Cross-Currents (ed. Inga-Stina Ewbank, Olav Lausand & Bjørn Tysdahl)
Aspects of Modern Swedish Literature (revised edition, ed. Irene Scobbie)
Paul Binding: *With Vine-Leaves in His Hair. The Role of the Artist in Ibsen's Plays* (2006)
Centring on the Peripheries: Essays on Scandinavian, Scottish, Gaelic and Greenlandic Literature (ed. Bjarne Thorup Thomsen) (2006)
A Century of Swedish Narrative (ed. Sarah Death & Helena Forsås-Scott)
English and Nordic Modernisms (ed. Bjørn Tysdahl, Mats Jansson, Jakob Lothe & Steen Klitgård Povlsen)
European and Nordic Modernisms (ed. Mats Jansson, Jakob Lothe & Hannu Riikonen)
Gender – Power – Text. Nordic Culture in the Twentieth Century (ed. Helena Forsås-Scott)
Nordic Letters 1870-1910 (ed. Michael Robinson & Janet Garton)
On the Threshold. New Studies in Nordic Literature (ed. Michael Robinson & Janet Garton)
Ellen Rees: *On the Margins. Nordic Women Modernists of the 1930s*
Michael Robinson: *Studies in Strindberg*
Michael Robinson: *Strindberg and Genre*
Freddie Rokem: *Strindberg's Secret Codes*
Turning the Century. Centennial Essays on Ibsen (ed. Michael Robinson) (2006)
Robin Young: *Time's Disinherited Children. Childhood, Regression and Sacrifice in the Plays of Henrik Ibsen*

Knut Hamsun: *Selected Letters*, Vols I and II (ed. & trans. by Harald Næss & James MacFarlane)
Erik and Amalie Skram: *Caught in the Enchanter's Net. Selected Letters* (ed. & trans. Janet Garton)
Edith Södergran: *The Poet who Created Herself. Selected Letters* (ed. & trans. by Silvester Mazzarella)

Victoria Benedictsson: *Money* (translated by Sarah Death)
Hjalmar Bergman: *Memoirs of a Dead Man* (translated by Neil Smith) (2006)
Jens Bjørneboe: *Moment of Freedom* (translated by Esther Greenleaf Mürer)
Jens Bjørneboe: *Powderhouse* (translated by Esther Greenleaf Mürer)
Jens Bjørneboe: *The Silence* (translated by Esther Greenleaf Mürer)
Hans Børli: *We Own the Forests and Other Poems* (translated by Louis Muinzer)
Suzanne Brøgger: *A Fighting Pig's Too Tough to Eat* (translated by Marina Allemano)
Camilla Collett: *The District Governor's Daughters* (translated by Kirsten Seaver)
Gunnar Ekelöf: *Modus Vivendi* (edited and translated by Erik Thygesen)
Kerstin Ekman: *Witches' Rings* (translated by Linda Schenck)
Kerstin Ekman: *The Spring* (translated by Linda Schenck)
Kerstin Ekman: *The Angel House* (translated by Sarah Death)
Kerstin Ekman: *City of Light* (translated by Linda Schenck)
Jørgen-Frantz Jacobsen: *Barbara* (translated by George Johnston)
P. C. Jersild: *A Living Soul* (translated by Rika Lesser)
Runar Schildt: *The Meat-Grinder and Other Stories* (translated by Anna-Lisa & Martin Murrell)
Hjalmar Söderberg: *Martin Birck's Youth* (translated by Tom Ellett)
Hjalmar Söderberg: *Short Stories* (translated by Carl Lofmark)
Hanne Marie Svendsen: *Under the Sun* (translated by Marina Allemano)

Northern Constellations:
New Readings
in
Nordic Cinema

edited by

C. Claire Thomson

Norvik Press
2006

A catalogue record for this book is available from the British Library.

ISBN 1 870041 63 1
First published 2006

Norvik Press was established in 1984 with financial support from the University of East Anglia, the Danish Ministry for Cultural Affairs, the Norwegian Cultural Department and the Swedish Institute.

Managing Editors: Janet Garton, Michael Robinson and C. Claire Thomson.

Cover illustration: *Halo* © Dimitri Grigoriev (d_a_grigoriev@hotmail.com). Please see the first paragraph of the Introduction (p. 11) for details.

Cover design: Richard Johnson
Layout: Neil Smith
Printed in Great Britain by Page Bros. (Norwich) Ltd, UK.

Contents

The map of the skies, that still, suspended ocean with the myriad islands, each its own world, was printed on a blanket for her cradle. The sun paints pictures for her; photography must give her playthings.

Hans Christian Andersen, 'The New Century's Muse'*

* Himmelkortet, dette ophængte stille Ocean med de Myriader Øer, hver en Verden, blev lagt aftrykt som Vuggeklæde. Solen maler hende Billeder; Photografien maa give hende Legetøi.
'Det nye Aarhundredes Musa', *Nye eventyr og historier*, Hans Christian Andersen, 1861.

Acknowledgements

The editor and publishers gratefully acknowledge the generous financial support of Norsk Filminstitut (The Norwegian Film Institute), Letterstedtska Föreningen in Stockholm, and the UCL Mellon Postdoctoral Research Programme at University College London.

This book has been a long time in the making, and I would, first and foremost, like to thank all the contributors very much for their enormous goodwill and hard work; those who came on board early exhibited much patience, and those I approached late in the day wrote with great efficiency. It is no exaggeration to state that this project, like so many others, would never have come to fruition without the practical help, ideas, patience and enthusiasm of Neil Smith, my friend and colleague. Many thanks to all at Norvik Press for supporting the project, to Pietari Kääpä, Daisy Neijmann and Annika Lindskog for advice on, respectively, Finnish, Icelandic and Swedish film and language, and to Dimitri Grigoriev for permission to use his wonderful photograph as the cover image. I am also grateful to colleagues at the University of Edinburgh, the University of East Anglia and University College London for the opportunity to teach various courses and seminars in Nordic and European film over the last eight years; I am sure I speak for all the contributors when I emphasise the importance of fruitful discussion with students and colleagues in the gestation of these essays.

On a more personal note, I would like to express my thanks to my parents, Catherine and Robert Thomson, for their unstinting interest and forbearance, and to Carol O'Sullivan, Jane Hjarl Petersen, Carsten Holm, Stephanie Millar, Catriona Murray, Jakob Stougaard-Nielsen and my very wise sister Elizabeth Thomson, who generously shared their words, ideas, time, coffee, flash drives and living space with me during this and other undertakings. And finally, a belated thank-you to Calum Brooks, who, in Edinburgh in the mid-1990s, first got me thinking about film.

C. Claire Thomson
London, February 2006

Introduction
Starry Constellations and Icy Fractals: Reading Nordic Films Past and Present

C. Claire Thomson

The photographer writes of the cover image: 'The photograph was taken in the interior of the Antarctic continent in Dronning Maud Land (75°00'S, 00°04'E, 2892 m above sea level) and illustrates a relatively rare phenomenon of the Halo and sun dogs or "mock suns" – light refraction caused by tiny ice crystals in the atmosphere when the sun stays low in the sky towards the end of the Antarctic summer. Sometimes two or even four sun dogs are seen, two on each side of their great original.' (Dimitri Grigoriev)

❄ ❄ ❄

This fleeting constellation of light, ice and camera, like the past for Walter Benjamin, 'can be seized only as an image which flashes up at the instant when it can be recognized and is never seen again' ('Theses on the Philosophy of History' V). The image is suggestive of the compass of *Northern Constellations* – not a history of the national cinemas of Scandinavia, but one possible crystallisation of readings of film texts through the lens of current criticism. Benjamin's historian recognises that facts and causes become historical 'posthumously', in the constellation of his own era with an earlier one ('Theses' A). Similarly, the themes and concerns that radiate most insistently in this book across and between essays, and which seem to illuminate and interrogate each other – and which are mapped out here – came to light after the event.

❄ ❄ ❄

This constellation of essays is also a firmament of stars in another sense: inevitably, the stars of the moment loom large in it. The figure of Lars von Trier – *enfant terrible* of Danish cinema – parades or lurks in four chapters,

Carl Th. Dreyer in three, and Ingmar Bergman in two. That the ballast of the book is provided by younger and less revered filmmakers is not intended as an exercise in tracing auteurial filiation or national narrative. It is the resultant unexpected couplings and promiscuous fusions of canonical and marginal film texts across eras and national traditions that will, I hope, prove illuminating. Several of the essays do, however, explore the varied ways in which younger filmmakers respond to the weight of cultural heritage and history, whether by intertextual allusion and parody (Bell, Tay, B.M. Thomsen), collaborative projects (Hjort, Rees), or textual adaptation (Bell, B.T. Thomsen). Benjamin might agree that Dreyer, Bergman and Sjöström would enjoy the company of their younger compatriots, for 'in every era the attempt must be made anew to wrest tradition away from a conformism that is about to overpower it' ('Theses' VI). The obverse, of course, also obtains, that the brighter stars (and more readily available film texts) of our present blot out many of the leading lights of past eras, because 'every image of the past that is not recognized by the present as one of its own concerns threatens to disappear irretrievably' ('Theses' V).

❄ ❄ ❄

The title *Northern Constellations* is also meant to echo Jürgen Habermas' seminal collection of essays, *The Postnational Constellation* (2001), which discusses the challenges of globalisation for the modern nation-state. Much research in Nordic cinema now centres on the production and circulation of films from the region in our transnational era, and on the imaginative response of small, wealthy, Northern European film cultures to the global and digital age (e.g. Nestingen and Elkington 2005, Hjort 2005). The focus of *Northern Constellations* is not this socio-economic context, though some of the contributors do discuss the transnational movement and reception of 'Nordic' films (Hjort, Koivunen, Iversen). Almost all the essays in the present volume are, however, informed by the tectonic shifts in the national imagination that Habermas maps onto the 'postnational constellation'. He sees both 'a hardening of national identities as different cultural forms of life come into collision' and 'the hybrid differentiations that soften native cultures and comparatively homogeneous forms of life in the wake of assimilation into a single material world culture' (Habermas 2001:72-3). In other words, we become more aware and protective of 'our' cultures at the same time as they are re-figured by demographic, technological and geo-political change. Narratives of homogeneous Nordic nations – and their corollary, narratives of Nordic national cinemas – burn away, revealing communities that are increasingly imaged and imagined in the arts as historically, ethnically and politically heterogeneous. For Habermas, democratic participation and human rights must replace the (majority) national culture as the glue of the political community. Indeed, some of the essays in *Northern Constellations* point to emerging forms of belonging, mediated through the film form itself, which are broadly affective and performative (Doxtater, Knudsen, Rees, Thomson, Iversen). At the time of going to press, the very real hurts and misunderstandings engendered by the publication in Denmark and elsewhere of cartoons depicting the Prophet Mohammed make painfully clear the urgency of new accommodations between civic and cultural nationalism, and of living, depicting and theorising intercultural encounters in innovative ways, using inherently transnational media.

❊ ❊ ❊

'The clocks of Western civilisation keep the tempo for the compulsory simultaneity of the nonsimultaneous' (Habermas 2001:75). The postnational constellation must be grasped as, precisely, a constellation because it encompasses the heterogeneous spacetimes of individuals and collectives, and the dynamical relations and hybrids that arise between them. For Benjamin, the special quality of the modern image was its ability to shock, not least its blasting through the everyday with 'the dynamite of a tenth of a second' (1999:229); but with the etiolation of the aura, so too went the temporal disjunction that disrupts linear time (Hansen 2002:45). The special potential of film to map spacetimes other than 'telling the sequence of events like beads on a rosary' ('Theses' A), and thus to subvert and re-tell narratives of identity and interaction, exercises several of the contributors to this volume (Sandberg, B.M. Thomsen, Doxtater, Thomson, B.T. Thomsen, Bell, Tay). While, for Benedict Anderson (1991), the imaginative spacetime of the modern nation-state was predicated on the 'homogenous, empty time' of history books, newspapers and novels, the lived time of the nation is (at least) double – the pedagogy of nationalist discourse and the performative iterations of the everyday – as Homi Bhabha (1994) has argued. As many of the contributors suggest here, film can approach the spacetime of contemporary communities as constellative, irruptive, and, above all, *felt*.

❊ ❊ ❊

The mock suns of the cover image, and the ice crystals through which they are refracted, are also suggestive of a third perspective on the figure of the constellation: the fractal. Coined by Benoit Mandelbrot in the 1970s, fractal geometry is the geometry of nature, the geometry of the fourth dimension; this is the dimension which lies between the three dimensions of Euclidean geometry, and which is apparent in the branchings of ferns and frost flowers, in the shape of coastlines, mountains and clouds – as well as the constellations of stars and galaxies, and the composition of snowflakes, as Mandelbrot's *The Fractal Geometry of Nature* (1982) makes clear. The apparently chaotic patterns of fractals conceal recursive self-similarity, patterns which are now beginning to be understood mathematically – but, crucially, can only be calculated by computer and represented graphically on the screen. Benjamin recognised early on that the camera, by altering scale and dissecting the moment, was privy to 'a different nature' than the human eye and could reveal 'entirely new structural formations of the subject' and the 'fractional second' of a movement ('The Work of Art in the Age of Mechanical Reproduction' 1999:230). It is striking that the spatio-temporal and social relations between bodies and communities that only film can reveal are explored by most of the contributors to *Northern Constellations*. But the potential of digital technology to build on this power in order to chart hitherto unknown kinds of space and to re-think reality – towards, we might venture, other ontological constellations – is also touched on by B.M. Thomsen, Knudsen, Thomson, and Bell.

✽ ✽ ✽

The first section of *Northern Constellations* – Spaces • Bodies • Skin – includes (but does not 'contain') the three essays which tackle most directly the relations between camera, space and body. In 'Mastering the House: Performative Inhabitation in Carl Th. Dreyer's *The Parson's Widow*', Mark Sandberg discusses Dreyer's distinctive approach to the film set as a space for inhabitation by his actors, and shows how the adoption of a quasi-authentic folk museum location for his film of 1920 blurs the line between fiction and documentary, rendering the film a multi-layered exploration of how to live with, rather than master, a given space. Bodil Marie Thomsen identifies the haptic image as the vehicle for Dreyer's actualisation of spirit in the flesh of his heroines in her chapter 'On the Transmigration of Images: Flesh, Spirit and Haptic Vision in Dreyer's *Jeanne d'Arc* and von Trier's Golden Heart Trilogy'; and she suggests new ways to understand Lars von Trier's custodianship of these bodily surfaces and senses in the digital era. In 'Bodies in Elevators: The Conveyance of Ethnicity in Recent Swedish Films', Amanda Doxtater adopts a different kind of vehicle to move amongst the bodies that jostle in the contemporary

Swedish filmic nation-space. The elevator is opened up as a site and stage of intercultural encounter, an often jarring meeting of bodies, narratives and spacetimes.

❋ ❋ ❋

The three essays in the section Local • National • Global are also deeply concerned with social and filmic space, mapping out the constellations and fractals of affective and political belonging in a postnational world. Britta Timm Knudsen excavates the space between documentary and fiction to explore contemporary Danish responses to the crisis in indexicality and the popular hunger for reality in her chapter 'Local Cinema: Indexical Realism and Thirdspace in Kestner's *Blue Collar White Christmas*'. The intimacy of everyday life becomes the stage for the dramas of globalisation, where the topographies of known and unknown, planned and affective, dissolve into each other, and the imaginative dimensions of space are rendered visible. Ellen Rees then considers contemporary Norwegian filmmakers' responses to the meeting of historical and political narratives of national identity with global business and culture. In her chapter 'Personal Ideology and Collective Cinema: *Folk flest bor i Kina* and Contemporary Norwegian Political Consciousness', she discusses how a collective approach to filmmaking practices and narrative form can re-align and subvert myths and discourses of the local, national and global. The strategies of the Danish film industry and of one filmmaker in particular – Lars von Trier – in the face of 'Global Hollywood' are the focus of Mette Hjort's chapter 'Gifts, Games, and Cheek: Counter-Globalisation in a Privileged Small-Nation Context. The Case of *The Five Obstructions*'. Von Trier's collaboration with the veteran director Jørgen Leth is discussed as an instance of individual agency in the service of 'gift culture', with the goal of transforming the odds for the small nation's film industry.

❋ ❋ ❋

Anu Koivunen's essay 'Do You Remember Monrépos? Melancholia, Modernity and Working-class Masculinity in *The Man Without a Past*' opens the section Memory • Reality • History. Koivunen unpacks the coalescence of sentiment, irony and political engagement in Aki Kaurismäki's *The Man Without A Past*, arguing that the film activates the twin national tropes of the alienated 'little man' and of a radical communitarianism. It affectively moves the reader by offering up, on the one hand, an embodiment of the crisis of masculinity and, on the other, an ironic narrative of national *ressentiment* rather than historical sentimentality. My own essay, 'Incense in the Snow: Topologies of Intimacy and Interculturality in Friðriksson's *Cold Fever* and Gondry's *Jóga*' also centres on the ambivalence of national memory, reading the encounter of a Japanese tourist with the terrain of Iceland in terms of embodiment and affect, an encounter which de-couples cultural intimacy from locality. In Friðriksson's film and Gondry's video, I argue, the national landscape begins to emerge as a postnational, posthuman geography. Gunnar Iversen's chapter, 'The Old Wave: Material History in *Cool and Crazy* and the New Norwegian Documentary', shows how the national peripheries can become the repository of national memory, and contextualises the documentary *Cool and Crazy*'s account of the meeting of individuals with national and global history alongside Norwegian television's response to the hunger for reality and community.

❅ ❅ ❅

The fourth section, Auteur • Authority • Subjectivity, brings together three essays which may be said to explore the encounters between voices, points of view and narratives. In 'Ibsen, Lagerlöf, Sjöström and *Terje Vigen*: (Inter)nationalism, (Inter)subjectivity and the Interface between Swedish Silent Cinema and Scandinavian Literature', Bjarne Thorup Thomsen returns to the early days of Swedish cinema, demonstrating how the tradition of filmic adaptation of literary classics could turn the film text into the disputed territory of figures from the cultural pantheon. But the case of Sjöström's *Terje Vigen* also shows how an adaptation's faithful and flexible relation to the source text, coupled with capitalising on the potential of the medium, could result in new constellations of seeing, of space, and even of the national imagination. Emma Bell proposes a re-evaluation of Lars von Trier's oft-criticised conflation of his twin alterities of madness and femininity. In 'The Passions of Lars von Trier: Madness, Femininity, Film', Bell draws connections between the director's experiments with cinematic form and his excursions into 'abnormal' states of mind and identities; the hyper-realism of the gaze of the madwoman, the wilful marginality of the idiots, and the imagination of the blind immigrant are privileged over documentary realism. Sharon Lin Tay also focuses on ways of seeing and telling in her essay, this book's closing chapter, 'Politics of the Auteurial Subject: Time, Narrative, and Intertextuality in *Scenes from a Marriage* and *Faithless*'. Weaving together readings of Ingmar Bergman's 1973 television saga and Liv Ullmann's direction of Bergman's screenplay twenty-seven years later, Tay reads the intertextual tensions between the two productions as symptomatic of gendered differences in the experience and representation of time, and their narrative corollaries.

❄ ❄ ❄

It has been argued that Benjamin saw in the starry constellations of the night sky a lesson in reading; a particular configuration is picked out by 'stargazes' (*Sternenblicke*) at a given moment (*Augenblick*), and ranged among unreadable intervals of sky, or the 'snow flurries' of the white page (Menke 2002). The scholars who have written the essays in this book in no way represent an established disciplinary community. As with all academic anthologies, the final constellation of essays is a happy product of professional chance: the vagaries of publishing schedules, teaching commitments, changes of employment and electronic communication conspired to determine the content of the finished product. Nevertheless, the demographic spread of contributors reflects my original aim to juxtapose essays by researchers situated – in terms of their institutional and disciplinary affiliation – both within and outside 'Scandinavia'. This has meant that not all the contributors wrote in their native language, and not all of them worked with Scandinavian source language material. Some essays are thick with quotations in a range of original languages, and some are much more concerned with the images themselves; inconsistencies in the treatment of Scandinavian-language material have been inevitable, though I have done my best to enforce the rule that, where possible, film titles are quoted once in the relevant Nordic language, and referred to thereafter in English. Similarly, the majority of contributors work across and between disciplines – literary studies, cultural studies, philosophy and political science – and their essays are marked by these fruitful border-crossings. Naturally, responsibility for any mis-steps is mine. The only remit provided, the vagueness of which the contributors accepted with good grace, was to 'read' a relatively well-known Nordic film in a theoretically-inflected way. The constellation of readings offered here is just that – a snapshot of current research, a set of *Sternenblicke* at the moment of readability.

References

Anderson, Benedict (1991): *Imagined Communities: Reflections on the Origin and Spread of Nationalism*. London: Verso.

Benjamin, Walter (1999): 'Theses on the Philosophy of History' and 'The Work of Art in the Age of Mechanical Reproduction'. In *Illuminations*. Introduced by Hannah Arendt. Translated from the German by Harry Zohn. London: Pimlico.

Bhabha, Homi K. (1994): *The Location of Culture*. London & New York: Routledge.

Habermas, Jürgen (2001): *The Postnational Constellation: Political Essays*. Translated, edited and with an introduction by Max Pensky. Cambridge: Polity in association with Blackwell Publishers.

Hansen, Miriam (2002): 'Benjamin and Cinema: Not a One-Way Street'. In Richter, Gerhard (ed.): *Benjamin's Ghosts: Interventions in Contemporary Literary and Cultural Theory*. Stanford, CA: Stanford University Press.

Hjort, Mette (2005): *Small Nation, Global Cinema*. Minneapolis: University of Minnesota Press.

Mandelbrot, Benoit B. (1982): *The Fractal Geometry of Nature*. New York: W.H. Freeman.

Menke, Bettine (2002): 'Ornament, Constellation, Flurries'. In Richter, Gerhard (ed.): *Benjamin's Ghosts: Interventions in Contemporary Literary and Cultural Theory*. Stanford, CA: Stanford University Press.

Nestingen, Andrew & Trevor G. Elkington (eds) (2005): *Transnational Cinema in a Global North: Nordic Cinema in Transition*. Detroit: Wayne State University Press.

Spaces • Bodies • Skin

Mastering the House: Performative Inhabitation in Carl Th. Dreyer's *The Parson's Widow*[1]

Mark B. Sandberg

Much is hidden in the cinematic notion of 'found location' in fiction films: a sense of unusual non-intervention, of documentary authenticity. By calling the space of a film 'found', one claims that it simply presents itself unbroken to production crew, actors, and spectators alike; the phrase reassures us that the physical world depicted in the film is simply happened upon. When emphasised in filmmaking, this attitude conveys the notion that aesthetic production is most creative when it emphasises a sense of fit. Of course, most location shooting does not foreground the act of finding, that lucky discovery that makes the existing space 'perfect' for a film. But in certain kinds of filmic practice, the found location plays a central discursive role in both the production of a film and in its aesthetic stance.

Such is the case with one of Carl Th. Dreyer's earliest works, *Prästänkan/The Parson's Widow* (1920). The release of the film on DVD (Film Preservation Associates, 2004) allows viewers today to appreciate anew a true classic of the Scandinavian silent cinema, but since many of the conceptual issues at stake here cannot be discerned from viewing alone, a fuller appreciation of Dreyer's idea of location requires some contextualisation and research beyond the filmic text itself. Dreyer's well-known emphasis on the painstaking process of filmmaking should prompt critics to treat his films as projects as well as texts: each film invokes a cluster of concerns revolving around his source-texts, his preparation of the milieu, the conceptual importance of scripts, and his interaction with the actors.

Throughout his career, from *Præsidenten/The President* in 1918 to *Gertrud* in 1964, Dreyer had a special, pragmatic obsession with the film set. Jean and Dale Drum identify three phases in Dreyer's practice of *mise-en-scène*: an early phase (the films of the late teens and early twenties) in which composition dominates, a middle phase of obsessive realism in set design (*Michael* and *Du Skal Ære Din Hustru/Master of the House* from the mid-1920s are the key films here), and a final phase initiated with *La Passion de*

Jeanne d'Arc in 1927, in which the realism is concentrated and abstracted into the minimalism for which Dreyer has justly become famous (Drum 2000:111). These observations are generally true, although the tripartite rubric deflects attention from what is otherwise a fairly consistent through-line in Dreyer's career. The best way to characterise Dreyer's use of the film set is to call it an ongoing ontological experiment, the goal of which was to explore the question of performative attachment: under what conditions might an actor be said to truly inhabit a space? What qualities of location, prop, and set design lead to that result? And to what degree can this ineffable sense of attachment be communicated (to the actors in the production process or visually to the audience in the projection of the film)?

Dreyer did have a set built for him in most of his films, but he himself demonstrated an interior decorator's passion for detail, often consulting closely with the set designer and contributing documents and images clipped from his famously obsessive pre-production research.[2] His experiments with sets were many, ranging from naturalist to minimalist, from the found to the built location, but throughout his career two notions dominate consistently: authenticity and inhabitation. The former is manifest even in the most famous later films like *Ordet/The Word* (1954) and *Gertrud* (1964), which despite their visually spare interiors began production with the same kind of detailed research and collecting projects as Dreyer's earlier films (Drum 2000:239, 260).

The most obvious emphasis on authenticity comes from Dreyer's silent film *Master of the House*, in which the set was based on a working-class apartment he had discovered in the Christianshavn area of Copenhagen (Kau 1989:112-13). Ebbe Neergaard, Dreyer's lifelong friend and first important Danish critic, elaborates on the unusual features of this set:

> Dreyer would have preferred to make the whole film inside a real two-roomed flat. But as this was impossible technically, a complete copy of such an apartment was built in the studio – not just a separate set for each room dotted round the studio with open sides like a doll's house, but a composite unit of four-walled rooms with doors between and gas and water and electricity laid on – everything was there. This may sound like exaggerated realism, but the emphasis was not on imitation; it was a question of bringing out the drama and its special intimate character. The confined working-space forced the director to keep close to his actors the whole time, and brought all the objects in the rooms into focus as well. (Neergaard 1950:17-18)[3]

The goal of this kind of authenticity was to create a feeling of substantial space for the actors. In fact, Dreyer was often more concerned that the space be believable for the actor than for the spectator, for there is in fact little of this unusually meticulous preparation that is noticeable to the spectator in viewing *Master of the House*. As Drum puts it, '... visually, the picture does not particularly benefit from Dreyer's fanatical realism: it looks no more realistic than a set usually did at the time' (Drum 2000:118). The key insight here is that it was something in the performance process that mattered to Dreyer – the actor's attachment to the set, not the spectator's. The set was the catalyst for an inner performance transaction in the actor, one produced by his or her confidence in the possible inhabitability of a set.

Dreyer's preoccupation with performative inhabitation is evident even in as stylised a film as *La Passion de Jeanne d'Arc* (1927). The non-perspectival contours of the set and the visual fragmentation of the editing (Bordwell 1981; Kau 1989) would seem to make this a strange filmic world for actors to make themselves 'at home' in, yet many production techniques – from the mammoth, 'wasteful' construction of the completely enclosed set depicting medieval Rouen (Drum 2000:134-35) to the intense silence imposed on the set, to the shooting of the film's scenes in sequence – were intended to have just that effect. Neergaard writes of this film, 'Not until a set is so constructed that it can be lived in, is it possible to work with the documentary authenticity which is the basis of filmic inspiration' (Neergaard 1950:23).[4]

A more recent assessment underscores the same aspect of Dreyer's method:

> This is a point that Dreyer has made time and time again, the importance of *being* instead of *acting* in films. This is why he so often used amateurs who fitted the roles naturally and could simply play themselves. This is why he insisted that sets be built completely – so that actors would feel utterly at one with the milieu of the film and become an integral part of it, forgetting that they were on a motion picture set. (Drum 2000:138-39, original emphasis)

If the kind of performance experiment described here sounds familiar, that is no coincidence. For Dreyer, there was early, direct contact with Stanislavskian acting techniques via the Russian emigrés from the Moscow Art Theater whom Dreyer used in his 1921 film, *Die Gezeichneten/Love One Another*, and throughout his career he made repeated reference to Stanislavski. Dreyer speaks approvingly of that kind of authentic performative emotion in his 1943 essay, 'A Little on Film Style', comparing the director's role to that of a midwife (Dreyer 1943:137). He also reports discussions with Ebbe Neergaard late in his career about Stanislavskian notions of 'mentality' in preparing for a role (Dreyer 1960:205). In a 1967 interview, Dreyer reported that an actor had told him, 'The secret is that you make us believe in the work' (Drum 2000:88).

It is important to point out that for Dreyer, however, this notion of authentic preparation was essentially an architectural issue; if the space was properly prepared, everything else followed. His was quite literally a technique of *mise-en-scène*, or perhaps better put, *'mise-en-milieu'*; that is, of inserting an actor into a meticulously constructed, believable environment. As Birgitte Federspiel, the female lead in *Ordet* put it, 'He didn't transform me – he just created the atmosphere in which we lived and the acting came involuntarily' (quoted in Drum 2000:88).

A special application of Dreyer's method of *mise-en-milieu* can be seen in the several films in which he did in fact use a found location instead of building a set himself. Of the three (*The Parson's Widow*, 1920; *Glomdalsbruden/The Bride of Glomdal*, 1925; and *Vampyr*, 1932), the first will be the focus of this essay since it puts into play both thematically and procedurally many of the performance notions discussed above, and does so at an early stage of Dreyer's career that predates his contact with Stanislavskian actors. In this film, one can find an early manifestation of a Dreyerian theme – 'mastery of the house' – that also gets articulated in varying degrees in both *Der var engang/Once Upon a Time* (1922) and *The Master of the House*.[5] The argument of this essay is that as Dreyer works out his notions of performance early in his career, mastering the house becomes a thinly veiled metaphor for an actor's performative mastering – or inhabitation – of the set.

The Found Museum

The Parson's Widow was the first of the several films Dreyer made for foreign production companies outside Denmark, in this case Svensk Filmindustri. His film is based on a humorous story of the same title by the Norwegian-American author Kristofer Janson. Published in a 1901 collection of three such stories, collectively entitled *Middelalderlige Billeder* (*Pictures from the Middle Ages*), Janson's 'Prestekonen' ('The Parson's Wife') is set in the time of King Christian IV (1588-1648) and is itself based on a published Norwegian legend called 'Præstekonen i Tysnes' ('The Parson's Wife in Tysnes') (Daae 1881:52). Both draw on the time after the Reformation in Norway when, for obvious reasons, the very possibility of a parson's widow presented itself for the first time along with the arrival of Protestant Christianity's married clergy. Custom had it that these widows were to be passed on with the parsonage and the position, so that a parson's successor would be obligated to accept the widow along with the call. The custom ended around 1630, when the individual congregations in Norway also lost the right to vote for their parsons.

The legend in question concerns a certain Margrete Pedersdatter, who in this way acquired three such husbands in series. Both Janson's Norwegian story and Dreyer's Danish shooting script seize on the comic potential of this situation and depict Søfren Ivarson, a young candidate for a vacant parson's position, who by winning the competition for the position is also obligated to marry the widow, approximately 60 years his senior. He is at the same time engaged to Mari, a much younger girl his own age. The two of them, calculating that the widow cannot have long to live, conspire to act as brother and sister so that they can both live at the parsonage while awaiting the widow's death. With a light, comic touch, the filmic story thus deals thematically with the difficulty of taking possession of space that belongs properly to another.

The actual physical set of *The Parson's Widow* had an intriguing resonance in this regard. The film was shot entirely on location at the Maihaugen folk museum in Lillehammer, Norway. Anders Sandvig, the museum's founder, began the building collection in 1894 by saving and relocating to his garden in Lillehammer representative examples of vernacular Norwegian architecture, often along with entire inventories of furniture, tools, textiles, and other traditional objects from central Norway's Gudbrandsdal region. In 1904, the collection was sold to the city of Lillehammer, moved to a nearby location, and incorporated as a public folk museum with the name Maihaugen. This museum was part of a larger movement across Scandinavia at the turn of the twentieth century that included museums like Skansen in Stockholm and the Norwegian Folk Museum outside Oslo, all of which were influential forerunners of what we now call living-history museums around the world.

The twin emphases of these Scandinavian folk museums were material collection – buildings were disassembled, transported from disparate locations, and meticulously reassembled at the central museum sites – and contextualised display. Objects and furnishings were displayed as if in use, inviting the spectator to perform an imaginary inhabitation of the preserved folk space while being allowed to wander through the museum homes. By all reports, the combination of scientific accuracy and lively presentation gave the museum's visitors powerful impressions of participation and physical immersion in folk culture.

This model of museum spectatorship was a perfect match to Dreyer's developing notion of performance in 1920. Dreyer intended his actors, like the folk museum spectator, to encounter in his sets a habitable space that would spark their imaginations and involve them intimately and materially in the depicted milieu. In an interview with a local Lillehammer newspaper in the late spring of 1920, just as shooting for the film was about to begin, Dreyer enthused about the possibilities the museum provided as a film set: '... jeg synes det er en prægtig samling. Det jeg forresten mest beundrer er, at man saa fuldstændig har kunnet undgaa at lave samlingen med schematiske opstillinger. Det er jo hele hjem deroppe!' (Dreyer 1920) (... I think it is a magnificent collection. The thing I most admire is the way they have so completely avoided schematic displays in the collection. There are entire homes up there!).[6] When the interviewer follows up by asking him if they would build any sets for this new film, Dreyer responded, 'Kulisser?? Nei unge mand, det arbeide slipper vi. Det er forresten et usedvanlig tilfælde, at der staar en prestestue fra 1650' (Sets? No, young man, we can avoid that business. It turns out that by an extraordinary coincidence there is a parsonage from 1650 at the museum).[7] Neergaard puts special emphasis on this fact in the revised edition of his book as well, italicising his main points: 'With that film he seized the opportunity to create a *completely* authentic milieu as the basis for the film's narrative. *There was not a single decoration or set built for The Parson's Widow*; every image was shot in the buildings and the terrain around the old Norwegian farm buildings with accompanying parsonage and church buildings ...' (Neergaard 1963:30).[8]

Before getting too swept up in this enthusiasm for authenticity, it is important to remember that despite the vaguely scientific collection methods, the museum's access to folk culture was not unmediated. In fact, many aspects of Maihaugen's public presentation of folk culture were already fundamentally theatrical – the carefully cultivated impression of intact, fully furnished, and inhabited buildings and occasional historical role-players blurred the line between curation and more traditional notions of theatrical *mise-en-scène*. It was in fact the affinity with theater and other popular entertainments that provoked criticism of the folk-museum movement by other Scandinavian museum professionals at the time (Sandberg 2001:237-39).

The mediated nature of the set in *The Parson's Widow* is further underscored by the problem of cinematic legibility: in order to make these dark, traditional folk interiors visually available to a film audience, the crew had to bring in strong artificial lighting (40,000 candle power) by running long electric cables from the power plant in town up the hill to Maihaugen. The light was so powerful that several of the actors injured their eyes (likely from the kind of temporary Klieg light blindness that often afflicted silent film actors of this time) and had to be treated by doctors ('Prästänkan' 1920:11). Eyewitness journalistic accounts also recount the strange impression it made to hear an electric motor humming outside a traditional Norwegian building several centuries old. Without the boost of modern lighting technology, however, the interiors would be useless on film. One reporter sums up the compromise thus: 'Nutidens kunst, forsynt med de mest moderne tekniske hjælpemidler, skal i forening med bevarte minder fra en gammel, traditionsrik tid forsøke at gi os et levende billede fra svundne tider' ('Filmselskapet' 1920) (The present generation's art, supplied with the most modern technical resources, shall attempt, together with preserved artifacts from an old, tradition-rich time, to convey to us a living picture of bygone days).

The necessity of artificial light exposes a fundamental contradiction of the found location, namely that not all places are as ready-made for filming as they might be for acting. This was especially true of Maihaugen's oldest buildings, originally designed as they were for warmth, not interior light. The extra lighting, in effect a technological prosthesis that makes the traditional interior spaces legible on screen, shows that even at this outer conceptual limit of 'found space', one can find evidence of the interface between finding and building that to some degree marks all location shooting.

In other words, the 'extraordinary coincidence' of finding a Maihaugen building dating from approximately the same time as the setting of the source story needs to be examined for the assumptions it entails. Any notions of Maihaugen's 'given' space, miraculously discovered, do not hold up well under scrutiny, but the real point for Dreyer was to inspire confidence in the substance of the set among his performers. What better way to do that than to rely on the museum's own presentation of the buildings as original, unmediated locations? The marks of centuries of inhabitation, the human wear and tear on the surfaces of the building that the museum so carefully preserved, must certainly have made acting in this performance space feel different from acting in a three-walled studio set. And for some viewers at least, that ineffable confidence seems to have carried over. Neergaard again: '*This documentary authenticity in the milieu and character types* gave the film a character remarkable for its time. One believed better in the action and the actors' performances because one had to believe in what one saw around them' (original emphasis, Neergaard 1963:31).[9]

As should be clear, the rhetoric of authenticity that is activated by the talk about the found location makes this film difficult to distinguish from straightforward documentary filmmaking. The review of the film in *The New York Times* nine years later calls it 'chiefly interesting for the information it depicts of old Scandinavian customs' (Hall 1929:32). Furthermore, the printed programs for the film in Swedish, Danish, and Norwegian all include a short cultural-historical commentary on the customs depicted in the film. There is also an interview with Maihaugen director Anders Sandvig in the Norwegian program material in which he notes an important shift in the idea of the film set: ' – Jeg maa si jeg anser dette for noget helt nyt paa filmens omraade ... Her staar vi jo overfor et kulturhistorisk arbeide som har faat saa egte omgivelser som det er mulig at skaffe tilveie. Hver ting er original' ('Prestekonen' 1920:12) (I must say that I see this as something completely new in the area of film ... Here we are of course presented with a cultural-historical work that has been given a setting as authentic as is possible to obtain. Every object is original). Clearly, the film was marketed as more than a fictional feature film; it was regarded as having special access to the past and to traditional culture through its choice of location.

The blended nature of the film is apparent during the several scenes in which Dreyer focuses on the same kind of folk customs that the museum emphasised in its own presentation to the public. For example, Dreyer expands the wedding scene between Søfren and Margrete to include a wealth of ethnographic detail not present in Janson's story, which surprisingly (given its other interests in cultural-historical detail) does not dwell on the form of the actual wedding at all. But both the typewritten script and the final film include the kind of typical scenes that would be role-played or demonstrated at the museum: fiddlers, bridal processions, folk costumes, dancing, and special customs at the bridal feast. This narrative dilation, in reality an ethnographic detour, is repeated at the end of the film for Margrete's funeral. Again, Janson's source story dispatches that event in less than a sentence, but the film devotes an extended sequence to the visual detail of how funeral rituals in the area would be conducted, including folk superstitions carried out to prevent haunting by the deceased (more on this point later).

The line between fiction and documentary was further complicated by the fact that Dreyer's production company also filmed a separate two-part documentary at Maihaugen that summer immediately after completing the shooting of *The Parson's Widow*. The film is entitled *Maihaugen: Arbeide og Fest/Maihaugen: Work and Play* (Svensk Filmindustri/De Sandvigske Samlinger, 1921), and was apparently filmed by Dreyer's crew as thanks for use of the location (the lighting arrangements already in place for the feature film clearly presented the museum with an unusual opportunity to make its own film of the building interiors). Intended as useful supplements to lectures about the museum, these two 'cultural-historical films' (as the contemporary press referred to them) gave an overview of the architectural development and work methods on display at the museum. In some cases they even used the same objects for work demonstrations (such as the loom) that had been used as significant props for the story in *The Parson's Widow*. More intriguingly, the narrative voice shifts in the second film to something more like fiction, as a historical wedding scene is recreated at the Bjørnstad farm. While role-playing actors act out the scene, an oddly juxtaposed group of spectators dressed in modern 1920s clothing can be seen filing by the historical spectacle, which proceeds along unaware of their presence. The convergence of the fictional and the documentary modes that summer at Maihaugen seems complete: the same film crew that made a feature film in a cultural-historical mode, boosted by the rhetoric of authenticity, also made a documentary film that lapses into fictional role-play and historical recreation.

Mastery of the House

At the conceptual interface between these two films lies the performance issue that fascinated Dreyer: how to inhabit a ready-made, given physical world. With the sense of location intensified by the Maihaugen museum's guarantees of authentic space, Dreyer could proceed to explore the notions of attachment between actor and space that would preoccupy him throughout his career. More importantly, in Janson's story Dreyer would find a narrative scenario that foregrounded that issue thematically. The discussion that follows here will concentrate on several key scenes from the film in order to show how this works on several conceptual levels.

The main narrative obstacle in the plot deals with the fact that the space of the parsonage does not give way for easy inhabitation by the likeable young couple. Instead, there is an awkward remainder at the site in the form of old Margrete, who in effect haunts the space by stubbornly hanging onto her place there, seemingly out of proper time. As she explains at one point early in the film:

> My lot is not an easy one. This is the fourth time I must be handed over like a piece of furniture to whomever claims me. But I am attached to this place, to every chair and candlestick, and if you part with what has become so important to your life, your innermost heart gets torn open. And you die ...[10]

Despite the apparent pathos of her situation, a major comic element of the film is the tenacity with which she hangs on and counters all attempts of the young couple to make the space habitable for them (that is, to meet each other romantically).

The humour of the film is heavily dependent on the idea of improper substitutions of one character for another. Søfren mistakes the old servant maid for Mari on two occasions, both in the comic scene at the loom and in bed at night, and in another plays a flute to flirt with Mari, whom he has seen duck around a corner, only to find Steinar, the grumpy, hulking servant, working there instead. More dramatically, the accident upon which the plot turns at the end is the result of a tragic switch of Mari for Margrete in the loft when Søfren removes the ladder from its place. All of this can be seen as development of the main premise, namely that Søfren himself is being improperly substituted for the parsons who have preceded him. The main conflict of the film is thus established as that of finding a proper place, of fitting in – and on what terms.

The fact that the problem of fit develops along an axis of extreme age and extreme youth in this film allegorises the problem of tradition more generally, a problematic that operates on several levels in the film. How can the new be reconciled with the old? Making a modern film at a museum full of old buildings is also a problem of fit, and as we have seen, entailed awkward

Figure 1: Søfren tries out his new surroundings.
Frame enlargement, *The Parson's Widow* (1920).

compromises with electric lighting. Janson's source story plays out a similar tension, being a then-modern (1901) collection of stories entitled *Pictures from the Middle Ages*. Likewise, the young couple of Dreyer's film struggle to find a new place in an old world that can't seem to accommodate them. And finally, this is also the problem the actor faces when presented with a ready-made location, or any set for that matter: how does one make oneself 'at home' in pre-existing space and come to inhabit it as one's own?

When Søfren first arrives at the parsonage, there is an important scene where all of this is played out. While Margrete is out of the room preparing the evening meal, Søfren is intoxicated by the luxury that would await him if he accepted the call. He looks at the furniture and valuable objects in the room, trying out the chair as he imagines himself in the role. There is a telling phrase from Janson's story preserved in the Danish film script at this point:

> Then she asks him to have a seat and make himself at home. She herself disappears into the kitchen. Søfren stands nailed to the spot, dumbfounded. What a comfortable room! There is a fire in the stove, so it is cozy there. The light shines through the oven door onto the floor. At the end of the table stands a tremendous armchair. 'There they had sat, his predecessors, because a depression had formed in the seat.' – He tries out sitting in the chair – it's almost impossible to get up again. (Dreyer 1920, 'Prestekonen' 1920:23)[11]

Figure 2: Søfren playing master.
Frame enlargement, *The Parson's Widow* (1920).

The quotation marks in the script indicate that the phrase is intended as a direct citation from Janson's story (67-68). In the context of the scene, the physical evidence of his predecessors at the parsonage is supposed to be tempting for Søfren; it is because they were so well fed that the permanent depression in the seat is so pronounced. But it also creates a Goldilocks scenario in which Søfren tries out the space while trying to imagine his own fit within it.

Figure 1 (p.32), a frame enlargement taken from this scene, conveys some sense of the physical presence of Søfren's predecessors, as he examines the chair before sitting down. The script's citation of Janson does not make it into the intertitles of the final version of the film; instead, the idea is conveyed visually by having Søfren first ease himself into the chair with obvious delight, and then inspect the valuable objects in the cupboard, weighing their value in his hands. 'All of this could be mine', we imagine him to be thinking, if only he could bring himself to accept the marriage match.

After the wedding, Søfren attempts to make this a reality by asserting what he takes to be his new authority over the parsonage and its servants (*Figure 2*, above). He storms into the room, slams a chair onto the floor for attention, and tells Margrete: 'In the future, I suggest you and your companions be less high and mighty. For I am master of this house.' In response, Margrete coolly calls in the servant Steinar to give Søfren a drubbing. After seeing him properly cowed, she adds, 'I suggest you concentrate on prayers and sermons. Do not play master here. I am master of this house!'

There are several interesting aspects of this sequence beyond the obvious resonance this line has for the English title of Dreyer's later 1925 film. The idea of 'master of the house' went through several redactions before ending up in the intertitle translated into English here. In the original Janson story, Margrete's retort reads like this:

> Pas han sine bønder og sine prædikener, døb han bøndernes børn og tal dem tilrette, reis han i sognebud og bind folk i den hellige ægtestand – men kom ikke her og ager husbond og herre. Thi riget her er mit, og jeg ved, hvorledes det skal styres. (Janson 1901:85)

> (You take care of your prayers and sermons, baptise the farmers' children and preach them into shape, travel around the district and bind people together in holy matrimony – but don't come here and play husband and master. Because the kingdom here is mine, and I know how it shall be governed).

The word Janson uses for 'playing' husband (*ager*) is a term with theatrical resonances of acting or pretending, conveying the sense that Søfren is attempting a role that he cannot authentically inhabit. The last line here adds a further echo from the Biblical Lord's Prayer (transformed into 'Mine is the kingdom'), indirectly augmenting Margrete's claim to authority.

Dreyer modifies this slightly in his Danish shooting script. Margrete's line is shortened to, 'For Fremtiden vil jeg raade ham til at passe sine Bønder og sine Prædikener – og kom ikke her og spil Husbond, thi Riget her er mit!' (In the future I would advise you to concentrate on your prayers and sermons – and not to come here and play husband, because the kingdom here is mine!). The last phrase is then crossed out in Dreyer's handwriting, to be replaced with the phrase 'det er mig, der er Herre i Huset' (I am master of this house) in the final film and in the intertitle list that accompanied it. The effect is striking; instead of calling up a religious resonance in their duel for ownership of the space, Dreyer makes it purely a material issue. Mastery of the house is recast as a question of command of objects and servants, and Søfren is told plainly that he has no access to that kind of relationship to the space of the parsonage. As long as Margrete is there, the most he can do is act the part inauthentically.

Dreyer's last-minute, material turn in this line of dialogue opens up some interpretive space to read 'mastery of the house' as a performance issue about the relation between actor and set. *All* of the actors, that is, were in Søfren's position when introduced to the location at Maihaugen for the production of the film, not just Einar Rød (who played the young parson). Like the fictional Søfren, each of them was presented with a space 'owned' by tradition; each of them was invited to make themselves at home in it, to personalise it for the duration of the shooting. In short, due to the specific plot configuration of Janson's source material and the evidence of previous inhabitation in Maihaugen's buildings, Dreyer was able to explore a story situation that resonates with the challenge every actor faces when confronted with a film set.

The scenes immediately following this showdown between Søfren and Margrete function as further development of the problem of inhabitation. A narrative bit included in the Swedish intertitle list (as well as in Janson's story and the Danish script, though redacted out in the final Danish and English intertitles) at the start of this series of scenes reads: 'Time passed. As for Dame Margrete, she sorely tried the patience of the young couple, in part because she wouldn't die, in part because she seemed omniscient and omnipresent ...'[12] Søfren cannot seem to find Mari alone, no matter what trick he attempts. When the final plan of removing the ladder while Margrete is in the loft backfires – a trick that pushes the limits of the comic, to be sure – and Mari is injured instead, Margrete seems to be an absolute narrative obstacle.

It is at this point that the ultimate secret of the plot's substitutional logic is revealed: Margrete herself had been in Mari's position when she was first engaged. Her fiancé too had been obliged to marry into the position, and the young couple had waited five years for the previous parson's widow to die and yield her place before marrying and enjoying thirty years of happiness together. Her story compels Søfren and Mari to admit their deception, but Margrete's reaction, difficult for us to read for only a moment, quickly turns to empathy: 'Poor children, poor children!' she says to them. And from that moment, she is changed. No longer a narrative obstacle, her thoughts turn to her first husband and a world beyond the farm and parsonage. In a genuinely moving scene, she makes the rounds of the farm, saying goodbye to both the animals and objects that had been handed down, as she herself had been, from generation to generation. *Figure 3* (p.36), an image taken at the end of this farewell sequence, shows Margrete taking off her cloak, echoing Søfren's earlier scene of trying on the clothes of his new calling ('Never in his life had he been so well dressed!'). Soon after, the film implies, she goes to bed and simply releases her hold on the place and dies. It is a death that resonates on the level of the film's production as well, since the terminally ill Hildur Carlberg died almost immediately after production was completed, thus in effect saying goodbye to both the film set and the world with her own passing.

The nature of the fictional Margrete's final detachment from the parsonage was something Dreyer worked his way through in stages of the project. Janson's story and Dreyer's Danish shooting script both initially made it more clearly a suicide, introducing the plot device of a magical elixir that can either prolong or shorten life. When Margrete goes to bed in the written versions of the story, she drinks the elixir and as a direct result is dead the following morning. She leaves

Figure 3: Margrete saying goodbye to the parsonage.
Frame enlargement, *The Parson's Widow* (1920).

a note saying that she has done this willfully and out of love for them, not wanting them to suffer as she has done, and asking forgiveness for not having died sooner. Dreyer must have changed his mind at some point, because this specific explanation is crossed out in the Danish script and omitted from the final film, leaving the means of her death a more open question. One can thus get the impression from the film that she simply decides to die and lets go, making way for the 'proper' inhabitation of the place by Søfren and Mari.

The Haunted Set

Any possibility of Margrete remaining a narrative obstacle is removed by her insistence that Søfren carefully follow the funeral protocol in order to prevent her from haunting the place. As the Norwegian program for the film states,

> Da fru Margretes støv bæres bort og hendes nærmeste mandlige slegtninger ved terskelen har uttalt hendes farvel til hjemmet, sænkes baaren tre ganger til tegn paa at hver av personerne i treenigheten blir tat til vidne paa at hun for altid har git avkald paa dette hjem. Og efter hendes eget raad strør Søfren linfrø efter hende, for det var kjendt av hvert barn som et av de sikreste midler mot gjengangere. Den døde kunde ikke paany komme ind i sit hus, før hun hadde talt hvert eneste frø. ('Prestekonen' 1920:11)

Figure 4: A 'horrifying' image?
Frame enlargement, *The Parson's Widow* (1920).

(When Dame Margrete's mortal remains are carried off and her closest male relative pronounces her farewell to the home, the casket is lowered three times as a sign that each member of the Trinity is called as a witness to the fact that she has given up all claim to this home. And in accordance with her advice, Søfren strews the floor with linseed, for as every child knew that was the surest way to prevent ghosts (*gjengangere*; lit. 'those who walk again'). The dead person couldn't re-enter her house until she had counted every single seed.)

It should be clear by now that the plot problem all along has been that of *gjengangere*, of the dogged persistence of tradition, bodies, and objects that do not make way for the new. The funeral procedures that Dreyer adds to the story shows that he had a particular interest in this as an architectural-performative problem of inhabitation, and that his further intellectual interest in the story was in finding a way out of simple repetition of the past.

One of the final images of the film, coming as it does shortly after the funeral sequence, bears quite directly on this issue. *Figure 4* (above) shows the young couple, finally ensconced as the rightful pair of the parsonage, with Mari dressed for the first time in the clothes of the parson's wife. The tone of the sequence is mournful, contemplative, and overtly religious in the final iris that frames the couple in the shape of a cross. The final intertitle reinforces that impression: 'We owe her a great debt, Mari. She taught you to keep a good home, and taught me to be an honorable man.'

Interestingly, this final scene feels quite different from the 'thirty happy years' that Margrete said began for her when she finally got her own turn as the parson's wife; what seem to be the prospects now for Mari and Søfren? Most critics, picking up on this disparity, have found this image extremely troubling. Jean Sémolué reads their final postures as 'petrified' and sees Mari and Søfren as two characters entrapped by a cross (1962:28). Andersson and Hedling concur (1987:53): 'Ungdomens frihet och naturlighet har förbytts i den mogna ålderns anpassning och tvång. Genom att den avslutande irisslutningen görs i form av ett kors visar Dreyer att den repressiva strukturen bär korsets signum' (The freedom and spontaneity of youth have been exchanged for maturity's compromise and coercion. By forming the concluding iris-out in the form of a cross, Dreyer reveals that the repressive structure carries the sign of the cross). Drouzy calls the last image 'nearly tragic', and states, 'Dreyer antyder på denne måde, at det hele begynder forfra. Intet nyt under solen. De to unge mennesker er allerede indfanget af systemet' (Drouzy 1982:71) (Dreyer suggests in this way that the whole thing is starting over again. Nothing new under the sun. The two young people are already trapped by the system). Kau takes the claim one step further. The 'happy' ending, he argues, 'bliver ... lagt ind i et uhyggeligt, spøgelsesagtigt gentagelsesmønster, som bogstavelig talt giver filmens sidste indstilling gyserperspektiver. Man ser for sig rækken af døde præster og ulykkelige enker. Nu er det Søfrens og Maris tur. Og de er ikke de sidste...' (Kau 1989:50) (... is placed in an uncanny, ghostly pattern of repetition, which literally gives the film's last shot a hint of horror. One catches a glimpse of a series of dead parsons and unhappy widows. Now it is Søfren's and Mari's turn. And they will not be the last...).

To slightly restate the critical consensus about the outcome of the film: there can be no mastery of the house since the house, in the shape of tradition, masters all. The power of the given world is such that only uncanny repetition is possible. But to assign this pessimistic critique to Dreyer himself, as several of these critics have done, is to put him at odds with what I earlier called his 'ontological experiment' of performative inhabitation. To be sure, Dreyer demonstrated a consistent thematic interest in oppression by the social order throughout his career; his fictional protagonists consistently find themselves hemmed in by social norms and laws. But as I have suggested, he had an equally enduring interest in the aesthetic yield that comes from his own creative submission to pre-existing narrative structures. By consistently choosing to work within the 'givens' of source texts, sets, and locations, Dreyer foregrounds the ways in which constraint can inspire as well as coerce. On the fictional level, the effect of that acceptance of constraint cannot help but look like a kind of 'entrapment'. But Dreyer himself, by cultivating a notion of performance as attachment in *The Parson's Widow* and other films, suggests that there might be other ways to think about making oneself at home, ways that involve neither mastery *of* nor mastery *by* the house.

Here is a hint in that direction from much later in Dreyer's career. In an interview entitled 'Thoughts on my Craft' for *Sight and Sound*, Dreyer extols the value of a temporary submission to the constraints of the material world, but emphasises the eventual power of art:

> Every creative artist is confronted by the same task. He must be inspired by reality, then move away from it in order to give his work the form provoked by his inspiration. The director must be free to transform reality so that it becomes consistent with the inspired, simplified image left in his mind. Reality must obey the director's aesthetic sense. (Dreyer 1955-6:129)

The model of artistic creation offered here – an initial meticulous immersion in reality, followed by a casting off – resonates with old Margrete's voluntary farewell at the end of *The Parson's Widow*. Like Dreyer's 'creative artist', Margrete is initially bound to a material reality to the point where she both masters it and is mastered by it (recall her comment about being handed from parson to parson like a piece of furniture). But the fact that she detaches from her embedded role as a simple act of will – again, an effect made possible by Dreyer's last-minute elimination of the suicide elixir as a plot device – leaves a way out of this binary logic of mastery or subjugation.

Those who are familiar with Dreyer's later career trajectory will recognise the transcendant aesthetic behind this gesture of relinquishing one's hold at the crucial moment, and in just the right way. It is nevertheless important to recognise how doggedly and sincerely Dreyer performs his inhabitation of the real, however temporary and strategic it might be. Perhaps the critical discussion of the final shot, with its emphasis on the 'constraint of the cross' and 'uncanny repetition', has lost sight of the end point of this inhabitative performance trajectory, as exemplified by Margrete, the one who got away. The idea of thirty happy years of earthly pleasures, followed by a graceful release, comes much closer to approximating the model of performance as Dreyer develops it.

As for Mari and Søfren, perhaps we should not be so concerned about their fateful, tragic repetition of existing patterns, nor with their entrapment in the old houses of Maihaugen in a long line of unhappy parson's widows. We might instead put our trust in the efficacy of linseed (and art) to keep the dead at bay, to keep tradition in its proper place, and to allow for a meaningful performance of inhabitation.

References

Andersson, Lars Gustaf and Erik Hedling (1987): 'Tankar om ett äktenskap: Carl Theodor Dreyers Prästänkan.' *Filmhäftet* (May).

Bordwell, David (1981): *The Films of Carl Theodor Dreyer.* Berkeley: University of California Press.

Daae, Ludvig (1881): 'Prestekonen i Tysnes.' In *Norske Bygdesagn.* 2nd ed. Christiania: J.W. Cappelens Forlag.

Dreyer, Carl Theodor (1920): 'Prestekonen: Tidsbilledet fra det 17' Aarh.' Unpublished film script. Danish Film Museum.

Dreyer, Carl Theodor (1920): Interview. 'Maihaugen og filmselskapet "Skandia": Et interview med director Dreyer.' *Gudbrandsdølen* 6 May.

Dreyer, Carl Theodor (1943): 'A Little on Film Style.' In Skoller, Donald (ed.) (1973): *Dreyer in Double Reflection.* New York: Da Capo.

Dreyer, Carl Theodor (1955-56): 'Thoughts on my craft.' *Sight and Sound* 25.3 (Winter).

Dreyer, Carl Theodor (1960): 'Ebbe Neergaard.' In Skoller, Donald (ed.) (1973): *Dreyer in Double Reflection.* New York: Da Capo.

Dreyer, Carl Theodor (2004): *The Parson's Widow.* DVD. Film Preservation Associates.

Drouzy, Martin (1982): *Carl Th. Dreyer født Nilsson.* Vol. 2. Copenhagen: Gyldendal.

Drum, Jean and Dale (2000): *My Only Great Passion: The Life and Films of Carl Th. Dreyer.* Scarecrow Filmmakers Series 68. Lanham, MD: The Scarecrow Press.

'Filmselskapet "Scandia" paa Maihaugen: Optagelsen af "En prestekone" begynte igaar.' (1920): *Gudbrandsdølen* 22 May.

Hall, Mordaunt (1929): 'A Norwegian Story.' *New York Times*, April 8.

Janson, Kristofer (1901): *Middelalderlige Billeder.* Copenhagen: Det Nordiske Forlag.

Kau, Edvin (1989): *Dreyers Filmkunst.* Copenhagen: Akademisk Forlag.

Neergaard, Ebbe (1940): *En Filminstruktørs Arbejde: Carl Th. Dreyer og hans ti Film.* Copenhagen: Atheneum Dansk Forlag.

Neergaard, Ebbe (1950): Carl Dreyer: *A Film Director's Work.* Trans. Marianne Helweg. New Index Series 1. London: The British Film Institute.

Neergaard, Ebbe (1963): *Ebbe Neergaards Bog om Dreyer.* Eds. Beate Neergaard and Vibeke Steinthal. Copenhagen: Dansk Videnskabs Forlag.

'Prestekonen' (1920(?)): Cinema program. Kristiania: Kommunernes Filmcentral A/S.

'Prästänkan' (1920(?)): Cinema program. Stockholm: Svensk Filmskompaniet.

'Prästänkan' (1953): Unpublished intertitle list. Danish Film Institute.

Sandberg, Mark B. (2001): *Living Pictures, Missing Persons: Mannequins, Museums, and Modernity.* Princeton: Princeton University Press.

Schepelern, Peter (2000): *Lars von Triers Film: Tvang og Befrielse.* Copenhagen: Rosinante Forlag.

Sémolué, Jean (1962): *Dreyer.* Classiques du cinema. Paris, Éditions Universitaires.

Notes

1. Editor's note: The rich interplay of intertitles, screenplays and commentaries in Danish and Swedish associated with this silent film is so complex (see, in particular, notes 8 and 10 below) that some source language material has been confined to the endnotes.
2. For most of Dreyer's early films he is given either sole or joint credit in the set design. Jens G. Lind was his most frequent collaborator in art direction in the 1920s, but others

included Axel Bruun, Hugo Häring, Hermann Warm, and Jean Hugo. See Bordwell 1981:205-217.

3. The 1950 English translation cited here is based on Neergaard's original 1940 text, which reads slightly differently in the Danish: 'Helst vilde Dreyer ha optaget Filmen inde i en rigtig lille to-Værelsers Lejlighed. Da det af tekniske Grunde ikke lod sig gøre, blev der bygget en komplet Kopi af saadan en Lejlighed ude i Atelieret-ikke en Køkkendekoration og en Dagligstue og et Soveværelse og en Entré hver for sig rundt om i Atelieret med aabne Sider ligesom Dukkestuer, men en sammenhængende lille Verden, lukkede Værelser med Døre imellem og indlagt Vand, Gas og Elektricitet-intet manglede. Naturalisme? Ja forsaavidt. Men Vægten blev ikke lagt paa selve Imitationen af Hverdagen; Naturalismen fremhæver jo bevidst Kopien i Kunsten, og det var der ikke Tale om her. Det var Dramaet, der skulde fremhæves, og dets særlige intime Karakter. De snævre Dekorationer tvang Instruktøren til at gaa paa nært Hold af Personerne hele Tiden og bevirkede, at Tingene i Milieuet spillede med.'

4. Original Danish text: 'Først naar en Dekoration er lavet saadan, at man kunde leve i den, kan man arbejde med den dokumentariske Ægthed, der er Fundamentet i filmisk Inspiration' (Neergaard 1940:43).

5. Admittedly, the 'master' idea is only emphasised in the French (*Le maître du logis*) and English titles of the latter film, not in the original Danish, *Du skal Ære din Hustru*, which translates as *Thou Shalt Honour Thy Wife*.

6. This and several following translations from Scandinavian-language print sources, unless noted in the bibliography, are my own.

7. The 1650 date of Maihaugen's parsonage would technically place it after the widows' custom had ceased in Norway, so despite Dreyer's passion for authenticity, he showed some flexibility with the cultural-historical facts here.

8. I have chosen to cite my own translation of the 1963 (revised) Danish edition here, rather than the published English translation, because I found it interesting that in this later version italics were added to give special emphasis to parts of the 1940 text (parts that were important for my argument) : 'Med den film greb han chancen til at skabe et helt ægte miljø som grundlag for filmens fortælling. *Der blev ikke bygget een eneste dekoration eller kulisse til Præsteenken*, hvert billede blev optaget i stuerne og i terrænet omkring de gamle norske bondegårde med tilhørende præstegård og kirke ...'

9. Original from revised 1963 edition: '*Dette dokumentarisk reale i miljø og typer* gav filmen et for den tid aldeles enestående præg. Man troede bedre på handlingen og skuespillernes spil, fordi man måtte tro på, hvad man så omkring dem.'

10. Citations from the film will for the sake of consistency rely on the English intertitles from the DVD released by Film Preservation Associates in 2004. Since the film began as a Danish-language script written for a Swedish production company, there is some variation in the intertitles used in each language. I have carefully compared the versions so as not to overemphasise a particular turn of phrase, and will comment on translation nuances when applicable. This sequence of English intertitles corresponds to the following versions in the bilingual title list prepared in 1953 that is available at the Danish Film Institute. Swedish: 'I må tro, att min lott icke är behaglig. Det är nu fjärde gången jag får finna mig i att överlämnas som ett husgeråd till vem det vara månde som kommer och vill ha kallet – men när man så som jag växer samman ed en plats, så faster man för varje dag, Gud giver, ett stycke av sig själv vid varje bord, varje stol og varje ljusstake – och skiljas man från alla desse ting, slitas hjärterötterna av, och man dör.' Danish: 'Min Lod er ikke behagelig. Det er nu fjerde Gang, jeg skal gaa i Arv med Embedet som et Stykke Husgeraad – men skilles man fra det, der er blevet en del af ens liv, rives Hjerterødderne over – og man dør.' (The sequence of titles in the original Danish script is closer to the

Swedish given here than the shorter version that ends up in this later title list.)

11. Original: 'Saa beder hun ham tage Plads og lade som han er hjemme. Selv forsvinder hun ud i Køkkenet. Søfren staar betuttet igen paa Gulvet. Nej, for en hyggelig Stue. Der er Ild i Bilæggerovnen, saa der er lunt derinde. Fra Døren i Ovnen lyser det ud paa Gulvet. For Enden af Bordet staar en vældig Armstol. "Der havde de siddet, hans Forgængere, thi der havde dannet en Fordybning i Sædet." – Han prøver, hvorledes det er at sidde i den Stol – det er næsten ikke til at komme op igen.'

12. Original: 'Tiden gick. Vad fru Margarete beträffade, satte hun de ungas tålamod på hårt prov, dels emedan hon icke ville dö, och dels emedan hon var likasom alvetande och allestädes närvarande.'

On the Transmigration of Images: Flesh, Spirit and Haptic Vision in Dreyer's *Jeanne d'Arc* and von Trier's Golden Heart Trilogy

Bodil Marie Thomsen

In Lars von Trier's Golden Heart trilogy – *Breaking the Waves* (1996), *Idioterne/The Idiots* (1998) and *Dancer in the Dark* (2000) – pure-hearted female heroines appear in the leading roles. They either become victims of their own unconditional love and goodness (Bess in *Breaking the Waves*) or their own passion for doing the right thing concerning the future, not the present (Selma in *Dancer in the Dark*). In the case of Karen (in *The Idiots*) her authentic virtue of honesty cannot be appreciated in her own family, who cling to convention and normality, even in the midst of crisis. Karen leaves her family after playing out their innermost fear: she convincingly plays a malfunctioning child or an idiot. In order to be able to live on after the loss of her newborn child, Karen actively decides to take the position of an outsider. Bess, whose husband loses his ability to make love to her, sacrifices her own lust and even life in order to give the life force back to the paralysed husband. Selma also sacrifices a love and a life of her own in order to give her son the possibility to gain a life (that is, the ability to see). Both Bess and Selma suffer death as a clear result of their almost inhuman beliefs in doing good for others.

This is of course not a very modern representation of women. Many film critics and feminists have been offended, scolding von Trier for letting the woman bear the burden of both passion and sacrifice, identifying how closely his films follow the representation of women in outmoded melodramatic *weepies*, where the women actor's sacrifices are only rewarded by the female spectator's tears, and not within the fiction frame (cf. Alyda Faber's reference to this discussion, 2003; and Bell in this volume).

For von Trier, melodramatic gender roles were not his central concern in the making of the Golden Heart trilogy. As is well known, he is elaborating on Carl Theodor Dreyer's themes and characters from *La*

Passion de Jeanne d'Arc (1928) and *Ordet/The Word* (1954). In Dreyer's films the passion of the heroines is almost always situated within their bodies, but the filmic style does not deliver the body as a visual representation of ideas, one of the melodramatic genre's most common traits. Instead the body and the face become flesh, concrete and real through the preference for extreme close-ups of skin and facial expressions. With this in mind I will take a closer look at the filmic style used by Dreyer as well as Trier in the films mentioned. Instead of looking at the Golden Heart trilogy as a revitalisation of melodramatic loss (and passion) in the confrontation with the ruling norms of society, I want to consider the passions of Joan, Bess, Karen and Selma as showing close relationships between bodily senses and spiritual (com)passion. So although most people seem to recognise von Trier's trilogy as melodrama, I would at least add that it might be melodramatic, but that it in some ways is closer to the genre of tragedy as its pathos is inspired by ethical values rather than moral issues. Von Trier stated in interviews in 1996 that he with the Golden Heart trilogy wanted to test whether the power of goodness and miracles like the ones in Dreyer's films would actually still have resonance – that is, in a climate where ironic gesture and mix of genres were the established norm (cf. Industry Central 1996 and Lumholdt 2003:110). Knowing this, we also must acknowledge that melodrama is only indirectly concerned with those higher issues of the tragic form: the laws of gods versus the laws of humans, life forces versus death forces, etc. To find some of those archaic concerns in the films of von Trier is refreshing in a (post)modern era. In a time where digital manipulation makes every illusion possible, von Trier challenges the dominance of optical sovereignty of classical Hollywood narration by way of haptic imagery inspired by Dreyer.

Although only *La Passion de Jeanne d'Arc* is actually a silent movie, all of Dreyer's films bear the mark of silent film imagery, where the emphasis on the body as *pathos* is confronted with the word as *logos*. This is indeed also a very melodramatic trait, but Dreyer insists that this body is connected to something outside itself that is not society. Some would call it religious spirit, others just spirit. It might even be the spirit of cinema itself that makes the bodies of Dreyer take part in miracles and beliefs outside the social law of humans. Dreyer does indeed insist on representing beliefs and passions belonging to the pathos of tragedies, although he is also a very modern film director. Trier inherits the ambition to connect body and spirit in the Golden Heart trilogy.

Transmigrations of Joan of Arc: from historic to mythic to cinematic figure of belief

Joan of Arc was born in 1412 in Domrémy in the region of Champagne. From the age of 13 she reported having visions from an angel telling her that the Englishmen (that is, Henry V and his forces) would lose the battle for France, and by the age of sixteen she enrolled in the army in order to get the French heir to the throne elected as King Charles II. She succeeded in her political and religious goals, sacrificing her life for a higher cause. She was captured in the territory of the Bishop of Beauvais, who delivered her to the Englishmen situated in Rouen. They let the French, in the person of theologians and doctors of the University of Paris, condemn her as heretic. She was burnt as a witch in the town square of Rouen on May 30, 1431.

In 1920 Joan was canonised a Catholic saint by Benedict XV, but earlier she had been depicted as a witch by Shakespeare in *Henry V* (1599), a romantic heroine by Schiller in *Die Jungfrau von Orleans* (1801) and a person of religious virtue by Thomas Carlyle and De Quincey. More films had been made about her life before Dreyer's, amongst them a film by George Méliès. By the time Joan of Arc was canonised, the world had turned its back on religious explanations leaving the modern subject responsible and alone with its own monsters and psychic flaws – from the line of Nietzsche, Kierkegaard and Freud.

Dreyer focused on the human nature of Joan of Arc, who was the illiterate daughter of a peasant. He based the film script on the actual trial documents, and the words used in the film are identical with the words spoken during the process. The Catholic Church certifies these documents as authentic:

> As regards the official record of the trial, which, so far as the Latin version goes, seems to be preserved entire, we may probably trust its accuracy in all that relates to the questions asked and the answers returned by the prisoner. These answers are in every way favourable to Joan. Her simplicity, piety, and good sense appear at every turn, despite the attempts of the judges to confuse her. (*New Advent Catholic Encyclopedia*)

Dreyer is also true to established assumptions about medieval style and texture of clothing, the naked faces wearing no make-up, etc. The copious use of extreme close-ups during the whole film is often mentioned. But no one has ever noticed that his style of filming clearly imitates the painting style of medieval times, in which what was crucial in the image was foregrounded. The central perspective of the Renaissance is denied us in *La Passion de Jeanne d'Arc*: we never get a full impression of the scale and architecture of the church, where part of the process takes place. On the other hand, faces and body parts are filmed very close up, and the rule of not transgressing the line of 180 degrees is broken, so the space becomes even more unstable and unsettling. Tactility dominates over optical mastery. Neither does Dreyer stabilise the spectator's position by giving an outline of Joan's story, her family background and reasons for her imprisonment. The spectator becomes a witness instead of an (aesthetic) judge. Everything is seen and perceived *in medias res* as if we were actually present in fifteenth-century France. By this method Dreyer makes us *both* witness the passion and death of Joan of Arc *and* witness the ability of the film to create images of belief, in creating passion and emphatic sensations in the act of seeing.

It becomes quite clear during the film that Joan would never be able to triumph over the theologians' eagerness to demonstrate their rhetorical superiority and skills in interpreting the Bible. She has no words, and she is outside the control of rhetoric. She is nothing but the bodily expression of passion. In this set-up we must surrender to identify with Joan of Arc, as she becomes a modern mediator between knowledge and belief. In turning to analyse *La Passion de Jeanne d'Arc*, I will focus on Dreyer's privileging of *tactile* or *haptic* imagery over optic perception. It is my point that the powers of monstrosity or grotesqueness in one period of time could later transmigrate to a positive power. I use the word transmigration instead of transformation to indicate that what might be considered a rather stable semiotic pattern of, for example, 'malice' in Medieval thought could, even unchanged, become a resource for a new creation of meaning today with an additional affective meaning attached to it. When, for example, the very unusual haptic imagery associated with medieval crude thinking (from the point of view of Renaissance perspective and Hollywood) is used consistently by Dreyer to portray the monstrous power of Joan's judges as well as the naïve passion of Joan almost five hundred years after her death, the power of monstrosity and extreme passion is both seen and felt. The unusual pictures demand another approach than the one we use when figures in the foreground act in the space of narration, created by the illusion of perspective. Dreyer challenges the modern idea of narration, where seeing a film is a matter of decoding it in the process of seeing. He uses film as a miraculous medium where the spirit of Joan can become actual and be sensed by a modern audience. The monstrous power of Joan's story and its many layers of interpretation become a virtual, spiritual resource in the close-up image of Marie Falconetti's face, challenging our most limited definitions of words like subject, knowledge and experience. Falconetti's open, passionate face must be sensed by every spectator as the site where sense and meaning coalesce, where the spirit or belief of Joan is made flesh by way of the film screen. This is the miracle of Dreyer: he actually is able to make us believe for one split second – and this by way of the film medium, and even film tricks, as when he in *Ordet* lets Inger awake from the dead. This is what film can do: make the dead return to life, make the once-filmed come to life again and again. This understanding of the special power of the film medium is what von Trier inherits from Dreyer.

Far from interpreting Dreyer's film in a religious context, French philosopher Gilles Deleuze sees his and Artaud's, Rosselini's and even Godard's ambitions as a search for a new ethical belief in this world, a belief in the body, in the immanence of life as becoming. He states:

> We must believe in the body, but as in the germ of life, the seed which splits open the paving-stones, which has been preserved and lives on in the holy shroud or the mummy's bandages, and which bears witness to life, in this world as it is. We need an ethic or a faith, which makes fools laugh; it is not a need to believe in something else, but a need to believe in this world, of which fools are a part. (Deleuze 1989:173)

According to Deleuze, film art demonstrates how our remembrance of things in our private and our culture's past are virtual but real, just as the house we are leaving is still standing and not just fiction in our head, when we're not in. The virtual is real and can turn actual. The challenge for modern philosophy and film is to activate a sense of pure time or virtuality instead of images of utopia or a science-fictional future. This is the philosophical challenge of film, according to Deleuze.

Dreyer was a master in showing this by way of mad people, ghosts, double incarnations, mummies and the naked face of Falconetti. Lars von Trier is doing the same thing in his *Riget/The Kingdom I & II* (1994 & 97), describing transmigrations between living and dead, remembered, dreamt of and present figures, creating excesses of monstrosity, that are not in the least horrifying. Everybody laughs at the grotesque and hybrid figures. Von Trier is also paying his tribute to Dreyer in the first scenes of *Breaking the Waves*, where even the camera angles of Joan's and Bess' faces are the same. Both Joan and Bess are figures of pure goodness, trying to reconnect the split between spirit and body still intact in Medieval Europe. Bess is like Joan filmed in extreme close up, and she is even looking directly into the camera, transgressing the once prohibited direct camera look to secure the story line for the spectator. So the spectator is forced to sympathise or identify with Bess, only to learn, later, that her direct look is (also) directed towards her internalised God. The spectator becomes a kind of witness and God at the same time – and must laugh once again or (in some sense) become responsible for Bess's God leaving her.

The haptic vision of Dreyer

In my opinion, Dreyer prepared detailed drawings of each take because he wanted a correct recreation of medieval iconography for everyone to see and experience – and yet this has not been commented by film criticism. His film is praised everywhere, but no one has ever gone into a meticulous study of this visual style, aligning it with the authentic fifteenth-century written documents.

For example, the French film critic André Bazin, who wrote about Italian neo-realism and became a spiritual leader for the group of *nouvelle vague* directors in France in the sixties, is very precise in his description of how Dreyer's *La Passion de Jeanne d'Arc* combines the real and the mystical, but without mentioning the medieval art of portrayal:

> With the exception of a few shots, the film is almost entirely composed of close-ups, principally of faces. This technique satisfies two apparently contradictory purposes: mysticism and realism. The story of Joan, as Dreyer presents it, is stripped of any anecdotal references. It becomes a pure combat of souls. But this exclusively spiritual tragedy, in which all action comes from within, is fully expressed by the face, a privileged area of communication.
>
> I must explain this further. The actor normally uses his face to express his feelings. Dreyer, however, demanded something more of his actors – more than acting. Seen from very close up, the actor's mask cracks. As the Hungarian critic Béla Balász wrote, 'The camera penetrates every layer of the physiognomy. In addition to the expression one wears, the camera reveals one's true face. Seen from so close up, the human face becomes the document.' Herein lies the rich paradox and inexhaustible lesson of this film: that the extreme spiritual purification is freed through the scrupulous realism of the camera as microscope. (Bazin 1998)

To further describe this iconography we must go to the Austrian art historian Alois Riegl's writings on the late Roman art industry (Riegl 1901 & 1927). He presents the shift from a physical, tactile art (Egyptian art, textiles, ornamental art) to late Roman art and architecture as a loss of tactile connections between the objects and the surface. This, on the other hand, creates a possibility for separating figure and ground, the condition for the development of a fictive depth, known to us since the Renaissance. Riegl invents the term 'haptic' to indicate that our eyes are able to sense softness or hardness as well as contoured structure without touching the material by hand. Haptic is the tactility of vision, so to speak. We use haptic vision when seeing an object in extreme close-up: the structure of the skin seen in a mirror, for example. Haptic vision excludes outlines, profiles and figurative isolation from the background. This discussion about the optical and the haptical was, according to Riegl, very much related to the fall of the Roman Empire, and the struggles on whether or not the body could be a vehicle to divine grace. The outcome of this we have all experienced: the body had to be transcended in order to gain a more spiritual point of view. So what is at stake here is nothing less than the relationship between our body and the body's visual preferences. Optical abstraction from the body gained sovereignty via Renaissance art, fashion and architecture.

Nowadays we have difficulty even sensing this abstraction from the physical sense involved in seeing illusionary depth. We are used to inhabiting an optically secure position, where lines of sight guide us to separate foreground and background. This perspective of depth gives the ability to control and to identify a distinct figure in a manageable space privileging abstraction and contour. Cinema, of course, also depends on these visual schemata, making it easy for us to identify moving figures acting within a diegetic structure, functioning as the background for interpretation.

The haptical and physical-sensational relation between body and vision did not totally disappear with modern visual distance and control, as can be seen in art historical movements like expressionism, fauvism and even pointillism. Recent developments in the relationship between optic and haptic have been discussed by Gilles Deleuze in his book on Francis Bacon (Deleuze 1981). He talks about 'the gothic line' where form and ground are diffusing into a kind of deformed realism attributed to animalistic as well as to human formation. This is opposed to 'the idealism of transformation' (Thomsen 2001:238-39), where the senses of the body are excluded. But his two books on film, *The Movement-Image* (1986) and *The Time-Image* (1989), also touch upon haptic forms of images. One of the directors he mentions in the chapter on 'Thought and Image' is Carl Th. Dreyer, who, says Deleuze, created images of a certain kind enabling the spectator to experience something outside the image frame, outside homogeneous conceptions of time and space. The visual space is reduced to a 2-dimensional 'flat image, cut off from the world' (Deleuze 1989:178). The abstraction of depth is hindered so that another 'spiritual' or 'trans-spiritual' dimension is reached. This method is called 'ascetic' by Deleuze, relating it to the description of a flat surface in the images of *La Passion de Jeanne d'Arc*, the portrayal of Gertrud in *Gertrud* (1964), Inger in *Ordet*, Mr. Gray in *Vampyr* (1932) etc. Deleuze names them mummies, and this term is positive:

> [T]he more the image is spatially closed, even reduced to two dimensions, the greater is its capacity to open itself on to a fourth dimension which is time, and on to a fifth which is Spirit, the spiritual decision of Jeanne or Gertrud. (Deleuze 1986:17)

And further in *The Time-Image*:

> Dreyer's mummy was cut off from an over-rigid, over-burdensome, or over-superficial external world: she was none the less permeated by feelings, by an over-fullness of feeling, which she neither could nor should outwardly express, but which would be revealed in consequence of the deeper outside. (Deleuze 1989:178)

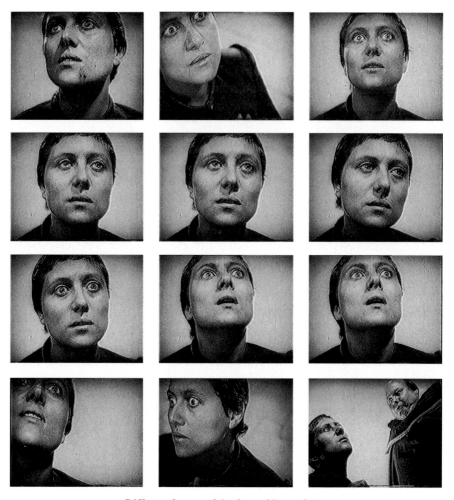

Different frames of the face of Joan of Arc

This feeling of something outside the image frame is reached by way of the haptic imagery (not Deleuze's word – but mine here).

Having had the opportunity to look a little closer, we can move on. Dreyer's insistence on not separating the figure from the ground denies us the normal distance granted to the object of our vision. As mentioned, Dreyer grants us the position of witnesses to an almost incomprehensible fight between Joan's insistence of a (for the priests) monstrous relationship between body and holy spirit, and Dreyer's depiction of the really monstrous bodies of the theologians, who insist on the bodiless representations of the holy spirit and God. We experience how the positive monstrosity of Joan's divine visions are debased in a Catholic register not allowing bodies, and

Different frames of faces of theologians and judges

especially women's bodies, and we experience how this in turn makes the priests and monks turn grotesque in Dreyer's vision.

They are filmed demonically from the ground up. Their fat and wrinkled faces are seen in extreme close-ups as well as Joan's face, but they are seen from ever-changing perspectives, faces in profile often cut in halves by the camera or placed in the corner of the frame. They are often portrayed as a group in conspiracy and, in spite of their interesting facial traits, they never seem to obtain any individuality (except for the young priest played by Antonin Artaud, who is genuinely interested in Joan as a person). The face of Joan is often filmed in frontal close up situated in the middle of the frame showing wonder, openness, sorrow and even joy.

The relationship between frontal and profile is closely related to the relationship between haptical and optical. This is not an observation Deleuze makes, although the description of the profile/frontal distinction is his (Deleuze 1986:87-101). The face in profile gives us the impression of will and action; to reach the contour of a profile, we have to be able to distinguish the face from the background. The frontal face, on the other hand, does not show any kind of force or action. It is, rather, associated with the background as well as the surface of the film screen. The frontal close-up invites us to pure compassion, wonder and identification. The profiled faces of the theologians underline the impression of conspiracy, and they belong very much to their surroundings and are granted some kind of perspective depth. They belong to the time and place where they are depicted, whereas Joan is almost always depicted alone in the frame as if belonging to another time and space. Her forces seem not to belong to this place and time. In the last section of the film, filmed in the town's square, female spectators are depicted as compassionate witnesses to the sufferings of Joan, as flames cover her. And there is no doubt as to where Dreyer puts his sympathy. Even as the body of Joan is slowly transformed to a corpse by the flames in a vertigo of fire, smoke, sky and houses, moving as by an external or internal force of vision, the identification and compassion with the body and face of Joan persists – and is immediately transformed to a spiritual force of belief and rebellion against the English oppressors.

The text is also very clear on emphasising the human and religious perspective of Joan. Dreyer's excerpts from the documents, where the theologians are questioning the male clothing of Joan as well as the looks of St. Michael (Was he naked? Did he have wings?) ridicule them rather than Joan. They are depicted as curious, gossiping, vain and too concerned with worldly matters to be able to judge anybody in the name of God. Dreyer radically mocks their questions, which, though they might have had some relevance in their own time, a modern audience could never take seriously. In this sense Dreyer is very much speaking from the point of view of the twentieth century, mocking the beliefs of medieval time, but rescuing the body and soul of Joan of Arc by way of his compassionate depictions.

The witch processes in Europe brutally stated the Christian norm, that the body should be excluded from the religious text. The so-called witches could not prove their innocence in verbal *logos*, since the crime clearly was the learned theologians' visual projections on the poor women's bodies. Those bodies had to be sacrificed in order for the Christian norm to stabilise in each local town. In Denmark at Midsummer Night (called the night of Saint Hans), when we gather around the open fire with a witch made of straw at the top, we still sing:

Hver by har sin heks
og hver sogn sine trolde.
Dem vil vi fra livet med glædesblus holde
vi vil fred her til lands
Sankte Hans, Sankte Hans!
Den kan vindes, hvor hjerterne
aldrig bli'r tvivlende kolde.

Each town has its witch
And each parish its trolls.
We'll keep them away with our bonfire
We want peace in our land
Saint Hans, Saint Hans!
It can be won where hearts
Never get cold from doubting.
(my translation)

With this film, Dreyer not only breaks with the exclusion of (female) bodies from the written, dry *logos* of history. He links this obvious critique to the dominance of optical perception and gives us an extraordinary film, still very powerful today, where passion and belief are linked to the haptic images. The haptic is mostly associated with the horrible sight of the monster – known to us by the difficulty in creating an outline, in selecting the figure from the ground: an overwhelming sight, and short-sightedness. He transforms the haptical monster into a human face filled with divine spirit – contrasting it with the weak power of human law. He exhibits the patriarchal, Catholic and body-haunted norm dominating us since the end of medieval time. Joan of Arc is depicted as the figural 'place' of passion, in the foreground, belonging to an invisible presence outside of time, outside of optical controlled space. The extreme frontal flat shots of her face register every passion, every minimal affect. And this haptic surface becomes the vehicle for the spiritual outside of the image, registered by the audience.

The face of goodness – Bess breaking the frame of fiction

This is also the case with the close-ups of Bess in *Breaking the Waves*. She can easily be seen as a modern image of Joan of Arc, mimicking the camera shots of Dreyer. Bess can neither be fully described as idiotic good person (in Danish, *tossegod*) or as bad (mentally unstable). She is both: good and bad, body and spirit. She is thus a figure who transcends the well-known scheme of melodrama. Both Bess and Joan believe in the spirituality of bodies, heaven on earth, the virtual in the actual. This is heretical in the eyes of the theologians/psychiatrists and they try to convince the women to decline their faith in order to save their life on earth. Joan and Bess both refuse to follow this conviction, based on so-called knowledge, since in Joan's and Bess's eyes their advisers have lost their faith. Bess dies believing spiritual belief and carnal love could unite. The psychiatrist is clearly a modern version of a theologian, who condemns her to exile and death. He does not believe in the spiritual body, visions and miracles. Both kinds of advisers/judges ask the heroines questions about their knowledge (of the Bible, of mental illness) instead of about their belief – and the film leaves them with no answer. Belief does not belong to the realm of arguments, it belongs to the realm of passion, and the act of dying is for both Joan and Bess decisive and done in order to change the minds of people. Both Dreyer and von Trier let their heroines die in order to affect the audience, letting them know the feeling of passion, the haptical vision outside melodrama and optical conventions of seeing. Human fragility is shown through the haptic surface of sensation – the vivid sensitivity of Maria Falconetti's and Emily Watson's faces – very far indeed from voyeurism, often offered to us by melodrama. And von Trier's ostentatious use of the direct gaze into the camera is a statement that really punctures the illusion of depth and reaches out for another dimension of haptic and erotic passion, that has always been the offensive force of cinema, denied by Hollywood in order to still stabilise the optical image and the illusion of control of the spectator. So while Dreyer is reaching out for the spiritual, von Trier is reaching for the passionate image in every aspect of the word, since his purpose is higher: to obstruct the optical control of the digital image in our time. I do not argue that von Trier is hostile towards digital media as such. He used digital video in filming *The Idiots* and he used digital editing in *Dancer in the Dark* and in *Dogville*. But I think his interest in following the spiritual and ethical path of Dreyer is to explore the strength of the haptical image in a digital time – renewed by the hand held camera, the jump-cuts and the camera-looks – and the whole ambition is to affect the senses and intellectual judgments of the audience, combining bodily senses and sense as meaning.

Digital film can avoid any reference to indexical material; it's flexible (Marks 2002:152). Lev Manovich suggests that the interest in reality and realism was just a short intermezzo in the long tradition of painting (Manovich 2001). So sensing by way of visual contact with indexical material, known from the period of photography and cinema, might not hold this particular relation to reality and truth in the future. The grainy structure of Falconetti's face in tears, the dots of images in newspapers, repeated in Warhol's images, the documentary style of *Cinéma vérité*, direct cinema and the new realism of Dogme 95 are possible styles amongst others today. In Jean-Pierre Jeunet's *Amélie de Montmartre/Amelie* (2001), in *Moulin Rouge!* (Baz Luhrmann, 2001) or in Peter Jackson's *Lord of the Rings* trilogy (2001-2003), optical and haptical elements mix without problem. Haptic and optic are not opponents as in the twentieth century. The clear message (or firstness, as C.S.Peirce would have it) of the close-up (Deleuze 1986) is one morph among other morphs of the image offered to the audience. Today we might feel the power of transmigration in the visual contact with extended space in computer games or in films using digital transformation rather than in a haptic figuring of the surface, and von Trier surely wants to take part in this development as an artist insisting on the basic purpose of film, according to him: namely to convey feelings to the audience. And this I believe he has shown better than any director in relating sensation (feeling) to sense (meaning), creating new events in every new film, and especially in the Golden Heart trilogy, where melodrama is renewed by traits of tragedy. Those traits of tragedy are, I think, related to the haptic image as well as to positioning the audience as witnesses affected in body and spirit by the happenings on the screen (Thomsen 2004).

Bill Viola and the simultaneity of spaces

Recently, Bill Viola, the famous video artist, has moved in the same direction as von Trier – without the ironic twist though. He has always been into depicting the body as a way of reaching spiritual transformation:

> The body is where awakening happens. It is the medium of transformation. Its sensations are the very language of myth, the place where spiritual domains intersect with the ordinary world of time and space. Myth and ritual are grounded in the body, making it the register of transcendence. (Morgan 2004:103)

And here at last we have a key to understanding the suffering of Joan of Arc or the heroines of Lars von Trier in the Golden Heart trilogy. It is not a masochistic glorification of pain inscribed on a woman's body in order to free someone else from his pain. Pain occurs to a body, but suffering happens in order to live with that pain – and pain changes the way we look upon our selves and the world (Morgan 2004:104). Sometimes this opens up a spiritual path of transfiguration of the artwork. This is certainly the ambition of Bill Viola.

In his recent works he seems to strengthen the ambition to show and affect pathos. He does that in two ways: by intensifying the movements of facial and bodily pathos and by showing the body as belonging as much to space as to time. Mark Hansen explains the digital method used in *The Quintet of the Astonished* (2000) and *Going Forth By Day* (2002):

> By exploiting the technical capacity, introduced by digitization, to shoot film at high speed and then, following its conversion to digital video, to project it

seamlessly at normal speed, Viola is able to supersaturate the image, registering an overabundance of affective information normally unavailable to perception. (Hansen 2004:6)

The affective information is intensified in those compositions, although they are not haptical in the normal sense of the word by producing a surface. But they give way to affective information. They are moving, but very slowly. We get neither a still image nor a moving image. We get something in between, where time is unfolding, so we can concentrate on passion as continuity and not something leading to action as in the normal language of Hollywood movies. As a viewer you become aware of your own vulnerability and might be inspired to pay greater attention to the expression of passions in bodies and faces. Medieval painting from fourteenth- and fifteenth-century Northern Europe, where you see a simultaneity of spaces in one painting, inspires the other new path of Bill Viola. In an interview for a BBC video production, Viola gave this very interesting statement:

This idea is lost in the age of the camera and the logic of imagery based on optics and how the eye sees the world. – We have lost this idea that someone could be in two places at once. (Kidel 2003)

The simultaneity of space has been lost because of photography and film where each frame is cut from space and later cut into movement as time by way of montage.

It is very interesting to notice this interest in space and its relationship with passion, since this is also the path Lars von Trier is taking in his new trilogy on America, of which two films, *Dogville* (2003) and *Manderlay* (2005), have already appeared. The whole idea of stripping the houses of walls and the landscape of light gives a Brechtian effect of *Verfremdung*, where the illusion of space is taken away from us. Instead we are left with the facial and bodily expressions and an idea of space that seems to look right through the idea of ordering and control inherited by the Renaissance perspective. The sudden change of light seems to make all the difference as well as the (limiting of) space the inhabitants are prepared to offer Grace, the heroine of *Dogville* and *Manderlay*. The background as an anchoring of perspective tends to disappear in both von Trier's and Viola's works. Instead we get an idea of simultaneity of spaces or limitless space, exhibiting hopes for the potential of the transmigrational force of art in the era of digital media.

References

Bazin, André (1998; 1952): 'The Passion of Joan of Arc'. Available at www.geocities.com/Paris/Metro/9384/films/passion_of_joan_of_arc/bazin.htm

Deleuze, Gilles (1981): *Logique de la sensation I & II, La vue, le texte.* Paris: Éditions de la différence.

Deleuze, Gilles (1986): *Cinema 1. The Movement-Image.* Minneapolis: University of Minnesota Press.

Deleuze, Gilles (1989): *Cinema 2. The Time-Image.* Minneapolis: University of Minnesota Press.

Faber, Alyda (2003): 'Redeeming Sexual Violence? A Feminist Reading of *Breaking the Waves*'. *Literature and Theology* 17:1, March.

Hansen, Mark (2004): 'The Time of Affect, or Bearing Witness to Life'. *Critical Inquiry. Art, Criticism and Interpretation*, Spring.

Industry Central (1996): 'Director's Chair Interviews. Lars von Trier.' First published in *Sight & Sound*, October. Available at: http://industrycentral.net/director_interviews/LVT01.HTM

Kidel, Mark (2003; 1996): *Bill Viola. The Eye of the Heart* & *Bill Viola and the Making of Emergence*. BBC in association with ARTE France.

Lumholdt, Jan (ed.) (2003): *Lars von Trier Interviews.* Jackson: University Press of Mississippi.

Manovich, Lev (2001): *The Language of New Media.* Cambridge, MA & London: The MIT Press.

Marks, Laura U. (2002): *Touch: Sensuous Theory and Multisensory Media.* Minneapolis & London: University of Minnesota Press.

Morgan, David (2004): 'Spirit and Medium. The Video Art of Bill Viola'. In Townsend, Chris (ed.): *The Art of Bill Viola.* London: Thames & Hudson Ltd.

New Advent Catholic Encyclopedia (2003): 'St. Joan of Arc'. Available at www.newadvent.org/cathen/08409c.htm

Riegl, Alois (1901/1927): *Spätrömische Kunstindustrie.*Wien.

Thomsen, Bodil Marie (2001): 'Alt stof udsender "billeder" – om det visuelle som begivenhed'. In Carlsen, Mischa Sloth, Karsten Gam Nielsen & Kim Su Rasmussen (eds): *Flugtlinier. Om Deleuzes filosofi.* Copenhagen: Museum Tusculanums Forlag.

Thomsen, Bodil Marie (2004): 'Realism of the Senses – on Ethics, Space, and Event in Lars von Trier's 1990s Trilogy'. In Oittinen, Vesa (ed.): *Spinoza in the Nordic Countries.* Department of Philosophy, University of Helsinki.

Bodies in Elevators:
The Conveyance of Ethnicity in
Recent Swedish Films

Amanda Doxtater

Hanging on the wall of the elevator that takes me to my office every day is a small placard displaying the contraption's safety permits and other important information. At the bottom is written an emphatic, 'This Permit Shall be Posted on *the Conveyance*' (my emphasis). The unexpected association of the word conveyance with an elevator did much to shape an otherwise intuitive association I had formed between the elevators I had seen in recent Swedish films and the depictions of ethnicity in those same films. A conveyance, according to the Oxford English Dictionary, is not merely a physical means of transporting people from place to place. A conveyance gives form to abstract thought and meaning. Definition number nine, for example, reads, 'The conveying of meaning by words; expression, or clothing of thought in language; disposition of material in a poem... b. Manner of expressing thought, form of expression or utterance, style.' Though a conveyance incorporates style and poetics into the expression of meaning, it is by no means a straightforward sort of communication. Conveyances can be secretive or private and are often ambiguous rather than transparent. Definitions eleven b and c even suggest that the operation of conveyance might include an element of deception, 'Cunning management or contrivance; underhanded dealing, jugglery, slight of hand... c. A secret or cunning device, an artifice...' (OED online).

In this essay, I want to exploit the ambiguity and expressive potential of the elevator to be a cinematic conveyance that gives form and meaning to issues of transnationalism and cultural diversity in several recent Swedish films. I read the elevator both as a poetic, filmic device for conveying experience and meaning, but also as a contraption or mechanism that does the heavy work of presenting and undoing stereotypes of various sorts. I will consider how elevators occur as specifically cinematic spaces in which to frame, shoot, edit together, and isolate the people of various cultural backgrounds who happen to step inside them. Also to be considered are those who remain locked outside of them or excluded. While mechanical elevators function to move people around, as cinematic conveyances they often function as a space of condensation, breakdown, and restriction of movement.

At the heart of the matter lies the question of how instances of cinematic conveyance can inform questions of cultural diversity and representation in Swedish films. While the elevator can, of course, be considered among the predictable sites of melodramatic conflict, along with other spaces of transition like the hallway or the staircase, the films I consider – namely *Svartskallen/Blackskull* (Barbro Karabuda, 1981, a television production), *Livsfarlig film/Lethal Film* (Suzanne Osten, 1988), *Hus i helvete/Hell Breaks Loose* (Suzanne Taslimi, 2002), and *Hissen/The Elevator* (Renato Olivares Macias, 2003) – re-inscribe this melodramatic tradition in new ways to convey diversely cinematic stories about living in an increasingly intercultural Sweden. Physical experience, ethnic and political stereotypes, cinematic expression, and artifice all coalesce in the elevator. I also offer *Kvinnors väntan/Secrets of Women* (Ingmar Bergman, 1952), as an example of a 'classic' elevator scene and point of comparison, particularly as an example of elevator as erotic space.[1] *A propos* comparison, the appearance of an elevator provides a concrete instance of commonality in films that are really quite diverse and in many ways resist being lumped under any umbrella term whether it be 'ethnicity', 'multiculturalism' or 'transnational identity'.

Rochelle Wright (1998, 2005) has written extensively on ways in which 'ethnic outsiders' have been represented in Swedish sound film since its inception. In addition to the thematic aspects of the varying modes of representation she addresses, she also takes into account socio-cultural factors related to film production in Sweden over the years including audience reception and state funding structures. In recent work she comments on how the narratives of several popular, mainstream films in Sweden reflect issues of transnationalism and present the stories of Swedes of immigrant background living in Sweden. She suggests that the non-native Swedish backgrounds of directors Suzanne Taslimi, Reza Persa, and Reza Bagher have brought into play a new kind of diversity to a national cinema that has always participated in negotiating Swedish ethnicities. My project seeks to complement Wright's work by exploring how the cinematic aspects of representations (or the seeming lack thereof) affect categories of ethnicity in stories about 'immigrant' or 'second-generation Swedish' experience. I see the elevator in these films as an aesthetic, artificial, and necessarily subjective lens through which to view representations of Sweden's multiculturalism. I have gathered these representational conveyances into four themes: elevator as bearer and parody of ethnic stereotypes, elevator as neo-naturalistic Petri dish versus space of imagined resolution, elevator as erotic, gendered space of social escape and entrapment, and elevator as dangerous (or at the very least ambiguous) spectacle.

Elevator as bearer and parody of ethnic stereotypes: *Blackskull* and *Hipp Hipp!*

The television production *Svartskallen/Blackskull* (Barbro Karabuda, 1981), taking its name from a highly derogatory racial slur literally meaning 'black skull,' offers a veritable cornucopia of stereotypes to which newly-arrived immigrants are subjected in a Sweden depicted as overtly racist. At worst, members of this Turkish family experience race-related violence, at best they are subjected to well-intended (if at times condescending) miscommunications. The main character of the film is Yasar (Yalçin Avsar), a young boy of about ten who encounters the elevator shortly after his arrival in Sweden when he is given a tour of the apartment house in which his family will live. His already-settled older cousin Kemal shows him which button to press to reach the sixth floor. 'Can you remember that?' he asks him as he jokingly pats him on the head. Coming from rural Turkey, Yasar has never seen an elevator before, let alone ridden in one, and later, when he attempts to operate it on his own, he becomes flustered and confused and in his frustration presses several buttons at once. The movement in the elevator of what should have been solid ground becomes the physical representation of the way that every stable point of reference from his life in Turkey has shifted beneath his feet. The elevator whirrs up and down and then comes to a halt. Being stuck inside exacerbates Yasar's feelings of disorientation, fear, and lack of control that he has experienced since his arrival, and he erupts.

In *Blackskull*, though the main character is actually a child, his struggles reflect the kind of infantilisation that the adult male protagonists in first-generation immigrant narratives in Swedish films often experience. Both young child and grown man find themselves isolated (and emasculated) by their inability to communicate in the language surrounding them. Laura U. Marks (2000) uses the term 'intercultural cinema' to describe a cinematic movement (albeit one rapidly transforming into a genre) that treats such frustrated communication, among other issues of displacement, hybridity and the politics and poetics of cultural representation:

> Intercultural cinema draws from many cultural traditions, many ways of representing memory and experience, and synthesizes them with contemporary Western cinematic practices. [...] many of these works evoke memories both individual and cultural, through an appeal to nonvisual knowledge, embodied knowledge, and experiences of the senses, such as touch, smell, and taste. In particular [...] certain images appeal to a haptic, or tactile, visuality. (Marks 2000:1-2)

Marks suggests that the symbolic and literal silence of incapacitation may provide the space in which colonial stories (in the context of Sweden, the term 'host culture' would certainly be more apt) break down. The language of a dominant culture cannot immediately represent the experiences of people new to it, but out of an initial silence a new, embodied language might emerge, a language capable of expressing the stories of immigrants to a new country. The transitional, temporary silence that she describes functions as 'an act of mourning for the terrible fact that the histories that are lost are lost for good' (Marks 2000:25). Yasar suffers something reminiscent of this loss of self, memory and history when he symbolically leaves his childhood behind in a series of flashbacks of his rural village and his beloved grandmother. But then he also begins to tell a new story of adaptation and learns to press one elevator button at a time.

While I would like to read the silent, liminal space of the elevator in *Blackskull* as a space in which dominant culture can be challenged in the name of new stories in which supposed cultural 'outsiders' position themselves as insiders and exert pressure on 'Swedishness' while still allowing for the real mourning of their own 'lost' stories, doing so is difficult. *Blackskull* suffers from a heavy-handed didacticism typical of many 'new immigrant experience' narratives of the 1970s and 80s that critique 'Swedish' narrow-mindedness and racism not only at the expense of formal or embodied innovation, but to a certain extent at the expense of the stories of its main characters. *Blackskull* arguably strives for a kind of bodily empathy with the young boy's plight; in many ways Yasar experiences Sweden through his body. He throws himself violently against the elevator door in his attempts to get out. He makes himself vomit after a bully classmate (upon discovering he is Muslim) tricks him into believing the meatballs he has eaten contain pork. And when his frustration at his situation becomes unbearable, he runs until he collapses from exhaustion. But ultimately Yasar's experiences are understood through its narrative, rather than by being embodied in the formal construction of the film's sequences. Though Marks admits that many of the characteristics of intercultural cinema, 'have become more mainstream, in theatrically released films that deal explicitly with the contemporary mixing of cultures in metropolitan centers' (Marks 2000:3) she continues to emphasise the importance of formal experimentation in intercultural films. The strength of intercultural film lies in its formal subversion and re-imagination of the narrative forms of dominant culture. The representation of struggle in *Blackskull* remains at the level of the kind of narrative communication in which Yasar cannot yet participate. In effect, this might be a filmic expression intent on communicating 'guilt' to a Swedish audience about its collective narrow-mindedness and racist attitudes toward immigrants. Paradoxically, because of its self-flagellating tendencies, a well-intentioned film might remain subtly disingenuous. Though *Blackskull* certainly must be appreciated as an attempt to raise awareness and sensitivity, the figure of the immigrant ultimately remains infantile and is problematically represented. When Yasir gets trapped in the elevator the camera stays with him through the sequence and poses as an insider intent upon relating his experience, but behaves as an observer interested in recording his struggle for the edification of a dominant 'Swedish' culture.

The didacticism of first-generation narratives like *Blackskull* are parodied by the Swedish comedy show *Hipp Hipp!* in a series of sketches in which a group of adult immigrants are taught Swedish by a goofy instructor who treats them like school children. As they attempt to master Swedish, they embark upon several short excursions through which they are comically initiated into the mystifying niceties of Swedish culture. A trip to Systembolaget (the State Liquor Store), for example, illustrates the passive-aggressive art of avoiding public confrontation. In Sweden, when an impertinent stranger pushes ahead of you in line, always wait until the offending party is out of earshot to deride them. Other important tips for negotiating one's way through Swedish society include: always bring chocolate to your Swedish host, drop your compulsory thank-you note in the letterbox as you leave a party, and always glance through your peephole before you open your door (to avoid chatting with neighbours). Among these scenarios is a brief scene in which the entire class, instructor included, squeeze into a tiny apartment elevator. Silence ensues as everyone, including the normally gregarious instructor, remains still and silent. After a few tense moments, the door opens and the instructor steps out. She grins and praises the class enthusiastically for not uttering a word or making eye contact in the elevator. To be Swedish, of course, is to be reserved, particularly when faced with the possibility of having to engage in awkward small talk with strangers. Though anecdotal, the sketch highlights the inscription of the presumably neutral, public space of the elevator with stereotypes about 'Swedish' society. Silence, to refer back to Marks' term, takes on another meaning in this hyper-Swedish context. In this case, it vibrates with exaggerated, yet unspoken understanding of how people are to behave together in Sweden. *Hipp Hipp!* replaces didacticism with parody as the mode of representation and in doing so subverts dominant narratives by addressing comically the infantilisation of immigrant experience.

Gender, Eroticism, and Entrapment: *Secrets of Women* and *Hell Breaks Loose*

Arguably, representations of ethnicity that communicate mainly at the level of narrative differ from ones that attempt to signify at the level of formal composition by consciously grappling with film's potential constrictions. As a medium, film must contend with categories of mobility and stasis in relating a story cinematically. From early on, theorists have noted how film's ability to combine motion (or the appearance thereof) with an expansive visual register distinguishes it from literary or theatrical productions. One of film's innovations involved its ability to incorporate shots from vastly diverse locations and temporalities. It could not only transport a spectator from the mountains of Northern Sweden to the centre of Malmö in an instant, it could effortlessly expand the theatre's necessary constriction of performance space-time. Footage from radically different locations could be edited into deceptively coherent, apparently contemporaneous action. Being able to represent movement in time was considered by many to improve greatly upon the representational power of the photograph or the theatrical production. At the same time, being a predominantly visual medium, film found itself intimately connected with what was indexically present in front of the camera during shooting. The seemingly unlimited capacity of film to represent was balanced by the impossibility of capturing what lay outside of the camera's frame (a limitation that is still hidden). Making a film thus necessitated a constriction of the seemingly infinite mobility and access to time and space of which a novel, for example, could avail itself. Like film, the elevator manoeuvres between mobility and stasis, expansion and constriction in order to convey meaning. Filming a scene in an elevator in which not only the protagonists of the film, but also the camera itself, remain deliberately limited to the spatial confines of the elevator becomes an interesting obstruction to film's ability to represent. Refusing to take advantage of the camera's mobility raises the question of what such an obstruction might contribute to the meaning of a film.

One example of an intentional limitation is the 'classic' elevator scene directed by Ingmar Bergman in *Kvinnors väntan/Secrets of Women* (1952) in which Karin Lobelius (Eva Dahlbäck) takes advantage of being stuck in an elevator with Fredrik Lobelius (Gunnar Bergstrand), her slightly tipsy workaholic husband whom she rarely sees, to spend a little time with him. The deftly choreographed episode allows for an elaborate and playful game of cat and mouse as the couple tease out each other's infidelities and seemingly re-kindle the spark in their marriage. In Bergman's extended elevator sequence, the camera finds itself trapped with the couple and gracefully spirals around them, always remaining out of sight of the mirrors in the elevator. Critics lauded the episode precisely for its lack of shots taken from outside the 'actual' elevator. Being trapped in the elevator with the couple enables Bergman's camera to play the role of an ignored, intimate voyeur. It becomes something of an intruder who gets in the way of the eventually amorous scene (perhaps even prompting Fredrik to unscrew the light bulb for some semblance of privacy?). It seals together the couple's formal, visual relationship to each other with their narrative marriage relationship by mimicking their playful jostling for the last word. As power relationships shift between them and first Fredrik then Karin dominates their battle of wills, each in turn dominates the high register of the frame. The formal composition of the sequence mirrors the rising and falling of their relationship and the rising and falling of the elevator all from its position of being locked inside it. In contrast to the spatial arrangement of the elevator, during the car ride home from the evening's dinner party, the couple are positioned in close proximity and engaged in banter that provides an introduction to their upcoming escapade, but their positions are fixed. Though the car might also be read as a conveyance of sorts, the fixed camera attached to the driver-side window of the car refuses the vertical movement that would indicate visually who is on top at any moment in their playful struggle. The sequence in the car figures Karin literally as the driving force behind their marriage, something that remains unacknowledged by Fredrick who is absorbed in his self-congratulatory monologue from the back seat. In choosing to confine the movement of his camera to the physical space of the elevator, however, Bergman explores how to represent movement that has been constricted. The denial of technological liberties enacts the elegant claustrophobia of the gender roles of the social class to which Karin and Fredrik Lobelius belong. Constriction affects Karin more than Fredrik, though he admits that she has always been the stronger of the two of them. (We eventually find out that he fails to keep his promise to take her along on his business trips as his real partner and secretary.) More than just cueing the foreplay engendered by the mechanical failings of the tiny elevator, the proximity of the camera mocks Karin's longing for intimacy in her marriage. After the couple emerge from their giddy night in the elevator and finally enter their apartment, the telephone rings and Karin's loving partner immediately reverts back to the company-man persona that she thought she had subdued the night before. Like the illusionary appearance of space and depth that the camera brings about when we see the couple reflected in the elevator's facing mirrors, the resolutions Fredrick has made the night before are also revealed to be illusory. In their home, the camera distances itself from her as her husband does. Through the open door of the next room we see Karin's realisation that the tenderness once again expressed by her husband has only been made possible by the artificial constraints of the elevator. The status quo of their gender roles and married life remain unperturbed.

In *Hus i helvete/Hell Breaks Loose* (Suzanne Taslimi, 2003), another couple gets stuck in an erotically invested elevator, but this time desire is complicated by understandings of how young Swedish women of Persian descent should behave before they are married. Whereas Bergman stalls upper-middle class gender relations only temporarily, the way that Taslimi conveys the lovers in her film through frames of romantic freedom and liberal Swedish society works to unsettle the status quo. The elevator sequence functions as one instantiation of the film's visual juxtaposition of themes of escape, freedom, and romantic choice with themes of oppression, exploitation, and confinement.

In this film, set in an apartment complex in suburban Sweden, three generations live together in one small apartment. The family, consisting of a grandmother, her son, his wife, and their three children are of 'utländsk härkomst' (foreign origin) and have been living in Sweden for at least one generation. With the exception of the grandmother, who speaks only Farsi, the entire family is fluent in Swedish; the mother and father of the family are bilingual, and their children communicate exclusively in Swedish. Serbandi (Hassan Brijany), the father and supposed head of the household, operates a catering company out of their kitchen and comically struggles to maintain his position of patriarchal authority amid steam, tensions, and seemingly endless familial bickering. His wife Nana (Caroline Rauf) chides him or completely disregards him and his mother laments having given birth to such a weak son. Minoo (Melinda Kinnaman), the eldest daughter and main character, is a young woman of around twenty-five who returns from America to attend her younger sister Gita's (Melize Karlge) wedding. Whereas Minoo overtly resists the suffocating protections of her father, Gita has made outward concessions to her father's moral uprightness, and attempts to maintain a façade of virginal purity for her father's sake.

The film hinges on intergenerational and intercultural conflict that arises between the independent Minoo and her equally obstinate father. Through a series of graphic flashbacks we discover that Minoo has spent the last few years in America, having been banished by her father for a pregnancy out of wedlock and an abortion. She has supported herself there as an erotic dancer and several flashback sequences in the film consist of disturbing, ominously repetitious handheld sequences of a man with a video camera shoving Minoo back onto a hotel bed.

About to be married, Gita finds herself caught between the 'traditional' values of her father and her sisterly love for the outlawed Minoo. She and her fiancé coordinate taking out the trash in order to have romantic pre-marital relations in, among other places, the elevator in their apartment building. In *Hell Breaks Loose*, the elevator becomes a space of stimulating escape laced with the titillating possibility of getting caught by neighbours and father alike. The elevator functions as a public space just beyond, but still precariously close to, the monitoring gaze of patriarchal authority *à la* Serbandi. The lovers take over the space, making it intimate and erotic. But when in their dishevelled excitement they attempt to squeeze in just one more quickie (up to the top floor and back), they get caught and are literally and figuratively exposed between storeys.

Taslimi constructs her elevator sequence using numerous overhead shots to establish the proximity of the lovers from above them. These paradoxically make the space of the elevator appear larger than the claustrophobic chaos of the family kitchen, where the camera bumps into bodies and hovers dangerously close to the bubbling pots on the stove. Taslimi intersperses these overhead shots above and down into the elevator with shots inside the elevator, and then from the space of the communal hallway outside. This juxtaposition allows us to track both the elevator and the conflict of the entire situation from a neighbour's point of view. As is the case with many elevators in Sweden, the door contains a window that allows its occupants to see out, but also to be seen. The interior positioning of the camera in the sequence situates us amid the erotically-trapped and jostling bodies in a manner akin to *Secrets of Women* (though perhaps less minutely choreographed), but whereas Bergman keeps the spectator decidedly within the aesthetic and social constraints of the real elevator space, Taslimi's inter-cuts outside and over Serbandi's hairy shoulder amount to a different, voyeuristic gesture. When Gita's comically frantic father hustles upstairs to reprimand them, his approach through the crowd that has gathered is shot with a destabilising hand-held camera followed by a jump cut of Serbandi's back repeated three times. Three times he is blocked, enraged and humiliated, by the elevator door he cannot open. The repetition emphasises his exclusion from the scene and foreshadows his position at the end of the film. Including the outside perspective allows Taslimi to edit the interior space of the elevator into a performative stage-space with the crowd of neighbours positioned as a nosy audience below it and the rhythmic alternation of interior and exterior perspectives emphasises the film's themes of escape and confinement.

The elevator suspends the couple momentarily between floors and thus dangles them symbolically between and within two sets of cultural behaviours. On one hand, their passion attests to their having fallen in love on their own (in contrast to the marriage that Serbandi attempts to arrange between Minoo and a Persian war veteran). On the other hand, the two feel compelled to hide their trysts in order to appease Gita's father. *Hell Breaks Loose* re-invests stereotypical scenes of romantic escape, of young Swedish lovers running out into nature, *à la Elvira Madigan* (Bo Widerberg, 1967), or *Sommaren med Monika/Summer with Monika* (Ingmar Bergman, 1952), with the ambiguously voyeuristic performance of desiring bodies enclosed in the metropolitan, mechanised space of the elevator.

The confluence of entrapment, release, desire, and performance, as evidenced by the elevator sequence, explodes in the dramatic climax of the film. On the day of the wedding, an ashamed Serbandi locks Minoo in her room. The virulent objections of the rest of the family have no outward effect on him; he is desperate to conceal her from the wedding guests. Inter-cut between shots of wedding festivities (including Serbandi's increasingly hysterical inebriation) are images of an equally desperate and strong Minoo who literally dismantles the room in which she is caged. She hacks apart the jail-like bars of her bed frame and then uses one to chop her way through the door. A final shot from the apartment reveals a sweaty and defiant Minoo walking out victoriously through the doorframe. Intent on exacting her revenge in the most public way possible, she makes her way backstage at the wedding reception and pre-empts the world-renowned belly dancer who has been hired for the evening. 'Den sköna Orientens farligaste orm' (The beautiful Orient's most dangerous snake), as announced by the tipsy MC, turns out instead to be Minoo performing a possessed strip-tease in front of her father and his guests. When Serbandi lunges toward her, Gita leaps on stage and defends her sister by wrapping her in the folds of her wedding dress, in response to which Serbandi stammers out his own retaliatory performance and reveals all the sweaty secrets kept by the women in his family. His wife is cheating on him with Leif the sewing machine repairman. Gita has long since given away her virginity (the one word he can unfortunately never get right in Swedish) and shouldn't be wearing white in the first place. Minoo he calls a whore. The shocked guests scurry home, muttering in shame and disbelief as they go, leaving only the 'disgraced' family in front of the camera. The wedding sequence culminates in a Last Supper-esque, mid-length shot of the family eating at the table of honour while the patriarch Serbandi is relegated off-screen where he remains invisible and excluded. For the first time in the film the family enjoys a peaceful meal together. As the film concludes, Serbandi's emasculation and humiliation are softened by his mother's invitation to come eat, to which he replies, 'Ja mor, jag kommer' (Yes mother, I'm coming). He never appears in the frame of the film again.

The visualisation of escape and constriction in *Hell Breaks Loose* performs a transgression of social roles and power relationships as they are figured in the beginning of the film. The film reclaims women's desire from stereotypical understandings of what that would mean in 'traditional' societies in which women conceal bodies in ways that differ from the ways in which they conceal them in Sweden (Serbandi constantly directs Minoo to put on more clothes and insists at one point that she wear Gita's more conservative attire to go out in public). The film works to bring women's desire out into the open to be acknowledged, affirmed, and flaunted in the face of a male position capable of disowning a daughter, and then hypocritically hiring a voluptuous, scantily-clad belly dancer for a wedding while demanding that daughters appear chaste.

Visuality or disclosure are not unambiguously positive categories in the film, however. *Hell Breaks Loose* remains critical of the objectification and exploitation to which exposed female bodies can be subjected in hypocritically 'free', 'western societies'. This position is represented by the American world of erotic dancing and figured in Sweden by Minoo's deadbeat Swedish boyfriend. In terms of the elevator sequence, Taslimi's editing strategy puts us everywhere around the couple, and might also implicate us as gawking observers in the spectacle of Gita's exposure. In an eerie parallel or foreshadowing of the video-camera violation in Minoo's flashbacks, the film opens with her younger brother filming Minoo's homecoming. The audience is implicated voyeuristically when he pans around to shoot directly into the film camera. The shot can be read as acknowledging that the audience is watching. In contrast to *Secrets of Women*, in which the couple escapes the elevator but remains within the frame of their social and gender roles, the women in *Hell Breaks Loose* both revel in confinement and then burst through it to push an ultimately loving, but utterly unreasonable, father figure out of the picture. In this film, the 'secrets of women' are performed, made public, and revealed to all, rather than remaining among women in the realm of a domestic living room conversation.

The Elevator and Ethnicity: Neo-Naturalistic conflict versus the Imaginary Space of Resolution

In addition to expressing the explicit and loudly perceptible tensions of a 'hus i helvete' (literally translated, a house in hell), by making use of techniques such as the close-up, film also conveys microscopic tensions and movements in situations that otherwise appear static. In gestures of realism, or in this instance, what verges on something like neo-naturalism, films (and filmic elevators) freeze, and then make perceptible, the interactions and conflicts that belie life's flow. In the case of *Hissen/The Elevator* (Renato Olivares Macias, 2003), these techniques are used in contriving a glimpse into intercultural Sweden. Aspects of this short film can be read as a kind of neo-naturalistic experiment in which people of different races and political affiliations are forced to interact (or duke it out, as the case may be). In this scenario, the film/camera both observes – and, importantly, magnifies – 'real life'. The interactions of large and diverse groups of people are condensed to the microscopic level of the two individuals trapped together. But the film also complicates the experiment by altering its variables. The way in which the film engages with binary systems, categories of mobility, stasis, proximity and distance remains ambiguous. It at once enacts binaries and offers the possibility of subverting them. Macias on one hand exploits the close-up and extreme close-up in a dissecting way and then on the other hand visually expands these with shots of an elevator set (a stage, if you will) that creates an imaginary, *resolutionary* space beyond the Petri dish.

The Elevator begins as elevator doors open onto an ambiguous space. It is not immediately apparent whether the camera is inside or outside the elevator. In contrast to the elevators in *Secrets of Women* and *Hell Breaks Loose*, there is no window to see in or out when the elevator doors are closed. Only when a young man in a hooded sweatshirt steps in and peers nervously behind him to see if he is being followed do we realise our position with the camera, decidedly inside the elevator. He presses the button to close the door. He is out of breath and panting softly. Faint sounds of a police siren and the inarticulate voices of a police radio are heard from outside. Suddenly a second man in a leather jacket squeezes in just as the doors are about to close. The camera pans left to follow him as he leans up against the wall. He too must catch his breath. In this movement left, the first man disappears out of the frame to the right. When the second man catches sight of the first he flashes a quick finger to his lips signaling their mutual interest in keeping quiet. Panning quickly right following his glance, we see the first man poised with his fist in the air on the verge of throwing a punch. They snarl at each other in tense silence, listening for the police footsteps outside to disappear. In a glowering close-up, the first man slips the hood of his sweatshirt off his closely-shaven head. This shot is followed by an extreme close-up in which the pores of the skin on his head fill the screen. The second man stares back at him as well, equally bald and equally furious. The first man in the elevator is a white neo-Nazi (from Stockholm, we find out later), the second a black anti-fascist (from Skåne). Though the elevator and the two protagonists in it hardly move in this sequence, the tension of the film has nonetheless been established as subtle movement. Béla Balázs theorises this aspect of film's potential for creating motion in a space in which motion is effectively, 'actually', suspended:

> By the movement of the camera or the flickering of the montage even the physical immobility of such static conditions could be mobilized and dramatized. This is a means of expression completely specific to the film. If for some reason or another movement is arrested in a scene on the stage or in the studio, then nothing moves there any more and there can be no question of tempo or rhythm. The film, however, possesses this possibility that the scene that is being shot may be completely frozen and motionless and yet the scenes projected on to the screen can nevertheless be in violent and varied motion. The characters may not move, but our glance may leap from the one to the other as it is carried by the camera. Men and things do not move but the camera shifts rapidly and excitedly from the one to the other and the movement of motionless pictures collated by the cutting may have a swift, wild rhythm, making us feel the inner movement of the scene in spite of its outer immobility. The scene in its entirety may be motionless in deadly numbness, like a stationary great machine. But the rushing close-ups show the throbbing of some tiny wheel of the clockwork. We see an eyelid twitch, a lip curl in the motionless figures, their immobility replete with utmost tension. (Balázs 1970:85)

At the level of narrative, *The Elevator* remains conventional in many respects as a film in which an odd couple find themselves stranded and must overcome their differences to make bearable their time together. At the level of formal representation, the film becomes more intriguing. Macias' juxtaposition of close-ups in the film (extreme and otherwise) with shots that extend the elevator into an imagined space provides relief from the oppressive performance of neo-naturalistic confrontation. Breaking the tense stand-off during which the camera panning back and forth is the only perceptible movement, a button is gingerly pressed, the doors close, and all hell breaks loose. The two men are immediately at each other's throats. The camera loses focus in the scuffle as the big, blurry forms of their bodies fill the screen with unsettling anger and violence. This initial, disorienting confrontation between the two men climaxes in a brutally palpable butting of their two shaved heads. This is captured in a high angle shot and then cut quickly with a mid-length shot in which the camera has shifted outside the 'real' space of the elevator and onto an elevator set, to show in slow motion the full length of their bodies as they fall onto their backs. These 'stage' shots are then quickly juxtaposed with high angle shots from close to each man's head as he shakes off the stunning blow. Back on their feet, though still visibly shaken, the neo-Nazi draws a knife which the anti-fascist then trumps by drawing a gun. Close-ups of the gun and of the faces of the two men in various degrees of focus again place the camera back in the 'real' space of the elevator but then continue to be inter-cut with shots of the staged space. While this might certainly be read as merely a practical solution to the challenges of making a film about an elevator (a solution that could likely be considered cheating by Bergman's standards), it also brings the film into dialogue with stage and theatrical representation by making a dialectical move between dissecting, limiting observation and a creative, imagined expansion. The film alternates between a closed-system of relationships (such as the two subjects in a closed experiment with a static, limited number of variables) and an opening for these relationships to be transcended imaginatively and visually.

Macias' premise of trapping his protagonists reveals the stilled space of the elevator to be alive with movement. In a similar way, the film freezes and isolates binary categories to reveal the fluctuation that persists underneath their deceptively immobile façade. *The Elevator* rehearses opposites at various levels of confrontation: white versus black, inside versus outside, primary versus secondary (as attested to in the dialogue between the two men when they argue like two children on a playground about who was in the elevator first), stasis versus movement (the camera creates movement even when the protagonists stand still), and even Muslim versus Christian. The final sequence of the film shows two women entering the elevator after the two men leave. One has brown eyes and a headscarf, the other has long blond hair. The formal rhythm and movement that animates the narrative also suggests the negotiability of these categories.

Balázs addresses the interaction between surfaces and underlying tensions in terms of the contrived conflicts of naturalism. In contrast to the naturalistic theatre, he claims, film provides a better microscope more capable of penetrating the surfaces of dramatic conflict. This is particularly the case in a drama such as *The Elevator* that lacks an apparent external event to initiate its conflict. The conflict between the two men originates in their hatred for one another, not in the mechanical malfunctioning of the elevator. Film's revelation of the minute workings of human interaction bests even Strindberg it seems. Balázs writes:

> The technique of the close-up which thus simplified the story of film and deepened and brought to dramatic life its smallest of details, succeeded in lending dramatic tension to a mere state or condition, without any external event at all. It was able to make us feel nerve-rackingly the sultry tension underneath the superficial calm; the fierce storms raging under the surface were made tangible by mere microscopic movements, by the displacement of a hair. Such films were unsurpassed in showing the Strindbergian moods in the savagely antagonistic silences *of human beings confined together in narrow spaces*. The micro-tragedies in the peace and quiet of ordinary families were shown as deadly battles, just as the microscope shows the fierce struggles of micro-organisms in a drop of water. (Balázs 1970:84-85, my emphasis)

In this passage Balázs references a film in which two robbers find themselves trapped in a time-released vault and the camera captures the men's every twitch and expression that on the stage would have remained imperceptible. The combination of cinematic claustrophobia and a performed survival of the fittest resonates with *The Elevator*, however, which, of all the films I consider, is the most explicit example of the elevator conveying the presumed tensions underlying Swedish multiculturalism.

Territorial boundaries and demarcation of space also underlie the narrative of the film. The two men compare their predicament to Robinson Crusoe, for instance, and bicker about who was first on the island/elevator and who would consequently have proprietary rights to it. They even decide to divide the elevator floor in two when it appears that they cannot share the space. They draw a line down the middle and then whoever crosses the line opens himself up to a blow of the other's choosing. Though bound by the limitations of the 'actual' walls of the elevator, they manipulate and rearrange it and make it meaningful to them. In contrast to *Secrets of Women*, in which the larger structures governing the relationship between the two people in the elevator does not change significantly after they leave it, in *The Elevator*, the space is altered by their presence. Magic-markered onto the walls alongside some tags and pictures of guns are windows through which views of bridges in Stockholm as well as other idyllic countryside vistas can be seen. The physical space of the elevator 'opens up' through these windows. Change is visualised in the graffiti the two men leave behind; the elevator into which the two women step at the end is not the same one that the two men stepped in the beginning. Formally and visually things have changed.

Though ending the film with the two women stepping up as the next 'contestants' might still be problematic in the sense that their encounter is still foreshadowed as automatically contentious (it is presumed that they will duke it out as well), overall *The Elevator* offers the possibility of seeing through and contending with claustrophobic stereotypes. The negotiations the two men undertake to endure their situation are eventually more comical than violent, despite initially attacking each other with fists and bodies and hands. The film can ultimately not avoid being about two cocky young men who argue, butt up against each other, trick each other into showing their weaknesses, and who are, equally, victims of their very human addiction to nicotine. They eventually almost get along – though they would never admit it.

Elevator as dangerous spectacle: *Lethal Film*

Livsfarlig film/Lethal Film (Suzanne Osten, 1988) offers a dystopic look at film's potentially destructive influence. It calls into question the innocence of the entire enterprise of making movies about the lives, bodies, and traumas of immigrants (and particularly of political refugees). The film is ambiguously set, 'Here somewhere – in a near future', in a shadowy post-apocalyptic hell in which the only films produced anymore are horror films, those being the ones that most approximate life. The film focuses on the nebulous intersection of film as entertainment, as representation, and as something like 'real life'. From the very beginning we are unsure whether the flame-filled, lawless world in which Emil (Etienne Glaser), the protagonist, finds himself has been directly caused by films or whether films just represent the horrors of the world as it is. In an opening scene, we watch the protagonist stare solemnly as a film expert is interviewed on the evening news in conjunction with a recent murder. The murderer has mutilated and positioned the victim's body in precisely the same pose as the victim of a recent horror movie. Film, the authority warns, resembles 'a bite from a poisonous snake – you can't get it out of your blood and it's a painful process to be brought back, back to reality'.[2] Cinematic representations seep into the bodies of their spectators. Film and reality are no longer distinguishable from one another and both will kill you. In other news that turns out to be central to the film, a group of political asylum seekers is reported escaped and on the run from authorities.

Emil has established himself as a reputable director of films that combine slapstick comedy with horror. Comic mutilation appears to be his speciality. Through *Lethal Film*, as in all of the snippets of films that appear in it, bodies nonchalantly explode and body parts are strewn everywhere. Shocking bursts of blood, severed limbs, and decapitations are simply a way of life. Human interaction has been reduced to gory rubble. It is a post-cinematic film, in the sense that the line between experience and filmic representation of experience has been exploded. The setting of the film resonates with Benjamin's oft-cited passage from his essay on art in the age of mechanical reproducibility in which he describes film's simultaneously destructive and revolutionary potential. No longer extricable from our bodies, film functions as a prosthetic device for understanding experience:

> Our bars and city streets, our offices and furnished rooms, our railroad stations and our factories seemed to close relentlessly around us. Then came film and exploded this prison-world with the dynamite of the split second, so that now we can set off calmly on journeys of adventure among its far-flung debris. With the close-up, space expands; with slow motion, movement is extended. And just as enlargement not merely clarifies what we see indistinctly 'in any case,' but brings to light entirely new structures of matter, slow motion not only reveals familiar aspects of movements, but discloses quite unknown aspects within them [...] (Benjamin 1999:117)

Emil's own journey of adventure begins when his twenty-something-year-old daughter Ella (Gunilla Röör), the child star of his early movies, condemns him for his complete inability to relate to the real world and leaves home. Their relationship has always been mediated by the camera, something for which she resents him. Ella has traded her life in show business for a job working with her boyfriend in a warehouse, a normal, 'real life' job with 'real' people. But the warehouse where she works exists on one of the lowest floors of a surreal department store full of old film props and movie paraphernalia. It is the underworld, filled with aisles of stacked crates and old film sets. The film explicitly rehearses the Orpheus and Eurydice myth as Emil follows Ella into the underworld into which she has fled. He must prove his faith in her existence apart from her image on film, apart from the mediation of the camera. As Orpheus, he of course doubts, and cannot resist pointing the camera on her as he has always done; and she vanishes. In his pursuit of Ella, Emil arrives at the idea for his next film. The particularly hefty bout of artistic malaise he has been experiencing is cured by the idea of eschewing 'fiction' film in the name of capturing the 'actual' lives of real people. He recruits his cast from the shadowy group of refugees who live and work in hiding in the warehouse. His producers agree to his bold new concept on the condition that he make it frightening enough to shock the audience. His footage and production techniques are eclectic. He films the gruesome stories of three South American women who have lost their children to dictators. A disturbed father tells of his son's self-sacrifice in Iran. A young man performs a moving first-person monologue recounting the demise of an innocent and mystified bull in a bull-fight. *Lethal Film* is quintessentially a meta-film about the spectacle of making films. To again cite Benjamin:

> The shooting of a film, especially a sound film, offers a hitherto unimaginable spectacle [...] In principle, the theater includes a position from which the action on the stage cannot easily be detected as an illusion. There is no such position where a film is being shot. The illusory nature of film is of the second degree; it is the result of editing. That is to say: *In the film studio the apparatus has penetrated so deeply into reality that a pure view of that reality, free of the foreign body of equipment, is the result of a special procedure – namely, the shooting by the specially adjusted photographic device and the assembly of that shot with others of the same kind.* The equipment-free aspect of reality has here become the height of artifice, and the vision of immediate reality the Blue Flower in the land of technology. (Benjamin 1999:115)

Emil exists in the grotesque state of trying to get enough distance from the camera to glimpse a reality behind it. The result is an awful spectacle as poignant episodes relating trauma coexist with wildly excessive scenes of the kind of passion and hysteria that Swedes supposedly repress, but which hot-blooded immigrants thrive on. There is crazed Flamenco dancing, a carnival parade, and absurdly directed attempts to record the everyday lives of these 'real people'. 'Just act like you'd normally act,' he says, 'Ok, now do it again, but more feeling this time.' Ultimately, Emil comes to the realisation that he has no control over the actions of his actors and that his attempts to script 'real life' have done more harm than good. He concedes that he has failed to represent the elusive complexity of their lives. In the end he gives up loading his camera with film.

Emil is conveyed to this underworldly spectacle set by a peculiar elevator. This elevator, its operator informs him as he steps inside, is a one-way elevator down. It never goes up again. In *Lethal Film*, the elevator symbolises Emil's desire to transcend technological artifice to achieve an immediate contact with reality. As he repeats several times throughout the film, he longs to just *live*. As the elevator descends past floor after floor of the department store, it tries to pierce layer upon layer of representation. But reaching an essential reality, a reality that Emil so desperately yearns for, is impossible, and the film continually reminds us so. Emil seeks immediate reality in the representation of political refugees, but finds that he is inextricable from the dystopic mechanical prosthesis that is his camera. But the supposedly dead-end elevator actually appears twice in the film, first on its way down, but then, toward the end of the film Emil and his sometimes lover Ingrid (Lena T. Hansson) ascend in it. The film revels in this ambiguous position.

In its sceptical gesture, *Lethal Film* exploits the slight-of-hand artifice of conveyance by pushing the director into the elevator. As a director of a film about 'ethnic' experience, Emil is held accountable for his selfish desire to represent stories of human trauma in an aesthetic form to be consumed by others. The film as a whole calls into question the reading of ethnicity in film as indicative of some understandable social reality. It remains a warning about the risks of depriving humans of their humanity by representing them. And yet, while simultaneously declaring the impossibility of making a meaningful film about human experience, *Lethal Film* nonetheless exists as such a film.

In conclusion

In some ways, writing about something as abstract as 'ethnicity' in these Swedish films echoes the risks addressed in *Lethal Film*: that condensing and representing enacts an objectifying violence on the people (and perhaps the films) it attempts to represent. Diverse, broad-ranging social contexts are necessarily isolated in order to be emphasised and explored. The movement of a large and complex body of films is halted and bound so that it can be pinned down for identification. However, it is the very difficulty of identifying exactly what and where elevators are that makes them an apt metaphor to express the experiences of people living together in small and increasingly diverse communities like Sweden. As a conveyance, the elevator disrupts fixed ideas of place and especially the connection between place and identity. Adapting to the close physical proximity of unfamiliar bodies assembled in a random elevator might suggest ways to address the challenges and sometimes uncomfortable adjustments necessary for diverse groups of people come to live together. Like people continually filling and emptying an abstract and imagined category like 'Sweden', the elevator is a place or category that is not entirely stable, but one which instead shifts and is not clearly at home anywhere. Elevators can be shifty, but also get stuck. They repeatedly fill up and empty out only to be filled up again. Like the nation itself, elevators give the appearance of stability and from an outside perspective look as though they are stilled – when, actually, they are often in transit from one storey – or story – to another.

References

Belázs, Béla (1970): 'The Face of Man'. In *Theory of Film: Character and Growth of a New Art*. Translated from the Hungarian by Edith Bone. New York: Dover Publications.

Benjamin, Walter (1999): 'The Work of Art in the Age of Mechanical Reproducibility', in *Selected Writings vol. 2, 1927-1934*. Translated by Rodney Livingstone and others; edited by Michael W. Jennings, Howard Eiland, & Gary Smith. Cambridge, MA & London: The Belknap Press of Harvard University.

Marks, Laura U. (2000): *The Skin of the Film: Intercultural Cinema, Embodiment, and the Senses*. Durham & London: Duke University Press.

Wright, Rochelle (1998): *The Visible Wall: Jews and other Ethnic Outsiders in Swedish Film*. Carbondale & Edwardsville: Southern Illinois University Press.

Wright, Rochelle (2005): '"Immigrant film" in Sweden at the Millennium'. In Nestingen, Andrew & Trevor Elkington (eds): *Transnational Cinema in a Global North: Nordic Cinema in Transition*. Detroit: Wayne State University Press.

Notes

1. My thanks to Mark Sandberg for bringing this film to my attention and for helping me with feedback in writing this article. I am grateful also to Tytti Soila who provided much guidance and encouragement at the early research stages of this project and the Fulbright Program for enabling me to see many films to which I would not otherwise have had access.
2. The English translation from dialogue is my own.

Local • National • Global

Local Cinema: Indexical Realism and Thirdspace in Kestner's *Blue Collar White Christmas*

Britta Timm Knudsen

The Danish filmmaker Max Kestner received two film prizes in 2005 (Årets Sær-Robert and the Dreyer Prize) for his staged documentary *Nede på jorden/Blue Collar White Christmas* (2003). This film is a documentary about a workplace, the lifeboat factory Viking in Esbjerg, a port on the west coast of Jutland. We follow four main characters in different situations at work and at home through a period of possible lay-offs due to outsourcing of part of the production to Thailand. Taking this film as an instance of the genre 'staged documentary', I want to argue that this genre presents reality through paradox – as being between the authentic and the performative – and, as such, is a development of the *cinéma vérité* from the sixties. I will also show that this genre offers the opportunity for the filmmaker to intervene in more obvious ways than those normally allowed in documentaries.

Apparently contradictory terms such as 'staged documentary', 'performative realism' (Gade and Jerslev 2005) and 'theatrical hunger for reality' (Knudsen and Thomsen 2002; Gran 2004)[1] express the transgression of oppositions which currently dominate the cultural sphere and its criticism. When it comes to documentaries we have an inherent quality of the genre which is now challenged: the 'indexical ability to document what is in front of the camera' (Sandbye 2005:120). Documentaries no longer simply document what is in front of the camera. The expression itself – 'staged documentary' – exposes theatricality as a postmodern condition (all is representation) and documentary as an expression of the longing for unmediated reality. The hunger for reality and theatricality are two sides of the same coin, so to speak. As early as 1959, the critic Goffman showed the performative presentation of self to be an inherent condition of the social sphere. We now have to take these insights into account and replace or deconstruct the contradiction into different modes or degrees of theatricality.[2] In today's media, *celebrity* as well as *ordinariness* are constructed (Moores 2004:23), but we deal with different degrees of construction. Celebrities –

actors, politicians and members of the royal family – are shown in private, backstage situations (the documentary impulse) and ordinary people are put into staged situations which have the potential of making celebrities out of them.

Blue Collar White Christmas is a classical documentary in the sense that it explores, explains and documents the others, 'the poor, the disadvantaged, the politically disenfranchised, or the "exotic"' (cit. Beattie 2004:107). It calls the seventies to mind because the people portrayed are the workers 'on the floor'. Documentaries, semi-documentaries and fiction films all share the socialist realistic themes so often used in this period.

In general, Danish cinema has an ongoing love story with realism, and Langkjær defines Danish postwar realism as movies with 'socially implicated themes, that is, the ability or lack of ability of the protagonist to react properly to or to manage his or her social situation' (Langkjær 2002:24). Other contemporary Danish feature films such as Per Fly's *Bænken/The Bench* (2000), or Anette K. Olesen's *Forbrydelser/In Your Hands* (2004) are also thematically socialist realistic and the filmmakers' gaze at the depicted world is an anthropological one, closely following the deterministic, downwards spiralling track of the protagonists, or investigating the micro-sociological relations in an enclosed space.

Thematically, the documentary is part of the contemporary nostalgia for the seventies, but aesthetically it comes closer to avant-garde experiments such as those performed by situationism in the sixties which, inspired by Lefebvre and Vaneigem, 'defied the alienation of capitalist society and defended the poetic qualities of everyday life' (Sandbye 2005:141) as well as the more formal experiments of Danish documentary filmmaker, poet and sports journalist Jørgen Leth in *66 scener fra Amerika/66 Scenes from America* (1982) and *Nye scener fra Amerika/New Scenes from America* (2003).

Indexical Realism

Staged documentaries, performative realist art (interactive forms), and cultural experiments (reality-tv) are all forms which challenge our concept of realism. How can we adequately conceive of realism in the light of postmodernism and the linguistic nature of our relation to the world?

In the influential work by the German literary scholar Erich Auerbach, *Mimesis. The Representation of Reality in Western Literature* (first published in English in 1953), we have a classical definition of mimesis as a re-presentation of everyday events in the lives of ordinary people. The classical definition of realism is iconic, pointing to a world the text refers to and of which the text is independent. Meanwhile, documentaries operate at the indexical level of the image, as John Corner points out (cit. Beattie 2004:14) because, in this case, the 'actors' in the scenes are in fact real workers at the factory Viking in Esbjerg; they do not simply act like them. Corner makes a distinction between realism in fiction and realism in the documentary-genres, a distinction which relates to the different impacts on the viewer. In fiction, a certain kind of '*imaginative* relationship' is provided between the viewer and the events on the screen; documentary, in contrast, provides an *inferential* relationship between the represented events and the viewer (Beattie 2004:15). Corner seems to advance the argument that documentaries primarily try to move the beholder logically through a convincing re-presentation of a situation. One must add to this that throughout the nineties we have witnessed a large number of documentaries (and reality-formats) which are increasingly aimed at producing sensual and emotional effects on the viewer.

This indexical realism can be seen as taking its point of departure in the essay by Roland Barthes on photography, *Camera Lucida* (2000; first published 1980). In this essay Barthes develops a contextual, phenomenological relation between the photo and its viewer. Barthes does not discuss the semiotic signification of photography as an abstract relation of signification to a disembodied viewer, but he points to the sensual, indexical relation beween a given photo and its viewer – meaning its direct and concrete sensual effects on an embodied viewer.

In contemporary realist artworks and genres the relation between the text and the viewer/reader is essential in at least three different ways:

1) a phenomenological realism which peacefully consolidates the emotional relation between viewer and work/text.
2) a second kind of realism, which conceives of the expressions as rebellious attacks on representation and the reading/viewing situation as an experience of the *limits of representation* (Deleuze 1985, Prendergast and Cohen 1995, Foster 1996). Prendergast sees this concept of realism also at work in the canonical realist texts (Balzac, Zola); Deleuze relates it to Italian neorealism and Foster points to the traumatic realism in the arts in the USA during the 80s.
3) a dynamical contextual realism which crosses the boundaries between work/viewer/context and points to the dynamical potential of such crossings.

A relational perspective considers both the relation between an artwork and its viewer and between an artwork and its surrounding context. These relations become dynamical. Indexical realism is a precise term for this because it points to a physically closer relation beween image and viewer and because the reality presented in the artwork could be a regular piece of reality (montage) in avant-garde artworks. Furthermore, I have argued that the nineties in Denmark saw a considerable rise of this kind of indexical realism in art and culture. Traces of reality and concretion of experience replaced the iconic representation of reality, just as different levels of theatricality replaced the simple dichotomy between authenticity and theatricality. What characterises art and culture in the nineties – although self-reflexive and in certain ways theatrical – is the hunger for reality (Knudsen 2003).

Realism in art and culture in the nineties dealt with traces of reality (closeness) at different levels. In that respect it is indexical and it demonstrates its roots in the avant-garde movements. The indexicality is seen at the three analytical levels: at the level of the author, at the level of the actor and at the level of the receiver/reader/viewer. In body-art performances – such as in the case of Elke Krystufek or Franco B. – all three levels interact.

The feature Dogme film *Idioterne/The Idiots* (dir. Lars von Trier, 1998) serves as a good example (and maybe the only one when it comes to movies) of the three levels being present simultaneously. The writer-director, Lars von Trier, is directly involved in and visible in the scenes as an interviewer in the 'simulated' semi-documentary interview-sequences with the actors. These sequences play a role as a second level of enunciation and function as a documentary frame for the story – but it is nevertheless, of course, only one level of the story. The actors are directly, bodily involved in the sometimes bodily disturbing scenes. The viewer is physically affected by the haptic images, not being able to achieve enough distance to identify with the images, but is, rather, immersed into them (Marks 2000:188). Thus, the boundaries between the film and the world are called into question thematically (the relation between being and playing is the theme of the film), structurally (by the semi-documentary interview-sequences) and formally/directly by the employment of actors with Down's Syndrome from 'outside' as an avant-garde element in the work as a whole. *The Idiots* as a work of art highlights the limits of its own representation, not as an attack on representation but as a dynamical way of conceiving the work/viewer/context relations.

In the nineties, different strategies were used in the arts in general to 'break down' the boundaries between the work of art and its context. You could *intervene* in the world like Superflex did with their Guarana Power soft drink, produced in Brazil and branded the American way. Or you could make *sociological investigations* of the social space by means of art (Sophie Calle pursuing people with her video camera, or Marco Evaristti putting small goldfish in a food-processor to see if people would press the button, or Susan Hinnum investigating the dating market). Or you could directly *copy* or *repeat* existing well-known environments, making the viewers very uncertain of the kind of project or world presented to them. This applies to Swedish artist Annika Lundgren's fake guided tourist tours or *Danes for Bush*, a satirical miming of an election campaign in the autumn of 2004 in the USA.[3]

In these examples, context is directly influenced by artful interventions, often in very direct ways (the Danish museum which exhibited the goldfish in the foodprocessor was sued, and the Brazilian guarana farmers felt the very concrete results of the art experiment), and often discursively, in discussions of the political role of the arts, sex, power and ethics.

Contemporary Danish Documentaries

The historical heritage not only of contemporary documentaries but also of certain *avant garde* experiments in the feature film (Lars von Trier) derives from the *cinéma vérité* (France) and Direct Cinema (Great Britain and USA) in the sixties. Direct Cinema is defined as 'a filming method employing hand-held cameras and live, synchronous sound' (Mamber 1974:1) and 'the act of filming real people in uncontrolled situations' (ibid.:2). The filmmaker is supposed to be an observer attempting not to alter the situations he witnesses. Non-interference, no added music and narration were key words in the Direct Cinema wave. Lots of documentaries on the contemporary Danish scene have adopted this fly-on-the-wall principle. *Cinéma vérité*, on the contrary, takes into consideration the performance and self-consciousness that the presence of the cameras provoke and the result is that '*cinéma vérité* is a practice which documents a performance *and* which has the capacity to take the subject (and the viewer) beyond or through performance to an authentic and truthful revelation of being' (Beattie 2004:93).

In this historical frame, staged documentary seems to be the adequate form of an indexical mode in which the kind of world presented to the viewer is already a result of the filmmaker's intervention in the referential world. In terms of American documentary theorist Bill Nichols' documentary 'modes', staged documentary seems to place itself between the reflexive mode and what we can call the performative mode (Nichols 1991, 1994). We must add the performative mode to Nichols' original four modes: 1) the expository, didactic mode with a voice-over expressing its clear-cut vision of an issue; 2) the observational mode played out in the Direct Cinema experiments beginning in the sixties; 3) the interactive documentary telling stories by the intermediary of witnesses; and 4) the reflexive documentary mode which highlights the representation itself. The performative documentary mode represents the historical world by means of poetic, expressive and rhetorical strategies.

Two of the grand old men in Danish documentary, Jørgen Leth and Jon Bang Carlsen, as well as the woman filmmaker Jytte Rex (with her *Veronikas svededug/Veronica's Veil*, 1977; Isolde, 1989; and *Silkevejen/Silk Road*, 2004), explore the mythological narrations as well as the sensuous, poetic quality of everyday life. They work with the crossing of the reflexive mode and the performative mode in their films, beginning with the brilliant *66 Scenes from America* (Leth, 1982) and ending with *Portræt af Gud/Portrait of God* (Carlsen, 2001). They explore the staging of reality represented at different levels. Leth enters a reflexive layer by letting his actors show they play themselves (and prefigures in that respect the situation of the reality-tv of the nineties). These documentaries explore identity as *presentation of self* (Goffmann 1990) or as performative identity in process due to the presence of the camera. Meyrowitz has used the term 'middle-region behavior' to describe the behaviour in-between an onstage public behaviour and a private backstage behaviour, a term which helps us to characterise the explorations undertaken in these films (Meyrowitz 1985:47).

Carlsen uses a more common meta-strategy by making the level of enunciation partly visible. Leth and Carlsen both usher in a global turn in Danish documentary, which continues throughout the nineties. Beyond these two characteristics – the meta-fictional impulse and the turning toward more global spheres – a last main trend must be mentioned (Bondebjerg 2002, Jerslev 2004): the great interest in the private, intimate spheres.

The private becoming public as a 'new dominance of various forms of first person speech' (Dovey 2000:103) is evident all over the cultural sphere but especially in new media and new genres (internet, video diaries, webcams, reality formats). All these forms of expression must be analysed as staged and authentic utterances at one and the same time. Authentic because of the indexical realism already mentioned, but authentic also because we as viewers/readers experience them as authentic. We can baptise the latter form of authenticity a symbolic authenticity, according to Jansson (Jansson 2002: 439).

The television series *Min.../My...* (2002) – in which six young filmmakers from the film academy were given the assignment of turning the camera towards themselves in order to produce intimate film statements – is a good Danish example of the tendency towards intimacy in the documentaries of the nineties. The documentary *Min elskede/My beloved*, by Dorthe Høeg Brask, about her own love story and break up with the lead singer of the famous Danish rockband Kashmir (he is a celebrity in Denmark) shows indexicality at three levels: the writer-director is directly implied, at the acting level she 'plays' herself, and the referential world is directly influenced by the represented world. The process is filmed in real time, an 'I' in process and transformation.

The very interesting thing about this project is the way Høeg Brask portrays her own vulnerability. She does not describe herself as a victim; but her self-portrait is far from flattering. It is this refusal of self-idolisation which makes the film interesting. The filmmaker Thomas Heurlin did the same thing with *Dømt til at være far/Sentenced to Be a Father* (2001), which is a self-portrait showing his difficulties in accepting the daughter he fathers as a result of a one night stand. Not to mention the Norwegian prize-winning documentary entitled *Alt om min far/All About My Father* (2002) by Even Benestad, which shows the enormous difficulties the son of a bi-gendered father has in accepting the alternating body-image of the parent. These projects put the actors depicted at risk socially, but their status as subjects of enunciation naturally saves them from total social condemnation. Exposing one's vulnerability and lack of perfection has become a sign of social power.

What Kind of Gaze?

Max Kestner has also produced a self-portrait, *Rejsen på ophavet/Max by Chance* (2004), about his own childhood in the seventies. He was an only child of hippy parents, who lived in strong opposition to the normative bourgeois society and preached solidarity with the workers. So much so that the father of little Max was disappointed with the promising intellectual skills of his son. He wanted him to become a real member of the working class! Visually, the documentary employs a lot of different kinds of images: private photos, press-cuttings, movie extracts, commercials etc.

Auditorily, the filmmaker uses extracts of music and his own voice as a deadpan, emotionally uninvolved voice-over commenting on the photos at a tremendous pace. Sometimes the voice-over points excessively to the images shown ('Under this table I have witnessed many family dinners'), or reveals something invisible ('This is a door just shut by my father') which, in spite of the excessive amount of speech and images, provides the documentary with aura and mystery.

The documentary develops the theme of belonging and becoming, but the point of departure is not similarity between clan members, but difference: 'How could I, as the voice-over declares, 'a normal person, have such a pair of parents who live in a commune, walk barefoot, sleep from time to time in the backyard, and see the world as black and white?' The relationship between Max and his parents seems to be random and not based on cause and effect, or deterministic liaisons. Nevertheless, in *Blue Collar White Christmas*, Kestner emerges as a politically engaged young filmmaker focusing on the eventual victims of globalisation and following in the footsteps of his socialist father.

What kind of gaze does Max Kestner aim at the world portrayed in *Blue Collar...*? The main 'character' is the workplace. The factory Viking, at Esbjerg, produces lifeboats, and the teams work in strictly gender-separated zones: we follow one female and one male team, on the job and at home. The female team consists of seven women, but our main focus is guided towards two of them, Anna and Lotte. In the male team the spotlight is on Henrik Tobiesen, the young apprentice, and Henrik Kragelund, his master. The dramatic plot in the documentary centers around the firing of twenty-three workers due to outsourcing to Thailand. Who will have to go?

Williams (1999) enumerates six types of gazes having to do with the relation between the filmmaker and the filmed world:

1) the clinical or professional gaze: e.g. the non-intervening gaze which the Direct Cinema-maker aims at his object
2) the accidental gaze: accidental live footage from crime scenes or catastrophes, e.g. the beating of Rodney King, and the terrorist attacks of September 11 2001
3) the helpless gaze: in which an intervention is desirable but impossible to carry out
4) the endangered gaze:[4] e.g. live footage from war or catastrophe zones, the recent Tsunami in South-East Asia
5) the humane gaze: e.g. in which the documentary focuses on an emotional response to a difficult situation
6) the interventional gaze: which places the filmmaker at the same level as the object.

Kestner's gaze is both clinical, humane and interventional. He comments on his own, slightly ironical, perspective by panning to a high-angle shot once the scene is set as a kind of staging of his own gaze coming from outer space. This formal feature relates to one of the final scenes in which Anna and her husband Henning are standing outside on a clear and frosty night watching the stars and contemplating the possibilities of life 'out there'. The documentary presents itself as visible proof of the gaze from above. 'The above' is opposed to the 'down here' as an ironic commentary on the divine as opposed to the earthly. The documentary focuses on certain oppositions between the earth and the sky, between a panoramic view of life and the rootedness in the everyday life, between visions/dreams and realities, between everyday life and leisure time. A formal characteristic of the documentary is to orchestrate these oppositions at the same non-hierarchical, pragmatic, horizontal level.

Blue Collar White Christmas is at one and the same time self-reflexive and performative. It makes use of poetic strategies (music, stills, and specific staged moments) in order to analyse the relation beween the small and the very big, but also of self-reflexive strategies – most of the time in a slightly ironic tone of voice. *To be able to see*, or *to be able to predict* or *guess* the future are very important issues throughout the whole film. At the strategic level, in the management discourse of the Viking-enterprise, it is called being visionary and making prognoses. The brand-concept *We Care* points directly to the ethical (social) responsibility of the enterprise. At the level of the 'actors', you can get yourself a pair of glasses in order not to be visually lost in space (as does Henrik, the apprentice), or you can get in touch with a clairvoyant who tries to predict what is coming in her crystal ball. The focus on the willingness to look into the future corresponds thematically to the opacity of the future in post-traditional societies. All the strategies, making prognoses, buying glasses and looking into crystal balls, are aimed at trying to cope with the *opacity of the future of the well-known place*.

As already established, Kestner's gaze presents itself as clinical, humane and interventional. But what kind of identity do the 'actors' perform in the documentary? Are they presented as helpless victims of globalisation? No, certainly not: they are represented and represent themselves according to the Butlerian idea of performativity as a citation of the law (Butler 1993:12) producing agency. In documentaries and in reality-tv the 'actors' involved perform as *themselves*. As already stated, the camera installs a performance layer. But the 'actors' also perform *as others* in satirical ways. At a Christmas party one of the main characters, Anna, a smart young woman, performs a gentle parody of the mid-level manager Jørgen to show how *he* would react to the women's idea of starting a production on their own. His remark – through Anna's slightly distorted voice – 'You cannot do without us' is obviously also a gender-commentary. But – perhaps more importantly – we also witness the 'actors' *performing* as themselves although *interpellated*.

Anna gives us a very good example of this. Having been told by the clairvoyant that 'you have a pair of shoes which your feet do not like' (which in the documentary seems to be an irrelevant observation) she puts all her shoes on display on her bed and finally picks the pair she thinks it is. This scene is a very tender and precise illustration of agency playing itself out in an oscillation between the unpredictable law and self-determination (finally she got rid of the pair of shoes *she* never liked). In this scene she performs as herself through the appropriation of the interpellated identity. It seems to be a very clear example of framed identity-making which is both *interpellated*, forcing us to become subjects of particular discourses, and *represented*, offering modes of representation in order to construct particular subjectivities (Storey 2003:80-81).

This oscillation between self-determination and interpellation is also played out in the film in terms of global and local identities. Glocalisation (Robertson 1995) – or the dynamical relation between global forces and local place – is without any doubt the main topic of *Blue Collar...* In the following I will claim that the documentary not only shows a global turn like the one Bondebjerg sees in the Danish documentary in the nineties, but the documentary also orchestrates the relation between local and global forces as a dynamical relation. Providing well-known places with poetic quality and being inventive of and with space are the formal challenges the documentary offers in return for the opacity of the future.

The Globalised Place

There is an ever-increasing focus on the relations between global and local forces in politics, culture and economics. The local and the global are no longer theorised as a dichotomy between the organic and differentiated (local culture) and the standardised and inauthentic (global economy and cultural impact). The global and the local are dynamically related and simultaneously produced as a result of their interdependence (Robertson 1995).

Globalisation is now understood as the correlation between connectedness, mobility and permeability of borders (Jansson 2004:15). Since the media-related time-space compression results in the world getting smaller, one could easily jump to the conclusion that physical location is of no or little importance in our world of saturated communication. This seems not to be the case. On the contrary, it seems to be a fact that place – as the phenomenological location of the body in the anthropological place (Augé 1992) – is more pertinent than ever due to globalisation. Places are no longer just local, they are phantasmagorical (Giddens 1990:24) because influenced by distant forces. Tomlinson, Morley, Appadurai, Featherstone and others have described globalisation as a de-territorialisation which means 'the loss of the "natural" relation of culture to geographical and social territories' (Tomlinson 1999:107). Tomlinson describes the ambivalence that follows upon the phantasmagoria of places: it brings cultural uncertainty but also an openness to the world which is new.

What happens to the appropriation of places when they become phantasmagorical? Can place be appropriated as mine, or others', or something in-between? We can try to get an answer to these questions through an analysis of *Blue Collar White Christmas*.

Just as the dichotomy between fiction and reality is left behind in the term of 'staged documentary', we do not witness a simple dichotomy between the standardised global and the diffentiated local in the documentary. Henrik the apprentice asks Henrik the master what to expect of the annual Christmas party at Viking and gets the answer: the usual, always the same thing. The predictability of local everyday life which ties a known past to a presumably known future has in fact come to an end because of the 'opacity' of the future due to global forces. My claim is here that the documentary stages the projection of the past into the future as a nostalgic mode – a past that we can kiss good-bye.

The distant forces dominating the local workplace of Viking are very present in the form of the threat of losing jobs, but the distant forces are also present through media representations. September 11 – and the images on tv of the burning towers – plays an overwhelmingly phantasmagorical role in creating the perception that the global threat has come closer to ordinary people's lives. In *Blue Collar...* the traumatic event is often said to have had such an impact that one would prefer to stay on the ground. Henrik the apprentice, saving money and gambling a bit, has a dream of going away for a while. His plan is not realised because he has to negotiate it with his terror-frightened girlfriend. Outsourcing and the threat of terror are expressions of the interconnectedness between the global and the local. The ambivalence toward this interconnectedness is clear: greater fear but also greater possibilities for mobility.

While Henrik is planning his long trip to the East and Henning and Anna are intending to spend their summer holidays in Turkey, the possibility of a company trip to Thailand is also suggested. We follow Anna and Henning in one of the most touching sequences of the film, on a one-day trip to the national capital. Henning has not been to Copenhagen for over twenty years. They go to Tivoli, reinforcing the fact that Copenhagen IS Tivoli for the tourist, a fairytale Capital, a nineteenth-century Disneyland for tourists. Entering the capital, it is experienced as a foreign landscape: exotic, impenetrable and aesthetically fascinating.

The camera takes close-up shots through the windscreen examining the faces of the explorers of the foreign country. The viewer closely follows travellers' reactions and we never see what they see. A panoramic view-point is never established, and we follow our social actors being bodily 'lost in space' and their difficult navigation in this wilderness. The street names are difficult to decipher (Nørre Farimagsgade hardly possible to pronounce), and the Esbjerg couple are obviously in unknown territory. Copenhagen is not experienced as something any more familiar than Marmaris or Bangkok – mentioned destinations for concrete travels – even if Copenhagen is so much closer culturally and geographically.

Esbjerg is directly connected to the global forces, which makes the distance to the national capital even greater. In this respect, the national level does not play a predominant role any more. Globalisation draws different borders between the familiar and the unknown. Copenhagen is experienced as just as exotic as any other big city, and it is the experience of it through local eyes that are communicated to us as viewers. Safely returned, Anna entertains her co-workers about the difference between 'out there' and 'back home', laughing out loud at this expression of her own experience. This is clear evidence that the relation between the familiar and the unknown does not have a fixed topography; it is a structural relation in which the familiar and the unknown have multiple combinations. The local can relate directly to the global, and the feeling of being at home can be linked to both, just as the linguistically and culturally close can appear infinitely strange. It is quite obvious that different audiences relate differently to the documentary, depending on whether they are from the provinces or live in the capital and find the Esbjerg couple themselves very exotic. The aim of Kestner is neither to point to the uneven timespace compression nor to the still great inequalities in the distribution of the power to master culture intellectually and bodily. His aim as a documentary film maker is not to treat the working class as powerless or exotic, but, on the contrary, as capable of mastering 'glocal' challenges.

The Invention of Space

Michel de Certeau (1984) analyses spatial practices such as walking in the city as a speech act which, beyond the planned intentions, adds more levels – mythological or utopian – to the city. To make use of something – a pedestrian activity is for example a certain use of the city – is a signifying practice which expresses an appropriation of space (in a phenomenological sense). We appropriate space through storytelling, memory and dream (de Certeau 1984:105). These are practices that invent spaces because the way concrete places are experienced is 'inseparable from the dreamed place' (ibid.:103). Places can be haunted by memory and legends, and they can be dreamt. *Blue Collar White Christmas* points to this inventive practice by taking the genre of staged documentary literally. On three occasions the documentary invents new space in well-known places.

Henrik the apprentice is a main character in the first scene. In his spare time he window-shops at travel agencies, looks through catalogues, plays the national lottery and one-armed bandits. On one occasion we suddenly see Henrik placed in a mute staged scenery – as a still life painting. He is wearing a Hawaiian-shirt and the background is a kitsch-painted beach motif with palm trees and blue water. Henrik leaves the scene and his fellow one-armed bandit players are suddenly dressed in Hawaiian-shirts without being aware of it. This demonstrates that distant exotic places are available technologically to a post-tourist (Urry 1990) or that mediated places are also appropriated in a concrete physical manner (Jansson 2004). The staged images not only show us that the local and global are interconnected but, equally, that the imaginary and the documentary impulse co-exist.

Henrik the master is the main character in the second scene. He is standing in his workplace looking up for a moment. The viewer experiences a sharp shift to an outdoor setting showing Henrik looking through the foliage of a withered beech in the last afternoon rays of sunshine. This image is aestheticised and shows a more diffuse longing, expressed through the poetic quality the documentary lends to everyday life. The final scene of the documentary is staged as a realisation of the nostalgic memory of the white Christmases of our childhood. Kestner is literally letting it snow – artificially – on the long tables at which the women are manoeuvering the large lifeboats without them noticing the snow. Kestner lets the dream come true for the viewers as if he were saying: Look, paradise is here and now.

Kestner constructs a kind of *Thirdspace* (Soja 1996) which shows us how the social actors connect mentally to the places. Soja uses the term to deconstruct the Lefebvrien categories of lived and conceived space (strategic forces and everyday forms of living). These intertwine and influence each other in dynamical ways. Soja links the dynamic forces – the becoming of a place – to their (re)appropriation of the memory inherent in the place in order to link has-been to becoming; memory to future. Thirdspace becomes what Lefebvre calls 'a possibility machine' (Soja 1996:81), a space at one and the same time *referential*, *remembered* and *utopian*.

In the final scene the image has a trialectic quality. The viewer witnesses the everyday, repetitive movements of the workers at Viking in the wintertime. At the same time, the snow falling down is an accomplishment of the wish of a white Christmas, which demonstrates that images documenting life do not have to be only referential but can also be imaginary and utopian. The images express the desire and nostalgic longings of the actors in the images. The final scene in Blue Collar White Christmas is at one and the same time a representation of a 'real' scene, a nostalgic memory re-staged, and the staging of a desire.

Conclusion

The realism of the staged documentary *Blue Collar White Christmas*, on the one hand, inherits the formal features of the *cinéma vérité* from the 60s by being performative realist; on the other hand, it transgresses the dichotomy between realism in fiction which installs an '*imaginative* relationship between the viewer and the events on the screen' and realism in documentaries, which 'in contrast, provides an *inferential* relationship between the represented events and the viewer' (Beattie 2004:15). Kestner transgresses the old dichotomy between the transparency and the mediated nature of the documentary as specific medium. A staged documentary is a third term, neither simply documenting, nor framing (and thereby altering) the real, but creating new images of the real. Kestner does not, as in the political seventies, want to make a statement about the world; he wants to evoke the poetic quality of a rather profane everyday life and to show how ordinary people develop agency in spite of the opacity of the future. They are not portrayed as political heroes, ideologically oppressed, or victims of distant forces, but just ordinary people living their subjected subjectivities.

Blue Collar White Christmas portrays not only a group of people but, even more, a group of places. The notion of place in the documentary is investigated phenomenologically at different levels: 1) the rootedness is seen through the relation of body to place as experiencing the well-known places or getting lost in the unfamiliar places; 2) as something one invests in emotionally and mentally, through memory, legends and dreams; 3) as something invented through the image-layer of the film. Technology and art are understood here as tools that help the viewer to experience places as pragmatic utopia.

References

Auerbach, Erich (1953): *Mimesis. The Representation of Reality in Western Literature.* Translated from the German by Willard R. Trask. Princeton, New Jersey: Princeton University Press.

Augé, Marc (1992): *Non-Lieux. Introduction à une Anthropologie de la Surmodernité.* France: Seuil.

Barthes, Roland (2000): *Camera Lucida.* Translated from the French by Richard Howard. London: Vintage.

Beattie, Keith (2004): *Documentary Screens. Nonfiction Film and Television.* London: Palgrave Macmillan.

Bondebjerg, Ib (2002): 'Det sociale og det poetiske blik. Den nye danske dokumentarfilm'. *Kosmorama* 229, 18-40.

Butler, Judith (1993): *Bodies That Matter. On the Discursive Limits of 'Sex'.* New York and London: Routledge.

De Certeau, Michel (1984): *The Practice of Everyday Life.* Translated from the French by Steven Rendall. Berkeley, Los Angeles & London: University of California Press.

Deleuze, Gilles (1985) : *Cinéma II. L'Image-Temps.* Paris: Minuit.

Dovey, Jon (2000): *Freakshow. First Person Media and Factual Television.* London: Pluto Press.

Foster, Hal (1996): *The Return of the Real. The Avant-Garde at the End of the Century.* Cambridge: The MIT Press.

Gade, Rune & Anne Jerslev (eds) (2005): *Performative Realism. Interdisciplinary Studies in Art and Media*. Copenhagen: Museum Tusculanum Press.

Giddens, Anthony (1990): *The Consequences of Modernity*. Copenhagen: Hans Reitzel.

Goffman, Erving (1990; 1959): *The Presentation of Self in Everyday Life*. Harmondsworth: Penguin.

Gran, Anne-Britt (2004): *Vår teatrale tid. Om iscenesatte identiteter, ekte merkevarer og varige mén*. Lyaker: Dynamo Forlag.

Jansson, André (2002): 'Spatial Phantasmagoria – The Mediatization of Tourism Experience'. *European Journal of Communication* 17:4, 429-443.

Jansson, André (2004): *Globalisering – kommunikation och modernitet*. Lund: Studentlitteratur.

Jerslev, Anne (2004): *Vi ses på tv – medier og intimitet*. Copenhagen: Gyldendal.

Knudsen, Britta Timm & Bodil Marie Thomsen (eds) (2002): *Virkelighedshunger. Nyrealismen i visuel optik*. Copenhagen: Tiderne Skifter.

Knudsen, Britta Timm (2003): 'The Eyewitness and the Affected Viewer. September 11 in the Media'. *Nordicom Review* 24:2, 117-126.

Langkjær, Birger (2002): 'Realism and Danish Cinema'. In *Realism and 'Reality' in Film and Media*. Copenhagen: Museum Tusculanum Press.

Mamber, Stephen (1974): *Cinéma Vérité in America: Studies in Uncontrolled Documentary*. Cambridge, MA & London: The MIT Press.

Marks, Laura U. (2000): *The Skin of the Film. Intercultural Cinema, Embodiment, and the Senses*. Durham & London: Duke University Press (especially Chapter 3: 'The Memory of the Touch').

Meyrowitz, Joshua (1985): *No Sense of Place. The Impact of Electronic Media on Social Behavior*. New York & Oxford: Oxford University Press.

Moores, Shaun (2004): 'The Doubling of Place: Electronic Media, Time-Space Arrangements and Social Relationships'. In Couldry, Nick & Anna McCarthy (eds) (2004): *MediaSpace. Place, Scale and Culture in a Media Age*. London & New York: Routledge.

Nichols, Bill (1991): *Representing Reality. Issues and Concepts in Documentary*. Bloomington & Indianapolis: Indiana University Press.

Nichols, Bill (1994): *Blurred Boundaries. Questions of Meaning in Contemporary Culture*. Bloomington & Indianapolis: Indiana University Press.

Prendergast, Christopher & Margaret Cohen (eds) (1995): *Spectacles of Realism. Gender, Body, Genre*. Minneapolis & London: University of Minnesota Press.

Robertson, Roland (1995): 'Time-Space and Homogeneity-Heterogeneity'. In Featherstone, Mike, Scott Lash & Roland Robertson (eds): *Global Modernities*. London: Sage.

Sandbye, Mette (2005): 'Performing the Everyday. Two Danish Photo Books from the 1970s'. In Gade, Rune & Anne Jerslev (eds) (2005): *Performative Realism. Interdisciplinary Studies in Art and Media*. Copenhagen: Museum Tusculanum Press.

Soja, Edward W. (1996): *Thirdspace*. Oxford: Blackwell.

Storey, John (2003): *Inventing Popular Culture. From Folklore to Globalization*. Oxford: Blackwell.

Tomlinson, John (1999): *Globalization and Culture*. Cambridge: Polity Press.

Urry, John (1990): *The Tourist Gaze, Leisure and Travel in Contemporary Societies*. London: Sage.

Williams, Linda (1999): 'The Ethics of Intervention: Dennis O'Rourke's The Good Woman of Bangkok'. In Gaines, Jane M. & Michael Renov (eds): *Collecting Visible Evidence*. Minneapolis & London: University of Minnesota Press.

Notes

1. *Performative realism*, (theatrical) craving for reality and staged documentaries – book titles and key concepts of contemporary cultural analysis – try to overcome the contradiction in terms between the two strivings.
2. Anne-Britt Gran enumerates three important degrees: the non-theatrical form, the explicit theatrical form and the implicit theatrical form (Gran 2004:93).
3. At the time of writing, the campaign still has a website at www.danesforbush.org (saving us from Old Europe).
4. I have myself in my article: 'The Eye-witness and the Affected Viewer. September 11 in the media' enumerated three categories of eyewitnesses. The documenting eyewitness is throwing an accidental gaze at the scenery. The second category consists of testimonies from the exposed body, which corresponds to the endangered gaze. The third kind of testimony comes from the affected body as it corresponds to the humane gaze (Knudsen 2003:19).

Personal Ideology and Collective Cinema: *Folk flest bor i Kina* and Contemporary Norwegian Political Consciousness

Ellen Rees

In 1996 the Norwegian film industry implemented a conscious program of support for collaborative film making spearheaded by Tom Remlov, former Executive Producer and Managing Director of the now defunct Norsk Film a/s. The initial idea was to produce four collective feature length films consisting of linked short films by various directors as a build up to the millennium celebration in 2000.[1] The marketing strategy of packaging short films within a feature format has previously met with success elsewhere, notably *New York Stories* (Allen, Coppola, Scorsese) from 1989. Only two films were actually produced for the Norsk Film millennium project, *1996: Pust på meg/Breathe on Me*, (released in 1997) and the Hamsun-inspired *1998: Tørst – fremtidens forbrytelser/Thirst – Crimes of the Future* (released in 1999) and neither of them received a large audience or a positive critical reception. Since Remlov's initial call for such films, however, an additional three similarly constructed collective films have been released, with the following box office results for all five films (all figures are as of 31 December 2003):

Title	Year	Number of visitors	Gross in Norwegian crowns
Folk flest bor i Kina	2002	35,400	2,160,856
De 7 dødssyndene	2000	10,542	562,619
1998: Tørst – fremtidens forbrytelser	1999	2,031	59,035
1996: Pust på meg	1997	n/a	73,395
Syndig sommer	1996	n/a	70,110

(Source: *Film og Kino* 4A, 2004:44-45)

Clearly *Folk flest bor i Kina* (whose English title for distribution was: *Utopia – Nobody is Perfect in the Perfect Country*) is the only such collective film to reach a broad audience, and even so it lags far behind the two most successful Norwegian films of recent years, *Elling* (2001), which had 776,359 visitors and grossed over 43 million Norwegian crowns, and *Heftig og begeistret/Cool and Crazy* (2001), which had 556,723 visitors and grossed over 29 million Norwegian crowns (*Film og Kino* 45). Nonetheless, *Folk flest bor i Kina* serves both as an interesting example of Norway's peculiar third way of collective cinema and as a forum for reflection on the status of contemporary political ideology.

The eight short films that make up *Folk flest bor i Kina* are linked by an over-arching frame narration about a Statoil gas station attendant and all take place just before a national election. Each episode has a different combination of director and screenwriter, as does the frame narration. The opening sequence, which together with the frame narration was directed by Thomas Robsahm, uses a montage of elements from each of the episodes to create a sense of unity in the film. Further, in most episodes small inserted elements from other episodes also help to create the unity that the producers and collaborators sought. The gas station attendant, Lasse (Trond Høvik), appears in all but two of the episodes.

Each episode attempts to point out the essential self-delusion that lies behind the specific political ideology the party it depicts espouses, while at the same time the film as a whole attempts a larger commentary on the state of Norwegian political consciousness today. The film contains an additional self-reflective tension, in that while Norwegian politics have moved further and further away from socialist and collectivist ideologies since the 1980s, the very collaborative nature of the film-making process itself is foregrounded, leading the viewer to question what function collectivism has in Norwegian society and Norwegian film-making in particular today.

In this chapter I will first discuss a few key elements of collaborative and collective film making, sketch out the backdrop of political change in Norway during the 1990s, and then analyse specific issues at play in *Folk flest bor i Kina*. I will focus in particular on three episodes from the film, 'Heimat (Senterpartiet)' ('Homeward (Centre Party)', distributed as 'Connecting People'), 'Redd Barna (Fremskrittspartiet)' ('Save the Children (Progress Party)'), and 'De beste går først (Arbeiderpartiet)' ('The Best Go First (Labour Party)', distributed as 'United We Stand'), which depict the three political parties that have experienced perhaps the most significant changes during the past two decades, and which have particularly interesting (and opposing) stances in relation to the notions of collaboration and collectivism within Norwegian society.

Collaborative and Collective Cinema

Historically the vast majority of film studies discourse has built upon the auteur as a conceptual model. Until recently, relatively little critical attention has focused on either the inherently collaborative reality of the production of film or on deliberately collective approaches to making films. In her study 'The Collective Voice as Cultural Voice', Christine Saxton describes the complexities of film economics and production behind the construct of the auteur in the following manner:

> the idea of the director as author of the film text has come under the scrutiny of theorists schooled in poststructuralist approaches to the text. According to this current school of thought, the voice emerging from the narrative, far from being the expression of an autonomous individual, is a very complex discursive phenomenon. (1986:19)

The well-known theoretical questioning of the construct of the author carried out by, among others, Michel Foucault and Roland Barthes spearheaded this important re-evaluation of auteur theory. Saxton points out the central irony of the auteur model, which fails to acknowledge both the contributions of the dozens of people actively involved in the making of each film, as well as the suppression of the essential economic considerations of film production. She suggests that the construct of the auteur functioned primarily as a method of conceptualising film as high art, reminding us that 'Films became authored texts if the auteur critics liked them, and authorless studio pieces if they did not' (21). Saxton argues further that all films, even the crassest of Hollywood commercial ventures, are in fact 'cultural collaborations' (20) dependent upon '[...] cultural knowledge and a certain foundational belief consensus on what is true and natural' (20) that is shared by both film producers and consumers. This focus on the viewers' power to imbue a work with meaning is an important theoretical development. However, there remains a vestigial bias against conceptualising film – any film – as a collaborative project, which Saxton seeks to undermine.

In contrast, deliberately collectivist approaches to cinema have remained on the margins of film-making, usually identified with specific ideological stances such as for example feminist or avant-garde artistic movements, in which non-authoritarian models of artistic collaboration reflect the larger transformative goals of the particular movement. For example, in the context of the United States, P. Adams Sitney claims '[...] the important stations of the evolution of the American avant-garde film were collective, and not the invention of any individual film-maker [...]' (2002:156). In these cases the cause or the aesthetic often comes before the careers of the individuals involved in film production and there is a tendency to subsume contributors. Such film collectives are frequently short-lived, and their products are almost without exception relegated to the outermost fringes of film culture. A rare example of collectivist work that has gained at least cult popularity are the collaborative projects undertaken by Andy Warhol and his Factory associates from 1963-1973 – but even in this instance Warhol has been granted status as auteur in critical reception of the films.

Projects like *Folk flest bor i Kina* need to be thought about outside the boundaries of the dichotomy of auteur cinema versus avant-garde collectivism. *Folk flest bor i Kina* resists both categories because it is on the one hand a series of short films produced conventionally with crew, cast and named director, while on the other hand it is structurally a collective endeavour in which each of the individual parts functions both autonomously (some have been released independently as short films) and in dialog with each other and within the film's frame. Rather than presenting an overt and largely irrelevant critique of the notion of the auteur along the lines of Dogme 95, where, despite the manifesto's admonishments and the lack of a visual credit in the film itself, the films are universally identified as products of an auteur (Thomas Vinterberg's *Festen*, for example, rather than merely *Festen*), *Folk flest bor i Kina* gives us a truly amorphous and viable alternative to the auteur.

An overview of Norwegian cinema history reveals surprisingly little avant-garde experimentation of this type, particularly given the innovation Norwegian artists have demonstrated in other art forms throughout the twentieth century – here I am thinking particularly of the Norwegian architectural firm Snøhetta, as well as postmodernist visual artists such as Odd Nerdrum and Vibeke Tandberg. Perhaps even more than most national cinemas, the film industry in Norway strove to emulate the Hollywood model, with the emphasis on feature-length, auteur-driven narrative film. Already marginalised linguistically and with limited resources, the Norwegian film industry apparently sought legitimacy through the aping of dominant cinematic conventions. Without a national film school until the 1970s, even the short film genre as a medium for art or experimentation failed to flourish until the middle of the 1960s. Although Norsk kulturråd finally began funding 'fri kunstnerisk' ('free artistic'), rather than purely documentary, short films starting in 1965, the long-standing practice of showing shorts before features in movie theatres was abolished soon after, in 1969 (Hanche et al. 1997:63). A marginal film club culture developed as the sole market for short films, but no major collective or collaborative projects appeared until precisely the historical moment – the mid-1990s – when collectivist political ideology in Norway appeared to have reached its nadir following upon the yuppie excesses of the 1980s. There appears to be a trajectory from individually produced short films, to the marketing of Norwegian short films – often packaged together as anthologies – as quality cinema at a time when Norway was producing few quality feature-length films, and then to the development of the collaborative, linked short film projects of the 1990s and today.

Norwegian Politics in the 1990s

Norwegian politics during the 1990s demonstrates a widespread shift away from traditional party loyalty on the part of voters toward a dramatically increased focus on individualism and independence from party organisation. Membership in all parties decreased and voter volatility from election to election increased. Knut Heidar notes that 'In the 1965 election, more than eight in ten stuck to their old party. In 1993 and in 1997, only four out of ten voted for the same party as four years previously' (2001:85). The increase in voter volatility is directly linked to the erosion of the Norwegian labour party's dominant position and ideology. New political issues, such as European Union membership, immigration, and environmentalism have shifted the alliances and coalitions within Norwegian politics away from the traditional divisions between socialist and bourgeois ideologies, making it harder for individuals to identify strongly with political platforms. Like voters elsewhere, Norwegians have substituted self-interest and issues for overarching ideologies.[2]

One of the most important political changes that took place during the 1990s was the increasing privatisation of the public sector, a policy that appears paradoxical given the fact that the most radical changes in this direction took place during periods in which Labour held the government. This was part of a larger trend in Europe as a whole, but it might be seen as surprising within the Norwegian context given its collectivist traditions. Perhaps the most significant example of privatisation, given the centrality of North Sea oil and natural gas production for the modernisation of Norway, was that of Statoil, the Norwegian nationalised oil and gas concern, in the early 2000s. In March 2001 the Norwegian parliament came to an agreement 'that up to 21.5 per cent of the Government's direct share of the Norwegian oil and gas resources (SDOE) may be sold to the oil companies' (Solholm 2001). The compromise decision was worked out between Arbeiderpartiet (Labour), Høyre (Right), Kristelig folkepartiet (Christian People's Party) and Venstre (Left).

The Statoil gas station, aside from being the subject of much derision in the debates from the early 1990s regarding the lack of concern for aesthetics in public space,[3] might also legitimately claim to function as the very symbol of Norway's collective wealth and progress – a signifier of the success and perhaps even moral correctness (in vaguely protestant or Calvinistic terms of justification) of the collectivist project undertaken by the welfare state. It is thus quite fitting that the collaborators behind *Folk flest bor i Kina* chose to locate their critique of Norwegian politics in a gas station. In Norway today, as illustrated in the film, the gas station has taken over the role of the corner shop, but with multinational and global undertones because of Norway's role in the petroleum industry that create an unresolved cultural tension. It is a site where global industry meets private use of space. I will now turn to three of the episodes in *Folk flest bor i Kina* in order to examine the ways in which they demonstrate and problematise the shift away from traditional political divisions.

'Heimat (Senterpartiet)'

The Centre Party episode portrays Marion (Kristin Skogheim), a highly urbane location scout, searching for a waterfall for a deodorant commercial. Her meeting with rural Norway and its traditional values represents an absurd loss of consciousness and contact with reality, a journey into an appealing but impossible fairytale land. Modern Maid Marion finds her way 'home' from the internationally-oriented city to the heart of Norway. The episode gives a complex reading of the rural-urban divide in Norwegian identity and reflects many of the rhetorical strategies Senterpartiet – the former Farmers' Party that claims to protect the interests of rural Norway – used during the build up to the 1994 referendum on EU membership.

After first venturing into the unfamiliar territory of rural Norway, Marion's cellular phone – her only link to what she perceives as civilisation – is swallowed by a cow. Marion exaggerates the fetishistic status of the cellular phone by calling it a 'Communicator' – the model name of a particularly advanced cellular phone produced by the Finnish company Nokia – but when trying to explain to a pair of local farmers what has happened, she feels obliged to translate from her high-tech jargon to the standard Norwegian word: 'Eller... øh... "mobilen". Den har spist mobilen min' ('Or... uh... "cell phone". It ate my cell phone'). Yet the stoic farmers do not skip a beat: one of them (Steinar Hammer) asks in a dialect typically maligned as the mark of a rube 'Var han vanntett?' (Schreiner *et al* 2002:39) ('Was he/it waterproof?'). Marion does not immediately understand the question, so the farmer supplements with 'Denne *Com*municator'en, var den vanntett?' ('This *Com*municator, was it waterproof?'), stressing the first syllable of the word according to the practice of his dialect and thus making the 'foreign' word his own. Her assumption that they cannot understand her is proven wrong. A wild cow chase ensues, and Marion knocks herself unconscious by running into a tree branch.

Language variation is important later in the episode when Marion regains consciousness. In the episode she has already established herself as a speaker of an urban *Bokmål*-based dialect, yet when awakened by a kiss she opens her eyes and proclaims in a rural *Nynorsk*-based dialect 'Eg er svolten' (ibid.:41) ('I am hungry' in *Nynorsk*). Marginalised in popular culture since at least World War II, *Nynorsk* has been under increasing attack in Oslo. Nowhere has the language been more ostracised than in the field of advertising, making the 'conversion' of Marion, who works for the 'New Wrapping' advertising agency, particularly ridiculous. Marion herself takes on a new language 'wrapping' in a sense. Furthering the joke, she asks (again in a *Nynorsk*-based dialect) 'Kor er eg no?' ('Where am I now?') and receives the answer 'Du er heime no' ('You are home now'). The dialect she adopts differs completely from the farmers', adding to the humor of the scene, and perhaps erasing the traditional importance of regional difference and variation – in a sense rural Norway becomes one homogenous 'other' in opposition to urban culture. Dressed in a lacy but modest white cotton nightgown, it is clear that Marion will reject her impure past and find her true Norwegian identity. Marion's new 'home' is a farmhouse filled with absurdly romanticised symbols of an imagined and idealised Norway. Director Arild Frölich calls it 'bonde-heaven' (Farmer-heaven) in his commentary to the film. The extended family (complete with a young mother nursing her baby, but oddly minus the actor Jan Gunnar Røise who plays one of the two farmers but has brown curly hair rather than blond) eats *rømmegrøt* (sour cream porridge) off Norwegian-produced Porsgrund 'Farmer's Rose' china as film composer John Erik Kaada's overblown rendition of Aaron Copland's 'Doppio Movimento ('Simple Gifts')' from *Appalachian Spring* (1944) swells in the background.[4]

Turning to the issue of the role of folk tales in the national imagination, the two farmers Per and Pål from the earlier scene, as well as their much more handsome brother Espen (Bjørn Rustbergard, the implied Ash Lad[5] who administers the awakening kiss to Marion) are actually nameless in the diegesis of the film (their names appear only in the screenplay and in the credits, although Espen has been changed to Ivar there), but the visual reference of the three rural brothers is so inculcated from childhood on in Norway that most viewers would immediately make the association to the folk tales published by Asbjørnsen and Moe in the 1840s. Frölich also refers to the third brother as 'odelsgutten' (first-born son) in his commentary on the film, and as such the third brother is the rightful inheritor of the land and a powerful figure in rural culture. The film assumes a 'knowing' national viewer schooled in the national heritage, but also 'knowing' in the sense that he or she has an ironic relationship with such icons.

One major element of the Norwegian folk tales that the episode references is precisely the kind of self-sufficiency, horse sense and disregard for authority that certain factions within Senterpartiet – particularly Storting representative Per Olaf Lundteigen, who was ridiculed for suggesting Norway should become self-sufficient in the production of washing machines – argued for during the 1994 EU debates. But perhaps the most significant element of Senterpartiet politics during the early 1990s was their rejection of the traditional divisions between socialist and bourgeois ideology. Heidar says 'The party vigorously claimed that the old left-right divide by now had become obsolete [...]' (2001:68) and instead conceptualised a new and revitalised Norway that drew its strength from the rural districts, traditional values and protectionist policies. The party attracted a significant number of urban voters with little or no connection to the rural districts primarily because its anti-EU platform emphasised 'the need to deepen national democracy (which was threatened by the EU and the bureaucrats in Brussels)' (ibid). Those who rejected this argument found it easy to ridicule urban Oslo-ites who planned to vote for the farmers' party, suggesting that only ignorant romanticism about the realities of rural life could motivate them. Yet the rhetoric of democracy and independence had a strong appeal in Norway, a European country that is only now in 2005 celebrating its first one hundred years of political independence.

'Redd barna (Fremskrittspartiet)'

Today's Fremskrittspartiet has by far the most colourful history of any Norwegian political party. Originally founded as 'Anders Langes Parti til sterk nedsettelse av skatter og avgifter og offentlige inngrep' (Anders Lange's party for strong reduction of taxes and fees and public intervention) in 1973, the party has from its inception combined populism and a remarkable awareness of the power of the media to transform itself from what initially appeared to be an absurd fringe protest party to a party capable of gaining fifteen percent of the vote in both 1997 and 2001. From 1978 to 2003, the spectacularly media-savvy Carl I. Hagen led the party. According to Heidar, '[...] the party played on popular sentiments against taxes, bureaucracy, and preferential treatment of groups like immigrants and welfare clients' (2001:70). We see these sentiments perfectly illustrated in the episode where two children first sell raffle tickets ostensibly to help blind children in Africa and then subsequently use the money collected on candy for themselves and (rather bizarrely) gasoline for their father's birthday present. Presenting herself as a much more worthy victim than the anonymous Africans, the young girl Eli (Rosa Engebrigtsen Bye) is in fact blind herself. The paradox is that despite her own handicap, she is utterly devoid of empathy for others and thus completely unsympathetic. The implication is that the party itself is blind to logic and reason. When called on her shameless extortion of people's pocket change by the gas station attendant Lasse, she bitterly places a few coins in the Save the Children collection box in front of him.

Lasse says: 'Folk flest setter ikke pris på å bli lurt på denne måten' (Schreiner *et al* 2002:54) ('Most people don't like to be tricked like that'). Eli's response serves as an example of the circular logic that Fremskrittspartiet is often accused of employing. Rather than addressing the moral question that Lasse raises, she attacks his vague generalisation, pointing out a technical inaccuracy that is irrelevant to the issue: 'Folk flest bor i Kina. Det sier pappa' (ibid.) ('Most people live in China. That's what daddy says'). The exchange leaves Lasse 'målløs' (ibid.:55) (speechless), which of course is the point of Eli's rhetorical strategy. Screenwriter Erlend Loe implies that the party's ideology is simple enough that a child can present it compellingly, or perhaps that the party is as boundlessly self-centred as a young child. In his commentary to the episode, Loe notes that the entire episode started with the idea of representing Fremskrittspartiet's ideology with children. Representatives of other Norwegian political parties have often found themselves as speechless as Lasse when confronted with the rhetoric of Fremskrittspartiet. In a discussion of the party's policies on immigration, social anthropologist Marianne Gullestad explains:

> Når politikere fra de andre partiene har problemer med å argumentere overfor Fremskrittspartiet og Carl I. Hagen, kan det skyldes at han hele tiden svinger mellom de ulike betydningene til ordet 'innvandrer', noen ganger rasemessig nøytralt (ordets denotasjon i ordboken), noen ganger rasemessig kodet (ordets konnotasjoner i mye av debatten). Den rasialierte kodingen er hele tiden underliggende, men når debatten blir for opphettet, svinger han til den mer nøytrale betydningen. (Gullestad 2002:90, note 27)

> (When politicians from the other parties have difficulty in arguing against the Progress Party and Carl I. Hagen, it can be attributed to the fact that he constantly alternates between the various meanings of the word 'immigrant', sometimes racially neutral (the word's denotation in the dictionary), sometimes racially coded (the word's connotation in much of the debate). The racialised coding constantly underlies the discourse, but when the debate gets too heated, he switches to the more neutral meaning.)

The fact that 'Redd barna (Fremskrittspartiet)' focuses on a form of foreign aid to Africans is no mere coincidence, since Fremskrittspartiet's policies on immigration, foreign aid, and race relations have been the source of much debate in Norway. Gullestad points out that in actuality the views of party members do not differ as much from other voters' attitudes as many would like to think, but by voicing anti-immigration views Fremskrittspartiet has made the argument that Norway's resources should be reserved for ethnic Norwegians an acceptable, if uncomfortable or embarrassing, part of public debate.

In the film segment, Eli shows complete disdain for the blind children in Africa that her campaign purports to raise money for because they are not 'here' and thus literally do not know what they are missing. Even more troubling, Eli employs the rhetorical strategy of tautology to argue that since these anonymous Africans are blind they would not have seen her actions anyway. The implication here is that the party ideology is completely self-serving and lacking in empathy for the plight of others. Given that Norway chooses to profile itself internationally as an important advocate for the rights of refugees and for enlightened development and foreign aid, the Fremskrittspartiet stance on immigration is very much at odds with the image that Norway wants to present abroad.

'De beste går først (Arbeiderpartiet)'

There is no question that the final segment of the film, entitled 'De beste går først (Arbeiderpartiet)', is the most important as well as the most individually successful short film within the *Folk flest bor i Kina* project. Director Hans Petter Moland's episode, distributed as a short film, had won no fewer than twenty-one prizes from various foreign festivals as of December 2003, according to Lars Ditlev Hansen. In comparison, Terje Rangnes' 'Redd Barna (Fremskrittspartiet)' had won four prizes. The importance of this segment – which after all features the single most dominant party of the twentieth century – is suggested in the introduction to the screenplay: 'Det er vanskelig å lage en film som dette uten at Arbeiderpartiet faller på plass. Vi har åpen "konkuranse" om hvem som kommer opp med den beste idéen' (Schreiner 2002:10) ('It is difficult to make a film like this without Labour falling into place (i.e. being presented in a clever way). We have an "open competition" for who comes up with the best idea'). The end product is decidedly nostalgic, and with its octogenarian cast hearkens back to the heyday of the Norwegian labour party.

The party's formative years have been described by Eric S. Einhorn and John Logue as having 'the evangelical fervor of a secular religion' (2003:101), and as the party organisation expanded and the party itself took control of government starting in 1928, its impact on individual members was enormously important: 'The labor movement was not just a matter of economic and political organization; it was a way of life [...] This helped to create and maintain a peculiar culture inside the labor movement that was characterised by the principle of solidarity' (ibid.:103). The success of the party's social agenda has also brought about its own decline as a political organisation in recent years, according to Einhorn and Logue: 'Although the party has retained its electoral preeminence during the last two decades, it has lost the moral certainty of the superiority of its vision of what society should be. Its voters have become middle class: They also own cars and summer houses and are concerned about high taxes and other bourgeois party issues' (ibid.:105). Few of the party's voters today live like the elderly men in the film, although they may find comfort in the ideals they represent. Characters like them have certainly been an object of fascination in Norwegian cinema in recent years, at least in films such as *Cool and Crazy* and Bent Hamer's *Eggs* from 1995.

The episode depicts a group of elderly men who depart from Lasse's gas station to take their annual hike in the district. Along the way they discover a charming young woman stuck in a marsh. They organise a rescue, but in the process end up stuck in the mud. Sensing they will not escape they expend their last breath singing Eugène Pottier and Pierre Degeyter's *L'Internationale* in Norwegian as they slowly sink beneath the surface. The episode functions as a metaphor for contemporary Norway on many levels. The men in the film represent a unique generation of Norwegians. They were in their twenties during the Nazi occupation and as party loyalists were the driving force behind the ideology of solidarity that built up the country after the war. They were also the last generation of Norwegians who were called upon to make sacrifices for the common good. Moland's short depicts their final sacrifice for the future, the massive expense of energy of a large political machine in order to save one individual that reflects the legacy of the welfare state. The film is bittersweet in that it portrays the old system as benevolent toward a younger generation that blithely does not recognise the sacrifice made on its behalf.

Although it has arguably never been a deciding factor in the actual voting habits of Norwegians, an ideology based on solidarity, participation and collectivism has been an important part of how twentieth-century Norwegian politics were perceived both at home and abroad. Arbeiderpartiet used a rhetoric of collectivism to advance its policies that supported industrial workers. In the outdated idealism of the elderly men's choir, we see an intertextual association with the communist members of the men's choir depicted in *Cool and Crazy* and their distress at the loss of their ideals when confronted with the reality of life in the former Soviet Union. It is the decline in the number of industrial workers, rather than a conscious rejection of Arbeiderpartiet ideology, that is behind the party's significant losses in voters during the 1990s. Moland's episode eulogises the labour class as a social phenomenon. In his commentary to the film he expresses great admiration for the men who played the parts (genuine members of a men's choir), while at the same time he clarifies that he himself did not grow up within the Labour movement. Moland offers no alternative to fill the gap that the demise of the Labour movement as a cultural phenomenon leaves.

The Norwegian Model for Collective Cinema

As I see it, *Folk flest bor i Kina* fits neither into the category of (unacknowledged) collaboration in mainstream or art cinema as discussed by Saxton nor into the kind of collectivist cinema developed from within underground ideological or aesthetic movements. The film goes beyond the necessary collaboration inherent in any film project because of its producers' conscious decision to involve multiple screenwriters and directors. At the same time, it remains a commercial venture and specifically does not represent a particular ideological or aesthetic movement. Instead, the film fits into a relatively new development in Norwegian film production that attempts to merge the creativity and flexibility of the short film with the marketing and financial opportunity of the narrative feature film.

To the extent that there is an ideological stance behind *Folk flest bor i Kina*, it can be said to be the lowest common denominator of Norwegian popular political consciousness. In their Introduction to the screenplay Karlsen and Sæther rather simplistically state 'Alle de politiske partiene har nedfelt et partiprogram som gir uttrykk for verdisyn, holdninger og mentaliteter som lett kan omsettes i handling og konflikt' (Schreiner *et al* 2002:8) ('All of the political parties have adopted a political platform that expresses values, attitudes and mentalities that can easily be translated into action and conflict'). The people involved in making the film consciously chose not to create political satire, but rather to '[...] i den grad det er mulig – skildre de politiske partiene med empati' (ibid.:8) ('to the degree that it is possible – portray the political parties with empathy'). It is perhaps not accidental that advertising, in particular the works of Roy Andersson (ibid.:9) was used as a source of inspiration for the creation of the eight short films, and the Introduction makes the connection between narrative and politics as explicit as advertising: 'Både politikk og historiefortelling handler dypest sett om det samme: Noe må stå på spill. Noen må oppnå det de er ute etter, andre må tape' (ibid.:9) ('Both politics and story-telling are on the deepest level about the same thing: Something has to be at stake. Someone must achieve what they're after, others must lose'). Yet the film does – perhaps paradoxically – succeed in presenting both recent fundamental changes in Norwegian political ideology in a nuanced way and a viable model for a kind of film making that is both collectivist and popular. Given the central role of the Norwegian labour party in Norwegian national identity during the twentieth century, and given the party's dual focus on precisely collectivism and mainstream appeal, the film may be viewed as a specifically self-reflexive project that mirrors the most central tenets of twentieth-century Norwegian political ideology in its very production strategy.

The structure of the film presents a de-centred national voice, using a strategy of self-irony that addresses the problematic nature of the demographic and cultural status of Norway, a nation of only 4.5 million inhabitants that has twice rejected EU membership. The film's structure also replicates the importance of consensus and collaboration within Norwegian society, since each of the segments is given equal weight to make up the whole, and since each ideological stance is subject to the same gentle irony. Rather than functioning as a linear, national historical epic such as Liv Ullmann's *Kristin Lavransdatter* from 1995, which appears entirely lacking in self-reflection and irony, *Folk flest bor i Kina* creates its sense of Norwegian identity through a narrative of an imagined community centred around a specific locus, namely the Statoil gas station. Locus here takes priority over history. Likewise, the film privileges local versus global knowledge on the part of the viewer, who must have familiarity with folktale traditions, political culture and even the norms of advertising in order to get the irony. *Folk flest bor i Kina* thus actively demands and constructs a 'Norwegian' identity for its viewer as part of a collective and localised community within the world.

References

Cowie, Peter (1999): *Straight from the Heart: Modern Norwegian Cinema 1971-1999.* Kristiansund: Kom forlag.

Einhorn, Eric S. & John Logue (2003): *Modern Welfare States: Scandinavian Politics and Policy in the Global Age.* Second edition. London: Praeger.

Film og kino årbok 4A (2004): 'Billettinntekter på norske filmer 1993-2003', 44-45.

Gullestad, Marianne (2002): *Det norske sett med nye øyne.* Oslo: Universitetsforlaget.

Hanche, Øivind, Gunnar Iversen & Nils Klevjer Aas (1997): *'Bedre enn sitt rykte': En liten norsk filmhistorie.* Oslo: Norsk filminstitutt.

Heidar, Knut (2001): *Norway: Elites on Trial.* Boulder, CO: Westview.

Saxton, Christine (1986): 'The Collective Voice as Cultural Voice.' *Cinema Journal* 26:1, 19-30.

Schreiner, Per, Nikolaj Frobenius, Marion Hagen, Kjetil Lismoen, Erland Loe, Thomas

Robsahm, Harald Rosenløw-Eeg, Ørjan Karlsen & Yngve Sæther (2002): *Folk flest bor i Kina: filmmanuskript*. Oslo: Cappelen.

Sitney, P. Adams (2002): *Visionary Film: The American Avant-Garde, 1943-2000*. Third edition. Oxford: Oxford University Press.

Soila, Tytti, Astrid Söderbergh Widding & Gunnar Iversen (1998): *Nordic National Cinemas*. London: Routledge.

Solholm, Rolleiv (2001): 'Political Majority Agree on Partial Privatization of Statoil.' *The Norway Post*. 28 March.
www.norwaypost.no/content.asp?cluster_id=15883&folder_id=5

Notes

1. In a sense the project might be viewed as a Norwegian counterpart to the Danish D-day collaboration between four directors associated with Dogme 95 and Danish national film and television organisations.

2. See Knut Heidar's *Norway: Elites on Trial* for a thorough discussion of recent developments in Norwegian politics.

3. The debate was initiated by the Minister of Culture Åse Kleveland and her advisor Peter Butenschøn in 1991 and according to Butenschøn resulted in 'Samarbeid og forhandlinger mellom 4 departementer og 6 oljeselskaper om retningslinjer for lokalisering og utforming av bensinstasjoner. Resulterte i publikasjon med anbefalte retningslinjer, som så i hovedsak er fulgt av selskaper og kommuner. Konkret førte det også til at ved sammenslåing av Hydro og Texaco i Norge/Danmark utviklet de ny stasjonsdesign i samsvar med våre anbefalinger, noe som ga kvalitetivt et betydelig løft' ('Cooporation and negotiations between 4 departments and 6 oil companies regarding policies for the location and design of gas stations. Resulted in a publication with recommended policies, which to a large extent have been followed by companies and municipalities. At the merger between Hydro and Texaco in Norway and Denmark, this in practice led to the development of new station designs that followed our recommendations, which resulted in a qualitatively significant improvement') (e-mail to author, 31 January 2005).

4. Thanks to Margaret Hayford O'Leary for clarifying the source.

5. The Ash Lad is a standard character in Norwegian folk tales. Often named Espen, his cleverness is often overlooked by other characters. He is treated as a stupid fool, but usually triumphs in the end and wins the princess and half the kingdom.

Gifts, Games, and Cheek: Counter-Globalisation in a Privileged Small-Nation Context. The Case of *The Five Obstructions*

Mette Hjort

In *Small Nation, Global Cinema* (2005), I argue that the emergence of the New Danish Cinema in the course of the 1990s can be traced to various more or less ingenious strategies of counter-globalisation aimed at thwarting the workings of what Miller *et al* (2001) refer to as 'Global Hollywood'. The transformation of a previously moribund national cinema into a form of cultural production commanding considerable interest within a national communicative space and on a festival circuit with global reach is, I suggest, the result of initiatives on the part of what I call a hebephilic state. What I have in mind, more specifically, is a state that values creativity and innovation, with the qualities in question being attributed to young people who thus in principle become deserving of unique forms of state support. The successful globalisation of the New Danish Cinema hinges on two explicitly articulated strategies of counter-globalisation, the one originally rooted in concepts of shared culture or heritage culture, and the other in an understanding of the striking efficacities of what Greg Urban (2001) calls 'meta-culture'.[1] If heritage film on a transnational Nordic scale exemplifies the former approach, the Dogme 95 movement, devised by filmmakers Lars von Trier and Thomas Vinterberg, is a clear instance of the second approach. A third, less clearly coordinated process of counter-globalisation is apparent in the creative appropriation of genre formulae constitutive of Hollywood crime and action films in a process of glocalisation that derives much of its interest from the way in which it incorporates the newcomers of Denmark's changing ethnoscape into the worlds, textual and other, of film.

The aim of the present discussion is to look more closely at the meta-cultural strategy (which involves framing specific cinematic works in terms of manifestos or rules) so as to draw attention to the crucial role that key individuals can play in processes of counter-globalisation. While many instances of globalisation have an emergentist and unsystematic quality, strategic, means-end deliberation on the part of especially corporate leaders clearly figures centrally in other cases. Disney's reach and penetration around the globe have, for example, respectively expanded and intensified over the last decade, and this fact was until recently attributed to policies devised and implemented by Disney CEO Michael Eisner. Yet individual agency, as an explanatory concept, is relevant not only to the analysis of neoliberal or corporate globalisation, but also to various attempts to articulate alternative globalisations. In the Danish case, some of the strategies of counter-globalisation that made the emergence and globalisation of the New Danish Cinema possible can be unambiguously assigned to a very specific agential address. More bluntly, the New Danish Cinema, and the successful instance of small-nation counter-globalisation that it represents, would not have occurred were it not for the efforts of certain very specific individuals who can be easily identified. The task at hand, then, becomes one of trying to define the type of agency that is decisive here. My sense is that we are dealing with individuals who self-consciously refuse the more than likely possibility of ultimate success in what Robert H. Frank and Philip J. Cook (1995) call 'winner-take-all-markets' in order instead to generate the dynamics of a gift culture that effectively transforms, and thereby psychologically expands, the small-nation context. In an effort to refine and substantiate this intuition I shall look closely at Lars von Trier's most recent attention-grabbing project, the collaborative experiment with veteran filmmaker Jørgen Leth, entitled *De fem benspænd/The Five Obstructions* (2003).

Generosity, Globalisation, and the Welfare State

I shall have the occasion in some concluding remarks to point to the rich literature on gifts and gift culture that finds its origins in Marcel Mauss's classic work (1970) on the topic. At this point some general comments about the place of generosity within contemporary Danish society are necessary, for it is important to understand the extent to which the filmmakers under discussion here are responding to deeply rooted national mentalities, and in ways that converge with a number of recent developments that are beginning to challenge the mind-sets in question. Let us begin by briefly evoking some of the standard meanings of 'generosity.' The *Oxford English Dictionary* identifies three distinct meanings of the term: 1. 'Excellence', which is said to be archaic usage, 2. 'high spirit' or 'courage', identified as obsolete, but continuous with the idea of a 'willingness to lay aside resentment', and 3. 'readiness or liberality in giving'. Generosity, these definitions remind us, encompasses (in addition to acts of material giving) charitable dispositions towards the other that resist the dynamics of envy and ressentiment. Commenting on the gift in sixteenth-century France, the historian Natalie Davis underscores the extent to which gift giving itself articulates a certain intersubjectivity, the modalities and extent of the practice being variable across time and in different cultures:

> Though there are big shifts in systems of gift and exchange over time, there is no universal pattern of evolutionary stages, where a total gift economy dwindles to occasional presents. Rather, gift exchange persists as an essential relational mode, a repertoire of behavior, a register with its own rules, language, etiquette, and gestures. The gift mode may expand or shrink somewhat in a given period, but it never loses significance. (2000:9)

Beliefs having to do with the principal locus of generosity, or with expectations concerning the ways in which the relevant dispositions find typical manifestation, may well change, then, and this is indeed what is happening in small, privileged nation-states such as Denmark, where generosity is mediated by and delegated to the state.

In the Danish case, one of the most striking effects of globalisation has been the multicultural transformation of a previously homogeneous ethnoscape. The presence of newcomers is the subject of relentless debate and figures centrally in many of the controversial policy decisions of the right-of-centre coalition government led by Prime Minister Anders Fogh Rasmussen. The more interesting aspects of the ongoing discussions have to do with the viability of the welfare state, not least within the context of a significantly expanded Europe. A widespread view has it that the original model is essentially unworkable in a world where a commitment to certain basic human rights – be it a matter of the right to family re-unification or of the right to live in freedom from persecution – entails a certain porousness of national borders. Current arrangements, in which newcomers are institutionalised as the automatic recipients of various costly 'gifts', are beginning to seem unfeasible on purely economic grounds. State generosity, it is thus increasingly claimed, will inevitably have to be rethought once a critical threshold is reached of economically non-contributing citizens, be they recent refugees or immigrants, second-generation 'new Danes' existing on the margins of Danish society, or so-called 'ethnic' Danes with ancestral ties to a Danish *ethnie*. The left-wing perspective tends to accept the inevitability of increasingly porous borders, as well as the possibility that the welfare state may need to contract in certain areas in order to ensure continued state generosity in others. The more conservative position favours contraction, but with the aim of ensuring that the existence of mechanisms for state generosity does not produce long-term free riders as one of its systemic effects, or channel wealth produced by 'ethnic' Danes towards newcomers with no long-term attachments or commitments to Denmark. The political divisions, not surprisingly, manifest themselves most clearly in competing conceptions of the nation-state and its tasks, and in diverging views on the human rights implications of various boundaries designed at once to include and exclude.

The changing Danish ethnoscape and ongoing transformation of the Danish welfare state will no doubt affect the ways in which generosity is understood and practised in the relevant small-nation context. As the McGill sociologist, John Hall, once casually remarked, it is a well-known fact that, having contributed approximately two-thirds of their income to a state that is charged with redistributing wealth according to various principles of need and fairness, citizens of welfare states are disinclined to embrace generosity as a virtue to be nurtured in everyday life. In the Danish case, the displacement of generosity to the nation-state level combined in the past with the conformism of a peasant-based culture that is deeply phobic about difference to produce a national culture that is characterised by limited generosity, both in material terms and as a charitable stance towards the other. While the presence of newcomers has made a certain mean-spiritedness a feature of public discourse in recent years, it has also had the very positive effect of somewhat thwarting the tyranny of consensual thinking. More importantly, it has broken the stranglehold that an everyday philosophy of sameness once had on charitable dispositions involving a positive and open-minded attitude towards the other as an individual with a potentially unique voice and perspective, as a person with something new and different to contribute to a social exchange and larger community.

It is no accident that the new Danish cinema is associated with a highly self-conscious provocateur who makes a point, on a regular basis, of adopting politically incorrect views that fly in the face of various national pieties. What Lars von Trier (and others to a lesser degree) are resisting is precisely the tyranny of welfare-state sameness that makes envy, as a disincentive for social differentiation, a key feature of the social bond. To emphasise collaboration, as an intense, emergentist process that allows both for breakthrough works and for the transformation of the individuals who are involved in a given work's production, is, I believe, to begin to pry filmmaking away from corporate models of exchange culture, as well as from the indifference that is the inevitable risk of state-supported filmmaking, in order to nudge it in the direction of a gift culture where what happens between people in a given context of production is decisive. What is at stake is a quite different way of understanding the social bond, for while the 'gifts' being circulated or generated may at times be invidious and produce unsettling effects, they do rule out the defensive *indifference* that is the result of a banally envious relation to the other. Of equal, if not greater importance in the present context is the contribution that commitments to a sharing of prestige, talent, and insight (along with whatever neuroses and obsessions the filmmaker might possess) can make to a minor cinema's ability to remain visible on a festival circuit with global reach, as well as on at least some of the screens around the world, where the blockbuster results of Hollywood's globalising strategies are standard fare.

The idea that a preoccupation with generosity and with some concept of gift culture plays a crucial role in the emergence of the new Danish cinema, and in at least one of the counter-globalisations that it represents, is clearly suggested by the discourse that some of the key directors have chosen to adopt. In the following statements, we note, the absence of generosity is consistently identified as a typical small-nation problem with clear implications for the minor cinema in question. In an interview with Hjort in 1998, just prior to the success of *Dogma # 1: Festen/The Celebration* at Cannes, Thomas Vinterberg characterised Danish small-nation cinema as follows:

> Petty-mindedness, lack of generosity, claustrophobia and mendacity are traits that can't be avoided in a country the size of Denmark or in an industry as small as the Danish film industry. What we're talking about here are so many ways of protecting one's self-conceptions. There really isn't room for anything else; the pettiness is almost inscribed in the geography, which imprisons people, and that sense of suffocation is probably something that will always prompt certain reactions in Denmark. The fact that people constantly long to get out is probably something that fuels the flames of narrative desire in Denmark. (Hjort and Bondebjerg 2001:274)

The defensive petty-mindedness that Vinterberg equates with a lack of generosity is a trait that Danes generally recognise as a feature of their culture. When referring to any number of possible behaviours associated with the mentality in question, Danes will often use the word *Jantelov* (the Law of Jante), a term made famous by the Danish-Norwegian writer Aksel Sandemose (1899-1965). In 1933 Sandemose published *En Flyktning krysser sitt spor* (*A Fugitive Crosses His Tracks*), a work of fiction that was clearly intended to provide a scathing portrait of typically Danish attitudes and values and especially of the writer's birthplace, Nykøbing Mors. *A Fugitive Crosses His Tracks* describes life in a peasant community that is governed by the following rules, with the pronoun 'we' referencing a self-consistent and internally homogeneous community throughout:

1. Thou shalt not believe thou art something.
2. Thou shalt not believe thou art as good as we are.
3. Thou shalt not believe thou art more wise than we are.
4. Thou shalt not fancy thyself better than we are.
5. Thou shalt not believe thou knowest more than we do.
6. Thou shalt not believe thou art greater than we are.
7. Thou shalt not believe thou amountest to anything.
8. Thou shalt not laugh at us.
9. Thou shalt not believe that anyone is concerned with thee.
10. Thou shalt not believe thou canst teach us anything.

'Jantelov' is at this point accorded entries in more encompassing dictionaries, where a typical definition reads as follows: 'a situation in which the community attempts to keep someone down; nobody is allowed to excel' (*Politikens nudansk ordbog* 1990:519). *The Xenophobe's Guide to the Danes* (Harris 1997) includes a humorous account of the law of Jante and its continued centrality to Danish life, as do travel guides such as *Time Out Copenhagen*. A quick google search brings to light countless sites devoted to explaining or countering the law of Jante, oftentimes in the form of various counter-laws. Thus, for example, a bowling club in the provincial town of Nørresundby claims to be ruled by ten alternative and rather more positive commandments that must be embraced by members, presumably with an eye to fostering the pleasures of community. One of the sites lists five distinct anti-laws and a variation on one of the five, all of which can be consulted to the tune of Simon and Garfunkel's *Bridge over Troubled Water*. More scholarly works on the law of Jante emphasise the question of social reproduction in small nations with agrarian roots, envy as a mechanism of social control and integration, and the stultifying cultivation of a self-satisfied, but not particularly satisfying, mediocrity.

Vinterberg, a key contributor to the now globalised new Danish cinema, identifies collaboration, flamboyant experimentation, and a brazen emphasis on performance as important guiding principles within a small-nation context marked by misplaced egalitarianism, conformism, and envy internally, and by indifference and problems of access in relation to a larger world. The problems, Vinterberg notes, are by no means insurmountable if filmmakers can somehow learn to 'think [themselves] beyond typically Danish mentalities' (Hjort and Bondebjerg 2001:275). Reflecting on the systemic effect of Lars von Trier's activities within the relevant small-nation context, Vinterberg describes the lesson that collaboration with this provocateur teaches: 'my collaboration with Lars von Trier [as one of the four Dogme 95 brethren] has taught me that he is able to make Denmark big, without leaving Denmark, and this, for me, is the ultimate ideal' (Hjort and Bondebjerg 2001:275). When read alongside the following reference to von Trier as a type of circus performer or impresario, this comment begins to point to the dynamics that govern the effort at counter-globalisation that is embedded in the Dogme 95 initiative and in related experiments, such as *The Five Obstructions*: 'With regard to the role played by Lars and Bille [August, winner of an Oscar for *Pelle the Conqueror* in the late 80s], it's clear that they've significantly expanded the stage for Danish film [...] I think that at an unconscious level that has affected us all a lot; the fact that Danish film now figures on the world map. The claustrophobic feeling that accompanies the thought of being financed by the state, of being guaranteed only a tiny audience, and of being part of a small industry is compensated for by the *circus* [emphasis added] that those directors are able to generate' (Hjort and Bondebjerg 2001:271). Vinterberg's use of the term 'circus' is remarkably precise, and brings to mind a number of Trier initiatives: the Dogme movement, the creation of a Film Town (governed by its own manifesto) in former army barracks in the Copenhagen suburb of Avedøre, the collectivist and somewhat interactive millennium project known as *D-Day*, and the quasi-serious game behaviour of *The Five Obstructions*. In the case of *The Five Obstructions*, we shall see, an element of circus arises both at the level of the compelling metacultural rules that are constitutive of the project and in connection with the attention that these rules generate as several different cinematic texts, and one of the participating directors (Leth), are leveraged into a global cinematic arena by the impresario called Trier.

An exchange with Jørgen Leth – the experienced filmmaker associated with experimental documentaries (*Det perfekte menneske/The Perfect Human*, 1967; *Livet i Danmark/Life in Denmark*, 1971; *66 scener fra Amerika/66 Scenes from America*, 1982), remarkable sports documentaries (*Stjernerne og vandbærerne/Stars and Carriers*, 1973; *En forårsdag i helvede/A Sunday in Hell*, 1976), and with the annual coverage of the Tour de France for Danish television – brings into play a number of different ways of understanding the gift concept in connection with film. That it is the task of the Danish filmmaker somehow to take issue with the petty-minded effects of a culture of levelling is a view that underwrites the classic documentary called *The Perfect Human*, which Leth probingly describes as a polemic against the 'disturbing', 'sterile' and 'very Danish cultivation of mediocrity' (Hjort and Bondebjerg 2001:68). When the conversation shifts to Leth's more recent works, such as the lyrical documentary focusing on the poet Søren Ulrik Thomsen (*Jeg er levende. Søren Ulrik Thomsen, digter/I'm Alive. Søren Ulrik Thomsen: A Danish Poet*, 1999), the filmmaker evokes a conception of the cinematic work as the result of various gifts that participants bring to the creative process: 'The stories he [Søren Ulrik Thomsen] tells in the film, about his childhood and his method, he had those in his head right from the start. He outlined several of them for me in Haiti a year before we started. Those were things he wanted to give to the film, I clearly understood that, and I also regard them as a gift' (Hjort and Bondebjerg 2001:74). There is an almost mystical dimension to Leth's approach, and he readily admits that 'The idea of sacrifice or total commitment is a crucial element in' his films (73). 'Sacrifice' in this context refers both to the kinds of situations that warrant cinematic exploration, and to the qualities that agents participating in the making of a film bring to the creative process. In discussing his work, Leth also returns, again and again, to the idea of 'chance gifts' (e.g. 70, 72). *66 Scenes from America*, Leth recalls, includes a sequence in which Andy Warhol eats a hamburger and is captured on film with an almost sculptural fragility as a result of his having misunderstood the filmmaker's instructions: 'In the Warhol scene I received an involuntary and perfectly wonderful gift, which precisely makes me believe in the magical significance of chance' (70). Leth's philosophy of cinematic creation hinges to a very significant extent on creating the conditions of possibility for various gifts, be they a matter of chance, of specific intentions, or of agents reaching for, and achieving, what they ultimately have to give to the world. These various gifts are the key elements in a creative process that Leth views as somehow aimed at re-enchanting the world: 'The driving force here has been my conviction that reality can be charged that way, can be somehow re-enchanted, to use an old-fashioned romantic term' (63).

I have mentioned the names of several directors at this point, but it is time now to recognise that these individuals do not necessarily have the same status or efficacy within a global network of prestige. The new Danish cinema is unthinkable without institutional structures of opportunity or a certain critical mass of talented film practitioners. At the same time, it seems clear that the globalisation of contemporary Danish cinema (resulting, among other things, in the designation 'New Danish Cinema') would have remained a mere thought in some unlikely fantasy had it not been for the presence of a von Trier. While Vinterberg refers to Bille August and Lars von Trier in the same breath when he evokes the expansion of the small-nation context through a kind of 'circusification', it is in fact von Trier who is most closely linked to the phenomenon in question. Whereas the moments of breakthrough and exit were virtually coincident in August's case, as they so typically are in small-nation contexts, von Trier used success, at home and abroad, to transform the local and enhance the probability of its global reach. Lars von Trier is (and has been called) many things. The persona that interests me here is that of the (at times intense and neurotic) enabler who chooses to make a gift of his talent, name, and reputation to a national context, specific project, or particular collaborator, rather than exchanging these assets for the ultimate rewards that are so tantalisingly available to top performers within the 'winner-take-all' markets associated with the dynamics of a Global Hollywood.

Exit vs Commitment: The Lure of Winner-take-all Markets

In *The Winner-Take-All-Society* Robert H. Frank and Philip J. Cook contrast two standard accounts of income differences, the one centered on 'individual productivity and related qualities, including education, experience, unique talents, temperament, drive, and intelligence', the other on 'the structure of opportunities' that is available in a given context (1995: vii-viii). While both are said to capture aspects of the phenomenon of income differences, Frank and Cook opt for the second approach, as this is the perspective deemed most relevant to understanding the causes and effects of what they call the 'winner-take-all society'. The situation requiring explanation, they believe, is one in which minor differences in performance or talent translate into radical differences at the level of income or rewards: 'It is one thing to say that people who work 10 percent harder or have 10 percent more talent should receive 10 percent more pay. But it is quite another to say that such small differences should cause pay to differ by 10,000 percent or more' (17). Frank and Cook identify two features that are specific to winner-take-all markets as compared to other kinds of markets: the former involve 'reward by relative [rather than absolute] performance' and a striking concentration of rewards 'in the hands of a few top performers' (24). Winner-take-all markets, they claim, fall into one of two types, 'mass' winner-take-all markets and 'deep-pocket' winner-take-all markets:

> The large incomes received by leading actors, recording stars, and best-selling authors [...] result from the willingness of a large number of buyers to pay a little more for the services of one performer rather than another. We will call markets of this type 'mass' winner-take-all markets.
> Large prizes in many other winner-take-all markets result from a small number of buyers who are intensely interested in the winner's performance. Examples in this category, which we call 'deep-pocket' winner-take-all markets, include the markets for top painters and sculptors, for attorneys who are effective at keeping organized crime figures out of jail, and for geologists who are unusually good at finding oil. (26)

It is the contention of Frank and Cook that the increased prevalence of winner-take-all markets, particularly in the area of culture, has many negative consequences. There is a tendency, for example, for mass winner-take-all markets to 'degrade our culture' (19) as a Global Hollywood opts for what is tried and tested, for the already established formulae or stars, for the sequel, or for the sex and violence that is known to guarantee '*quick* market success' (19). Frank and Cook quote remarks by *New York Times* film critic, Janet Maslin, on the 'modern blockbuster era' that is deemed to coincide with the expansion of winner-take-all markets in the sphere of popular culture and corresponding contraction of alternative markets:

> [In the earlier era], risk taking was deemed more artistically valuable than commercially foolhardy, which is one good way of distinguishing between the creative climate of the early 1970s and that of today. Peter Bogdanovich, who made his reputation with the small, perfect film 'The Last Picture Show' in 1971, and whose latest film ('The Thing Called Love,' starring River Phoenix) went straight to video after it performed disappointingly in regional markets, recently speculated about whether he could ever have begun his career in a cutthroat, bottom-line oriented atmosphere like today's. The answer, he thought, was probably no. (Cited in Frank and Cook 1995:195)

The 'blockbuster era' is, of course, simply a different term for Hollywood's policy of globalisation, the 'ultra-high budget film' having been explicitly adopted by Hollywood from the late eighties onwards as a means of attaining 'a major presence in all of the world's important markets' (Balio 1998). It is clear, then, that there is an intimate connection between the rise of mass winner-take-all markets and globalisation in one of its possible incarnations, just as we are likely to discover a strong resistance to such markets in strategies of counter-globalisation aimed at generating alternatives to a neoliberal imaginary fuelled primarily by US interests.

Frank and Cook are not content to provide a purely descriptive account of winner-take-all markets and the societies to which they give rise, for their aim is to show that the systems in question find their origin in a moral vice – greed – and can be corrected or contained once this fact is properly recognised. The influential work of former Harvard President Derek Bok, entitled *The Cost of Talent*, is evoked in support of the idea that the moral failings of the winners who command most, and certainly a disproportionate percentage of the rewards, are an important part of the problem. What Bok identifies is the phenomenon of 'powerful elites who are insulated from competition and able to set their own terms in a world increasingly unrestrained by inhibitions about greed' (cited in Frank and Cook 1995:5). While Bok's driving concern is the academic superstar, the elites in question include top performers in business, sports, film, and many other areas. Frank and Cook seek solutions to the problems of the winner-take-all society in various cooperative agreements, which need not be initiated or even fully supported by the elites in question: 'In the winner-take-all society, cooperative agreements to reduce the size of the top prizes and curb some forms of competition need not lead inevitably to socialist squalor. On the contrary, such agreements are the key to a more equitable *and* more prosperous future' (viii). Yet, it is crucial to note that individual initiatives on the part of those belonging to the elites in question can result in very significant systemic effects and genuine progress. For example, some of the problems of recognition and access that typically confront small-nation filmmakers in relation to global markets governed by winner-take-all logics may be deftly circumvented or at least somewhat attenuated if highly successful filmmakers opt for a collectivist outlook rather than for purely individual success in the stratosphere of obscenely excessive rewards. Counter-globalisation in a small-nation context, the case of Lars von Trier clearly suggests, may be initiated and fuelled by top performers who self-consciously reject ultra-high-budget models of cinematic production (and the rewards they make possible) in order to expand a small-nation context through artistically self-validating collaborative ventures that allow individual prestige to leverage others into a shared space of recognition.

The argument I am developing hinges on seeing Lars von Trier as a top performer who prefers to contest rather than contribute to the dynamics of neoliberal globalisation. Let me briefly, then, evoke his contribution to cinema as well as a number of pronouncements or gestures that are suggestive of the political stance in question. Lars von Trier is the single-most important auteur to have emerged from the Danish film milieu since Carl Theodor Dreyer. The oeuvre of this filmmaker, who is now in his late forties, includes the Europa trilogy – *Forbrydelsens Element/Element of Crime* (1984), *Epidemic* (1987), *Europa* (1991), the Golden Heart trilogy – *Breaking the Waves* (1996), *Idioterne/The Idiots* (1998), *Dancer in the Dark* (2000), and the first two films in his 'Land of Opportunities' trilogy – the controversial *Dogville* (2003) and the more recent *Manderlay* (2005). The TV series entitled *Riget/The Kingdom* (1994) and *The Kingdom 2* (1997) was a popular success on a national level and something of a cult success internationally, while the Dogme 95 project significantly enhanced the filmmaker's visibility within various communicative networks. While von Trier's first trilogy betrayed an almost nihilistic rejection of humanistic pieties, his more recent projects bespeak a politically motivated commitment to collectivism, to a more inclusive world order, and to the countering of US dominance. Von Trier makes it clear, for example, that US film reviewers were right to see *Dogville* as a condemnation of US foreign policy under Bush Jr.:

> In my youth, we had some big demonstrations outside the World Bank and [against] the Vietnam War and we all turned out to throw rocks at embassies. Well, at one embassy [...] But I don't throw rocks any more. Now I just tease. I learned when I was very small that if you are strong, you also have to be just and good, and that's not something you see in America at all [...] I don't think that Americans are more evil than others, but then again I don't see them as less evil than the bandit states that Bush has been talking so much about [...] What can I say about America? Power corrupts'. (Official *Dogville* site)

A more recent controversy, arising in connection with the UNICEF 'Cinema for Peace' award that von Trier was to accept at a public ceremony in February 2004, was prompted by the filmmaker's accusatory acceptance speech (which appeared to target the wealthy and privileged members of the festival's audience), by the organisers' decision to edit the video-taped speech, and by Zentropa producer Vibeke Windeløv's irate response on seeing the unauthorised results. The unedited tape, which was deemed inappropriate by the festival organisers, has von Trier developing a contrast between two tribes in the world, the one living close to the well and thus with access to water and able to enjoy the luxury of being concerned with peace, the other living far from the well and being preoccupied as a result, not with peace, but with water. One last example of von Trier's engagement with broadly political issues suffices for present purposes. This time I have in mind an institution-building initiative, rather than the meanings of cinematic works or provocative pronouncements on occasions designed to celebrate contributions made through film. In 2003 Zentropa, the company owned by von Trier and his producer partner, Aalbæk Jensen, committed resources to a project involving support for a non-hegemonic cinema and, more specifically, for the creation of a Film House in Lagos, Nigeria.

De fem benspænd/The Five Obstructions

The Five Obstructions, an 88-minute film and collaborative experiment involving Lars von Trier and Jørgen Leth (and co-financed by Yeslam bin Laden), can be traced back to a dinner party at documentary filmmaker Tómas Gislason's home in the year 2000. Von Trier was getting ready to launch Zentropa Real, a Zentropa subsidiary that would be devoted to documentary filmmaking, and invited Leth to contribute a manifesto-like statement on documentary poetics to the festivities (to which von Trier would add his own manifesto-like statement emphasising the need 'to defocus ... [i]n a world where the media kneel before the altar of sharpness, draining life out of life in the process' (Danish Film Institute 2002:31). During these festivities von Trier suggested that he and Leth make a film together, and this led to the following email exchange between the two directors in November 2000:

> Dear Jørgen,
> The challenge/The Film you are supposed to solve/make is called: The five obstructions.
> As a starting point I would like you to show me a 10 minute film, you have made -- *The Perfect Human Being*.
> We will watch the movie together and talk about it -- then I will set up limitations, commands or prohibitions, which means you have to do the film all

over again. This we will do five times -- of this the title. I would find it natural
if our conversations became a part of the final movie -- with the six small films,
of course.

I hope you're happy with the assignment. Maybe the subject for the first
movie should be something we came to an agreement about? Of course we
would have the most fun if the subject is of a character that gives us as big a
difference as possible between film one and six?

Let me know how you feel about this. Please write.

Best regards,

Lars

Dear Lars,

I find the assignment tempting. I can see an interesting development between
film one and six, the route around the obstacles, the conversations, I'm sure
we'll get a lot out of this. It is exciting. I look forward to your obstructions.
I really like the idea of having to change, adjust, and reduce according to given
conditions in the process.

Best regards,

Jørgen (Danish Film Institute 2002:31)

The Five Obstructions shows the two filmmakers meeting at Zentropa in April
2001. They watch Leth's modernist, starkly minimalist, black and white,
experimental short film from 1967, which von Trier claims to have seen
twenty times. Having watched *The Perfect Human* with Leth, von Trier states
the ostensible purpose of the remake exercise: 'That's a little gem that we are
now going to ruin', which Leth claims to consider a 'good perversion' that is
worth 'cultivating' (Mark Jenkins' review for *The Washington Post* indicates
that the film is 'unrated' and 'contains a few brief sexually explicit scenes and
much film-theory perversity'). Much as in the case of Dogme 95, the guiding
principle is to pull the rug out from underneath the director's feet – in this case
Leth's – by imposing the opposite of what he requests or by prescribing
practices that are antithetical to his cinematic style or habitual modes of
filmmaking. Obstruction # 1 reads as follows: '12 frames, answers, Cuba, no
set.' Leth normally relies very heavily on a lingering gaze; to proscribe any
shot of more than 12 frames is thus quite literally to impose an alien
framework on the filmmaker. The original short film poses a series of
questions about the perfect human to which Leth is now to provide answers.
Leth admits that he has never been to Cuba, which makes his adversary
momentarily entertain and then impose location shooting on the island. And,
finally, Leth indicates that he would like a certain kind of set, and the result is
that von Trier 'obstructs' him by ruling out a set in this case. We are shown
shots of Leth on April 2, 2001 in which he insists that von Trier is 'ruining'
the film 'from the start' by imposing the 12 frame rule. The result, the usually

unflappable Leth quietly fumes, can only be a 'spastic film'. Documentary footage shot in Havana in November 2001 gives the viewer some sense of how Leth resolves the challenge posed by the obstructions, and subsequent images show him returning to Zentropa on March 21, 2002 to show his remake to von Trier. The latter notes that Leth 'looks great', which, he says, is a 'bad sign', for, had the obstructions functioned as they should have, Leth would be looking rather 'battered'. Having watched *The Perfect Human: Cuba*, von Trier indicates that Leth has passed his first test and offers him vodka and caviar.

Von Trier's second obstruction is designed to 'test' Leth's ethics. More specifically, the point is to challenge the distanced look or disengaged observer stance that characterises much of the filmmaker's work. The rules governing remake number two are: 'The most miserable place; Don't show it; Jørgen Leth is the man; The meal.' Leth is himself allowed to choose what he considers to be a truly miserable place and opts for the red light district on Falkland Road in Mumbai. The requirement that the misery not be directly shown is ingeniously met by Leth, who uses a translucent screen partially to block off the impoverished scene in which he, as the perfect man originally played by Claus Nissen in the 1967 film, eats a gourmet meal surrounded by poverty, exploitation, and illness. When Leth returns to Copenhagen to show the results to Lars von Trier on September 12, 2002, he is told that he has failed to follow orders, the use of the translucent screen being a clear violation of one of the elements in the overall obstruction. Von Trier underscores the extent of his disapproval and disappointment and indicates that he has no choice but to punish the disobedient Leth. The latter is initially told to return to Mumbai and start over, which Leth insists that he simply cannot do. The result is the worst punishment of all: a free-style film. Obstruction # 3 is finally articulated disjunctively ('Complete freedom or Back to Bombay'), but in fact provides no choice, since one of the putative options was ruled out in no uncertain terms by Leth. The guiding thought in von Trier's articulation of Obstruction # 4 is that Leth is a filmmaker who has only undertaken projects to which he was genuinely drawn and in which he could fully believe. Obstruction # 4, which involves Leth remaking *The Perfect Human* as an animated film, is thus designed to impose a task that would be absolutely unappealing, even loathsome, to Leth. Leth looks horrified on hearing the injunction and says: 'I hate animated films', which prompts von Trier to say 'I hate animated films', to which Leth responds with yet another 'I hate animated films', which elicits one final repetition of the phrase from von Trier. A subsequent image shows us Leth in a car, talking on his mobile phone to one of his collaborators and explaining that they are to make an animated film of the kind that they really dislike. Images from Port-au-Prince in December 2002 provide insight into

Leth's strategy in connection with the task at hand, as do subsequent sequences from Austin, Texas in January 2003, where Leth elicits the assistance of Bob Sabiston. Leth and von Trier watch Obstruction # 4 on two sides of the world (in Port-au Prince, where Leth lives much of the year, and in Copenhagen), communicating by telephone in order to ensure a perfectly synchronised viewing. Von Trier acknowledges that Leth has managed, yet again, to turn the obstruction to positive effect, and proposes as a result to take control of the final remake. Obstruction # 5 thus reads as follows: 'Lars von Trier will make the last obstruction. Jørgen Leth will be credited as director. Jørgen Leth will read a text written by Lars von Trier.' The text in question, which Leth is made to rehearse so that the emphases will be just right by von Trier's lights, takes the form of a letter, written as such things normally are, in the first person. The Leth persona constructed by von Trier begins with a 'Dear, stupid Lars' before going on to claim that he, Leth, had grasped von Trier's deeper motivations throughout. Lars, Leth's voice insists, was obsessed with the idea that Leth, much like von Trier, cultivates a provocative, perverse perfection as a filmmaker. In von Trier's mind, Leth's voice (still reading von Trier's textual attributions to Leth) continues, this perfection serves as a mask behind which the 'abject human' hides and thus amounts to a kind of dishonesty. The obstructions are thus ultimately an attempt to lay bare the truth behind the investment in, and performance of perfection. The letter from Leth to von Trier (written in its entirety by von Trier) concludes by stating that it was von Trier, not Leth, who was ultimately exposed in the game of obstructions, Leth having obstructed von Trier, rather than vice versa. Obstruction # 5, and *The Five Obstructions* as a whole, ends with the phrase 'This is how the perfect human falls', a citation from the original film.

Concepts of game behaviour, gifts, sacrifice, and therapy dominate the two filmmakers' meta-discursive comments, some of which are made within the context of the work that *The Five Obstructions* amounts to, others in discussion with film critics and the press. Leth, for example, provided the following characterisation of the game that he took himself to be embarking on with von Trier: 'So we are entering a game – but not a sweet children's game. It will be full of traps and vicious turns' (Danish Film Institute 2002:32). In many ways the game in question is a psycho-therapeutic one, with all of the attendant power plays, some of them quite poignant since it is a matter of the younger pupil, von Trier, adopting the role of therapist in relation to his former teacher, Leth.[2] As part of his response to one of Leth's remakes, von Trier explains his intentions as follows: 'It's similar to therapy. [...] Why go, if you don't give the therapist the cards? My plan is to proceed from the perfect to the human. That's my agenda. I wish to 'banalize' you. By finding things that hurt. The soft spots.' Leth, von Trier repeatedly insists, is stubbornly refusing to create something that is less than perfect, something that would be at odds with his preferred self-understandings as a filmmaker and artist. Yet, it is precisely some form of imperfection that von Trier seeks as a kind of 'gift' or 'sacrifice' from Leth. Leth remains unscathed and 'unmarked' by the obstructions, says his opponent, yet what the game requires is a willingness to be exposed, to be vulnerable, to fail: 'The greatest gift an actor can give you as a director,' von Trier insists, 'is to screw up. I want the same kind of gift as I get from an actor when he does a scene in a way that he hates.'

Yet, it is not simply a question of demanding gifts or sacrifices from Leth, for the project is in the final analysis itself a kind of gift from von Trier to Leth, or this, at least, is what the impresario would have us believe. In the concluding moments of the film, von Trier makes the following statement on the grounds of the Film Town in Avedøre, where the Zentropa offices are located: 'I have a certain expertise in a number of areas. And Jørgen Leth is one of them. I know more about him than he does.' The entire exercise, von Trier cheekily remarks, was essentially a 'Help Jørgen Leth project', a gift flowing from von Trier to Leth. That von Trier to some extent was operating with this particular view of the process throughout is suggested by comments such as the following in response to Leth's *Obstruction # 1: Cuba*: 'The 12 frames were a gift [...] It was like watching an old Leth film.' What was needed, he implies, was some kind of externally imposed set of constraints that would somehow return the aging, but still vital Leth to the creativity of his youth.

The Five Obstructions has gone on since its release to become a major festival success. The explanation is no doubt to be sought, among other things, in the duel-like and ethically Manichean quality of the interactions between a highly prominent filmmaker and his former teacher (the former performing the role of Evil, the latter of Good), in the inherent interest of the formal experiment, and, just as importantly, in the inventiveness and ingenuity of Leth's various 'solutions.' Leth has on numerous occasions drawn attention to the way in which the film that was to 'develop from a project having Jørgen Leth's fingerprints on it [the original *Perfect Human*] into a film carrying fingerprints clearly identifiable as Lars von Trier's' (Danish Film Institute 2002:32) has served to boost his reputation in remarkable ways that point to the strategic efficacity of such traces of personal prestige within a small-nation context. Leth recalls the standing ovation at the Venice Film Festival in 2003, the spontaneous clapping in the streets of the same Italian city as he made his way around it, and the film's enthusiastic reception at the Toronto film festival: 'People simply discover me in connection with their prior knowledge of von Trier. Some talk about a 'late career success', and I don't have a problem with that. I have otherwise been comfortable with my position in the documentary world where I have enjoyed reasonably high status – and with the couple of classics that I had to my name' (Wendt Jensen 2003: 26; my translation). There can be no doubt, however, that Leth perceives his significantly enhanced visibility as a kind of gift, arising through chance but also through an almost willful sharing of reputation.

Lars von Trier, we readily concede, is often vilified by journalists, most recently at the time of writing in an article in *The Independent*, which the editors of *The South China Morning Post* chose to reprint. Entitled 'His Wicked Way' (2004), the article relies on various kinds of Lars-lore to paint a picture of a sexist, manipulative, and quasi-sadistic director driven only by sordid and perverse inclinations. While this particular instance of journalistic discourse has all of the failings of the genre at its worst, it is important to underscore that we can recognise von Trier's contribution to a strategy of counter-globalisation – via various gifts and metaculturally framed collaborations – without committing ourselves to an impossibly simplistic view of the director as 'all good'. Gifts, Marcel Mauss (1970) clearly showed in his groundbreaking analysis of the Kwakiutl potlatch, can be instruments of power and manipulation. And Derrida's commentary (1992) on Mauss's work has served to foreground some of the difficulties involved in imagining pure gifts uncontaminated by the dynamics of exchange. A gift that is recognised to be a gift, Derrida contends, engenders a sense of obligation, which in turn functions as a kind of return that inscribes the gift within a network of strategic calculations. An element of exchange is present, or so at least the argument goes, even in those cases where the gift goes unrecognised, for the very fact of living up to certain preferred self-conceptions is sufficient to prompt a sense of satisfaction on the part of the giver.[3] Von Trier's metacultural collaborative projects are highly ambiguous affairs that, far from presupposing purity, make a virtue of the many different ways in which gift and exchange cultures can be imbricated. The collaborative experiments that von Trier stages are clever marketing strategies and effective tools of self-promotion, but they are also ingenious devices designed to profile the insufficiently recognised talents of small-nation filmmakers and to enhance the flow of reputation associated with a small-nation context. Von Trier's 'help a colleague' project is at once a matter of transferring prestige to a deserving filmmaker and of creating the conditions under which further prestige is likely to emerge. The surplus in question benefits not only the particular individual whose reputation (and thus range of creative options) has been considerably enhanced, but an entire network of small-nation filmmakers. The strategy of surplus as and through social effervescence serves to expand the small-nation context psychologically, but it also helps to define the relevant film *milieu* as a site of innovation and promise, making it that much easier for other small-nation filmmakers to become (or remain) players in the various games of filmmaking. Counter-globalisation in small welfare-state contexts need by no means be a State-driven or even regional affair with elaborate policies and special budget lines. The Danish case suggests that certain highly effective forms of counter-globalisation may instead depend on the presence of supremely talented directors who are self-respecting enough to reject the idea that success means exit and brazenly self-confident enough to believe that the structures of opportunity linked to visibility in a global arena can be significantly changed by a series of socially effervescent circus-like operations involving talent, cheek, honesty, trust, irony, wit, and a certain streetwise understanding of the pragmatic (and especially performative) dimensions of communicative processes in an age of globalisation.

References

Balio, Tino (1998): '"A Major Presence in all of the World's Important Markets": The Globalization of Hollywood in the 1990s.' In Neale, Steve & Murray Smith (eds): *Contemporary Hollywood Cinema*. London: Routledge.

Danish Film Institute (2002): *Film: Special Issue/Leth*. Copenhagen: DFI Publications.

Davis, Natalie (2000): *The Gift in Sixteenth-Century France*. Madison: The University of Wisconsin Press.

Derrida, Jacques (1992): *Given Time*. Translated from the French by Peggy Kamuf. Chicago: University of Chicago Press.

Frank, Robert H., and Philip J. Cook (1995): *The Winner-Take-All Society: How more and more Americans compete for ever fewer and bigger prizes, encouraging economic waste, income inequality, and an impoverished cultural life*. New York: The Free Press.

Harris, Steven (1997): *The Xenophobe's Guide to the Danes*. Oval Books.

Hjort, Mette (2005): *Small Nation, Global Cinema*. Minneapolis: University of Minnesota Press.

Hjort, Mette, & Ib Bondebjerg (2001): *The Danish Directors: Dialogues on a Contemporary National Cinema*. Bristol: Intellect Press.

Jenkins, Mark (2004): '"Five Obstructions": Filmmaker Faceoff.' *The Washington Post*: March 26.

Jenkins, Tim (1998): 'Derrida's Reading of Mauss.' In James, Wendy & N.J. Allen (eds): *Marcel Mauss: A Centenary Tribute*. New York: Berghahn Books.

Mauss, Marcel (1970): *The Gift: Forms and Functions of Exchange in Archaic Societies*. Translated from the German by Ian Cunnison, with an introduction by E.E. Evans-Pritchard. London: Cohen & West Ltd.

Miller, Toby, Nitin Govil, John McMurria & Richard Maxwell (2001): *Global Hollywood*. London: BFI Publications.

Politikens Forlag (1990): *Politikens nudansk ordbog*, 14th edition. Copenhagen: Politikens Forlag.

Sandemose, Aksel (1933): *En flyktning krysser sitt spor. Fortelling om en morders barndom.* Oslo: Tidens förlag.

South China Morning Post (2004): 'His Wicked Way.' June 20.

Time Out (2003): *Time Out Copenhagen.* Harmondsworth: Penguin Books.

Urban, Greg (2001): *Metaculture: How Culture Moves Through the World.* Minneapolis: University of Minnesota Press.

Wendt Jensen, Jacob (2003): 'International Hyldest til Leth.' *Danmarksposten* 84:10, 26-27, 29, 39.

Official *Dogville* site: www.tvropa.com/Dogville

Notes

1. Meta-culture, or culture about culture, is, in Urban's account, associated with the modern period. His view that meta-culture serves to give a certain 'accelerative force' to the cultural texts or discourses that it is about makes his concept highly relevant to the study of various types of globalisation. Whereas Urban takes film reviews to be a paradigmatic instance of meta-culture, I am more interested in the types of meta-culture that become constitutive elements of the very cultural texts that they are about. Manifesto-like pronouncements that define the rules of a given cultural game are thus central to my discussion, the intuition being that the accelerative force of meta-culture more generally is intensified by this kind of reflexive dimension.

2. Leth was one of von Trier's teachers during his years at the National Film School of Denmark. Like many of von Trier's teachers, Leth is on record as having found the student very talented but rather arrogant. Von Trier has acknowledged his debt to Leth's inspiration on many an occasion, particularly with regard to the connection between constraints (or rule-governed frameworks) and creativity.

3. See also Jenkins 1998 for a cogent interpretation of Derrida's engagement with Mauss's views.

Memory • Reality • History

Do You Remember Monrépos?
Melancholia, Modernity
and Working-Class Masculinity in
The Man Without a Past

Anu Koivunen

Aki Kaurismäki enjoys the status of being the only Finnish fiction film director who has achieved international fame. In many ways, Kaurismäki fulfils the dreams and decades-long expectations of a small European nation and its even smaller film culture. While being recognisably 'Finnish' in terms of cultural references and public image, Kaurismäki's films are exportable and appealing to an international audience. At the same time, however, public talk on Kaurismäki's films often involves a kind of guilt-tripping of the domestic film audiences. It seems that Finns should *like* them more than we actually do.

Despite a lot of public praise, despite a number of influential film journalists who underline the exceptional qualities of Aki Kaurismäki as a filmmaker, and despite the knowledge that his films since the late 1980s have been 'loved' by 'millions' in French and German art house cinemas – and despite him being hailed as a successor to Robert Bresson, Luis Buñuel, Jean-Luc Godard, Alexandr Dovzenko, Jean Renoir, Yasujiro Ozu, Vittorio De Sica, Douglas Sirk, Frank Capra, John Cassavetes, Samuel Fuller, Orson Welles and Ingmar Bergman, Kaurismäki has never had a broad popular appeal in Finland.[1] In my reading, this gap between Kaurismäki's international fame and the lack of national popular appeal is a result of the ambivalent affective rhetoric employed by his films.

In Finnish public reception, Aki Kaurismäki's Finland Trilogy (with *Kauas pilvet karkaavat/Drifting Clouds* from 1996, *Mies vailla menneisyyttä/The Man without a Past* from 2002, and *Laitakaupungin valot/Lights in the Dusk* from 2006), as well as the earlier Workers' Trilogy or the 'trilogy of the lost' (featuring *Varjoja paratiisissa/Shadows in Paradise* 1986, *Ariel* 1988, *Tulitikkutehtaan tyttö/The Match Factory Girl* 1990) have been framed as performances of national narratives and sentiments (whether nostalgia, melancholy, or shame), but also as timely political acts.[2] Especially for his *The Man without a Past* (winner of the Grand Prix du Jury, Cannes 2002) Kaurismäki has been praised as a voice of social consciousness, a bold critic of multinational, neo-liberalist capitalism.[3] At the same time, however, ever since the early 1980s his films have, in terms of actors, topics, set design and music, been associated with subcultural scenes and postmodern irony.

In this essay I will argue that this mixture of national sentiment, politics and irony characterises *The Man without a Past* resulting in a spectatorial address that is highly ambivalent for audiences in search of 'national sentimentality' (Berlant 1997). Appropriating Giuliana Bruno's (2002:8) notion of cinema as 'emotional cartography', I propose that *The Man without a Past* operates as 'affective transport' that alternates between nostalgia, melancholia, anger, and irony. In her *Atlas of Emotions*, Bruno elaborates on the etymological roots of both emotion (Latin *emovere*) and cinema (Greek *kinema*) that both connote motion as well as emotion. In Bruno's argument, cinematic space not only moves 'through time and space or narrative development but through inner space', and, therefore: 'Film moves, and fundamentally "moves" us, with its ability to render affects and, in turn, to affect' (Bruno 2002:7). Taking my cue from this thesis, I suggest that in its thematisation of late modernity, masculinity, and the working class, *The Man without a Past* stages a jarring movement between times, places, and emotions. In its rhetoric, it fuses sentimentality with irony and resentment with melancholia, amalgamating a minimalism of form with an abundance of affect, and thereby moving the viewers between senses of proximity and distance. On the one hand, historical references and nostalgic music invite a Finnish viewer into a feeling of familiarity and closeness. On the other hand, the comic, ironic and violent tones of the narration create a distance, blocking or hindering rather than encouraging national sentiments and nostalgic pleasures.[4]

This ambivalent affective rhetoric echoes the narrative and aesthetic strategies of the late twentieth and early twenty-first centuries, variously termed *pastiche* (Dyer 2001) or *retro* (Grainge 2000). The two concepts both highlight the presence of many temporalities, both imply a fluidity between surface and depth, style and experience, and both offer ambivalence and insecurity as key features of the aesthetic mode. Thus, they both comprise the alliance of irony and 'new sincerity' Jim Collins (1993) detected in new American cinema in the early 1990s. As for the affective transport of *The Man without a Past*, nevertheless, I would like to suggest a broader, historically specific framework. In my reading, the film serves as a relevant case for invoking Miriam Hansen's (2000:10) concept of 'vernacular modernism' as 'a cultural counterpart and response to a technological, economic, and social modernity'. Paraphrasing Hansen, I suggest that Kaurismäki's film constructs a particular 'sensory-reflexive horizon for the experience' of late modernity, the felt experience of 'post-industrial economic desperation' (Monk 2000:156), that is, the conflicts between individuals, the market, and the downshifting of the Nordic welfare state. In an era of what Wendy Brown (1999) has termed 'left melancholy', however, politics does not exist without a sense of irony.[5]

The Man on the Train

In its opening sequence, *The Man without a Past* reiterates a key trope of Finnish modernity. Since the early years of the twentieth century, the image of an arrival to Helsinki by train has condensed the affective and political complexities of the modernisation narrative. On the one hand, it implies a lack of choice, the economic necessity of leaving one's home region, whether agrarian or industrial, in search of work. On the other hand, it suggests a new start, a possibility of social and cultural mobility. At the same time, however, the beginning of Kaurismäki's film evokes the gendered meanings of this trope: both the 1950s popular culture as well as the 1970s political theatre framed the trope of train travel – and the modernisation narrative it evokes – as a male drama. In 1950s carnivalesque comedies, such as *Hei, rillumarei!/Hey, Rillumarei!* (1954), the trope was framed as an escape from the alienated and inauthentic life in an urbanised, modernised Helsinki and female-dominated relationships into a genuine, equal comradeship among male lumberjacks in the North (Koivunen & Laine 1993). In the lyrics of a famous political song from the 1970s, again, the train transports an anonymous, 'silent man', victimised by unemployment, and the song asks us to recognise his individuality: 'Who is this man and where is he travelling?'[6]

The Man without a Past thematises the question of identity both in its title and its opening sequence, but in the diegetic universe, the identity crisis is propelled by a scene of victimisation that evokes famous Hollywood male melodramas such as *Awakenings* (1990) and *Regarding Henry* (1991, cf. Lahti 2001:114): a man, M. (Markku Peltola), is beaten up by three petty criminals, and the act of violence calls forth a development of a new self. In Kaurismäki's version, the man is badly injured and declared deceased at a hospital. He, however, rises from the dead, like the Bride of Frankenstein, leaves the hospital, ends up lying on the sea bank, and there, his new life begins. The slapstick aesthetic of these shots switches abruptly into a serious mode as the man is found by two young boys who carry a water canister in a frame that for Finnish audiences evokes a famous painting by Hugo Simberg called the 'Wounded Angel' (1903). This citation enhances the rich symbolism of injury and resurrection of the scene and the whole film. It also suggests a possibility of reading the whole of the film narrative as a dream-like fairy-tale or a depiction of the after-life. Speechless, helpless and amnesiac, the protagonist is cared for by the Nieminen family living in a storage bin, in a kind of a container village in a deserted harbour area, a trace of once active industry. The landscape is, as usual for Kaurismäki, a liminal non-space between city and country, an in-between of the urban and rural boundaries which usually mark the narratives of modernisation. In the same way, liminality characterises the time of the narrative in which temporally specific markers are mixed with anachronisms and a sense of timelessness. As a viewer, therefore, one is constantly transported not only along the narrative, but also the different modes of narration, spatiality and temporality.

This opening sequence leads to the introduction of 'M.' as an amnesiac – a man without a past, the title of the film being an obvious allusion to Robert Musil's post-WW1 modernist novel *Der Mann ohne Eigenschaften* (1930-1952). Like Ulrich, the protagonist of Musil's novel, M. lacks identity. In the film, it turns to be a blessing: he is not constrained by a fixed self, but is a stranger to himself and to others and, hence, a *possibilitarian*. As in *Regarding Henry*, amnesia is here 'the precondition for creating a better male self', to quote Martti Lahti (2001:114), and with a lost identity, of course, the real historical power relations are also suspended. While the opening sequence suggests the blue-collar background of M. by showing the welder's mask in his luggage, for the time being he is not bound by a professional identity. Typically for the film's ambivalent narration, M. is both linked with historical identity markers (a working-class man arriving in Helsinki in search of a job) and detached from them.

The creation of a new male self is aided by two altruistic female characters. First, M. is nursed and nourished by Mrs. Nieminen, Kaisa (Kaija Pakarinen), a version of the fifties suburban housewife (even if living in a container village) and a guardian of her family and alcohol-prone husband. In a Salvation Army soup kitchen, M. meets Irma, the Salvation Army officer played by Kati Outinen, who helps M. by arranging a job and new clothes for him. Soon, he rents a container of his own. While M. lacks name, social security number, bank account and permanent address, he nevertheless needs a proper costume to 'go forward in life', as Irma puts it. 'The grace of God holds true for heaven, but here on earth one has to help oneself, too', she contends.[7]

And, indeed, M. goes forward. Entering the container village and the Salvation Army as an outsider, he functions as an agent of change for his surroundings, much like the strangers that in westerns and melodramas rearrange communities. As he, surrounded by kindness and respect, develops a new self, he aids in strengthening the sense of community among the dwellers of the container village and the urban outskirts. The Salvation Army band starts playing R&B and Finnish tango, gathering the dwellers to communal open-air *soirées*.

Ressentiment or communitarianism

> *Drifting Clouds* is classic Kaurismäki, a beautiful, melancholy work that all but restores humanism to contemporary cinema. Who but Kaurismäki could make a comedy about unemployment, and turn it into a soulful, transcendent statement about hope and survival?
>
> James Quandt, Cinematheque Ontario[8]

In many ways, *The Man without a Past* reiterates the themes of earlier Aki Kaurismäki films. Since the 1980s, his underdog protagonists have included garbage collectors, supermarket check-out girls, usually unemployed and homeless but always impeccably heterosexual men in search of a decent life. According to Peter von Bagh (2000:105), a Finnish film critic and the most lyrical spokesperson for Aki Kaurismäki, 'the workers' trilogy' and particularly *Drifting Clouds* (1996) 'rank internationally among the most recent of insightful and sensitive depictions of the workers' milieu or the proletariat self. They evidence in the depths and on the fringes of the cities a sort of colonialised Finland, a Third World Finland – and a powerful, inimitable humanism, seasoned with a sovereign humour and disdain for bureaucracy [...]'. In 2002, a German web magazine concluded that '[m]oralisch gestärkt und mit neuem Glauben an die Arbeiterklasse verlässt man das Kino' (Filmzeitung.de 13.11.2002) (one leaves the cinema feeling morally strengthened and with a new confidence in the working class). While the public persona of Aki Kaurismäki suggests either an absurd sense of humour or serious drinking problems, his films invite political commentary capitalising on political frustrations among European film audiences.[9] In my reading, the politics of *The Man without a Past* is two-fold.

On the one hand, the narrative of *The Man without a Past* constructs a sharp antagonism between individuals and the state as well as global capitalism. This contradiction evokes the 'from below' perspective of many Finnish 1950s popular comedies, where the political and cultural elites were recurrently revealed as shallow and inauthentic (Koivunen & Laine 1993; Peltonen 1996). In the carnivalesque *rillumarei*-comedies of the post-WW2 era, a male comradeship, a community of the people (*Volk*), was pitted against petty bureaucrats, social climbers and proponents of modernisation. In *The Man without a Past*, 'the little man' is pitted against state and the market who are shown doing their best to disempower citizens. At the employment agency as well as at the police station, M. is humiliated – without a past and registered identity he is nothing. After an incident at the bank, M. needs the renowned civil liberties lawyer Matti Wuori (a former chairperson of Greenpeace, and a former member of South African Truth Commission) to get him out of jail. As for the capitalist economy, it is the end of the world. Building sites recruit cheap workers from Kyrgyzstan, the bank M. contacts is being sold to North Korea and a bank director recommends a Swiss account as a solution to M's identity problems. This antagonism leads to the first of the two moments of revenge punctuating the film, a bank robbery, even if a parodic one. A business man (Esko Nikkari) whose enterprise the bank has ruined (a fate echoing many true stories of the 1990s economic recession in Finland) robs a bank in order to cash out his frozen assets – not a penny more, of course – to pay the workers he had to lay off. M witnesses the robbery, and agrees to distribute the wage packages for him.

This episode manifests Kaurismäki's 'heart of a Bolshevik' (Filmzeitung.de 13.11.2002) and a Nietzschean slave morality that permeates Kaurismäki's narrative world, a romancing of the 'little man' and a relentless hate of those in power. Even if they are criminals in the eyes of the law, there is nothing morally suspicious about the working-class in Kaurismäki's films. Quite the contrary, the characters show moral rectitude, economic continence, and self-sufficiency, thereby embodying 'a distillation of evangelical disciplines' (Skeggs 2004:38). In this respect, *The Man without a Past*, too, makes a good viewing for all critics of late global capitalism and corporate states – both in Finland and elsewhere. The film's narrative ethos echoes the politics of *ressentiment* described by Wendy Brown. As Brown (1995:69) argues in her *States of Injury: Power and Freedom in Late Modernity*, 'the late modern liberal subject quite literally seethes with ressentiment'. In late modern leftist (as well as feminist and gay and lesbian) politics, she identifies 'a tendency to reproach power [on moral grounds] rather than to aspire to it' (ibid.:55). *The Man without a Past* and many other Kaurismäki films certainly make, to quote Brown, 'a complaint against strength, an effort to shame and discredit domination by securing the ground of the true and the good from which to (negatively) judge it' (ibid.:44). Brown summarises this affectively engaging alliance of powerlessness and morality as follows:

> [P]owerlessness is implicitly invested in the Truth while power inherently distorts. Truth is always on the side of the damned or the excluded; hence, Truth is always clean of power, but therefore also always positioned to reproach power. (Brown 1995:46.)

On the other hand, *The Man without a Past* also constructs positive 'fantasies of a radical communitarianism' that 'are meant to gesture, at least, toward the possibility of reinvention of agency and community' (Kaplan 2003:5). This has been, perhaps, the most common reading of the film:

> Elokuvan keskeiseksi teemaksi nousee ihmisten välinen solidaarisuus ja avunanto, usko parempaan huomiseen ja onnen mahdollisuuteen [...] Rakkaus ja ystävyys rinnastuvat toveruuteen ja maailma esiintyy sellaisena kuin sen pitäisi olla. (Timonen 2002b, brochure for Sodankylä Film Festival)

> (The central theme of the film is solidarity and assistance among human beings, a belief in a better tomorrow and in the possibility of happiness [...] Love and friendship are paralleled with comradeship, and the world presents itself as it should be.)

The open-air *soirées* M. organises suggest a local sense of togetherness that gives rise to this reading. While the dance evenings may be read – affectionately and/or comically – as instances of particular Finnish togetherness (at least when Finnish *schlagers* are played), they also invite a more general, allegorical reading, suggesting an international community of those living at the margins of the nation-states. In any case, earlier representations of the 'ordinary people' are called forth. In the Finnish context, *The Man without a Past* invokes the many 1950s *rillumarei* films that championed a carnevalesque alliance of 'ordinary people' against 'overlords' (*herra*), suggesting 'a view from below' and a futurity in terms of horizontal relations among human beings (Peltonen 1996).[10] In terms of politics, thus, Kaurismäki's film is a peculiar mixture of pessimism and optimism. On the one hand, the poor dwelling conditions, joblessness and the social exclusion are taken for a fact (cf. Monk 2000:160). On the other hand, M. can easily employ himself, and the Nieminens are, ironically enough, very content with their container life.

The moral grounding of this communitarian utopia was suggested by the Economy Section of *Helsingin Sanomat* which in 2003 asked, in a whole-page analysis, whether Richard Sennett's recent book *Respect in a World of Inequality* (2003) could account for the international success of Kaurismäki's film (Raeste 2003). According to Sennett's analysis, lack of respect towards the disadvantaged is the greatest threat against the current societal structures. And respect 'cannot occur simply by commanding it should happen' (Sennett 2003:260). In *The Man without a Past*, respect is a recurrent gift. The scene where penniless M. enters a café asking for a free cup of hot water and ends up having a full meal illustrates this point. 'The food was left over, and it would be wasted otherwise', the café assistant tells M., careful not to show any pity. All moments of *giving* in the film are depicted with utmost restraint. No sense of charity or compassion is manifested (Raeste 2003).

During the 1990s, compassion was a hot political issue in a Finland undergoing a severe economic crisis with unprecedented unemployment and increasing poverty as a result. The crisis was symbolised in media imagery of growing bread queues: people queuing up for free groceries in front of Salvation Army offices or parish buildings. Hence, the trope of Salvation Army links *The Man without a Past* to specific events in recent history. While the title suggests that the man has no history, that the new life he lives is beyond history, the trope of Salvation Army evokes both the 1990s economic history and the post-war Finnish cinema as frames of reference. After the lost war, when social structures were gravely shattered, several films featured Salvation Army as a catalyst of amelioration, especially in social problem films. In this respect, *The Man without a Past* alludes to *Nokea ja kultaa/Soot and Gold* (Edvin Laine, 1945), a film set in a harbour landscape (shot by Felix Forsman with influences from French poetic realism) and a story of a man (Laiska-Jammu) who is morally reborn with the help of a female Salvation Army officer (Ansa Ikonen). In this manner, through the trope of the Salvation Army, *The Man without a Past* addresses its viewers – once again – in a double tongue, evoking both traumatic history and framing it as yet another version of cinematic representations.

Whether reaching towards the past or imagining a futurity, Kaurismäki's latest film connects thematically to the 'anxiety about the demise of the traditional working class (associated with work, community and an attachment to place)' identified in British 1990s cinema (Hill 2000:178). *The Man without a Past*, too, laments the 'decline and death of an old social and economic and political order' – but furthermore, it mourns (once again) the 'death of the working-class hero' discussed by Cora Kaplan (2003:1-2) as the framework of *Brassed Off* (1996), *The Full Monty* (1997) and *Billy Elliott* (2000). While the British films, however, according to Kaplan (2003:2), represent working-class men as 'men of feeling', Kaurismäki's men are classic examples of men of honour in search of respect and dignity – showing a restraint of emotion.

J.P. Roos (2000), professor of Social Policy, argues that *The Man without a Past* 'kuvaa mitä tarkimmin suomalaisen miehen ominaisuuksia' (is a most accurate description of the characteristics of the Finnish man): 'eleettömyys, hiljaisuus, tunteellisuus, rehellisyys, surumielisyys, yritteliäisyys, filosofisuus viinan avulla, väkivaltaisuus (hakkaajaporukka edustaa myös suomalaista miestä)' (artlessness, silence, emotionality, sincerity, melancholia, enterprise, becoming philosophical with the help of liquor, violence (even the beating gang represents the Finnish man)). However, psychohistorian Jari Ehrnrooth has suggested a diametrically opposed reading. In his view, Kaurismäki's characters are 'selkeästi epäsuomalaisia' (blatantly un-Finnish): whereas 'erakkomainen yksin pärjäämisen eetos' (the reclusive ethos of making it on your own) is, according to Ehrnrooth, central to Finnish mentality, 'vahva, vapaasti valitseva yksilö' (a free individual who makes choices) does not fit in (Ehrnrooth 1996:61-62.) As these quotes demonstrate, the discourses around *The Man without a Past* most evidently invoke debates on 'Finnishness' as a mentality and as a quality of the film and its characters. The differences between the two readings notwithstanding, 'Finnishness' is self-evidently associated with masculinity and, more specifically, with the fetishised, generic figure of the working-class man. As I have argued elsewhere, in the cultural memory of Finnish cinema, the nexus of nation, modernity and gender is often focalised on the man-in-crisis for whom male comradeship, escape or alcohol are offered as sole consolation (Koivunen 2003:195-246). *The Man without a Past* reiterates this trope in its portraits of both M. and Mr. Nieminen (Juhani Niemelä), solving their crises by suggesting that a life at the margins, in the container village, be a framework in which both heterosexual romances and male comradeship works. This reading, however, is by no means specifically 'Finnish': national narratives as a transnational genre tend to prioritise male protagonists, and the global aesthetic of modernisation regularly features anxious men in search of a meaning in life.

Melancholic pleasures

Having moved the viewer between national narratives, historical references, political agendas and parodic bank robberies, *The Man without a Past* ends with a sequence that frames the narrative simultaneously in terms of both revenge and melancholia. The sequence begins with M. returning – again by train – from his trip to his recovered past. No more a man without a past, M. has recuperated his identity and his name, returning to the container village as Jaakko Antero Lujanen. It becomes clear that identity is more than a bureaucratic issue or a removable coil covering a core self: instead, identity presupposes a narrativisation of both one's past and one's expected or desired future.

Having learnt that he is a divorced man, with an ex-wife now living with a new fiancé, Mr. Lujanen (the name connoting firmness and toughness) – the former welder, now the band manager – returns to Irma. On his way, he meets anew the gang that beat up him up in the beginning of the film. This time, he prepares to defend himself, but suddenly the scene converts into a second scene of revenge in the film. Here, the film's humanist emphasis on respect and dignity is overthrown as an army of other outsiders – alcoholics and cripples – emerges from the darkness, outnumbers the gang and indulges in a revengeful, comic but ultimately violent beating, which the security guard (Sakari Kuosmanen) who also arrives at the scene decides not to interfere with. 'If you don't mind, I won't hurry in calling an ambulance', he says to Mr. Lujanen.

In the next moment, however, a melancholic tone overtakes the violent revenge scene, as we hear and see Annikki Tähti – a well-known artist in Finland – singing her 1950s *schlager* hit, 'Muistatko Monrepos'n' (Do you remember Monrépos?). For Finnish viewers, the song itself opens up a memory lane: for some viewers, it is yet another old pop song that a film (and Aki Kaurismäki) uses to convey affective climax; some the song takes back to their own youth to remember the previous hearings of the pop song, whereas others are moved by the context-specific meanings of the song. In the post-WW2 situation, this song enabled and mobilised a politically incorrect mourning of Karelia, the Finnish province that after the Second World War was annexed to the Soviet Union. In 2002, performed – once more – by the aged Annikki Tähti with a fragile voice, the song re-frames the narration as melancholic and invites readings that focus on national identity. As suggested by Sigmund Freud in 'Mourning and Melancholia' (1917/1957:245-246), melancholia entails mourning 'a loss of a more ideal kind'. For him, melancholia is a grieving without an end, an enduring devotion to the lost object, place or ideal, and as such, a pathology. Recent cultural theory, however, has reinterpreted Freud, claiming that no work of mourning is possible without melancholia and that melancholia be better understood as 'a structure of feeling, a mechanism of disavowal and a constellation of affect' (Eng 2000:1276ff; Eng and Kazanjian 2003:2-4). On the one hand, then, the tunes of 'Do you remember Monrépos' read as a national, cultural pathology: the identity of Finland/Finns being dependent on incorporated lost objects, such as Karelia. On the other hand, the song suggests an allegorical reading of the whole film being about a loss of an ideal, be it the political project of the welfare state or the leftist revolutionary dreams. In this perspective, then, the discourse of amnesia that the title of the film, *The Man without a Past*, reads as 'left melancholia' (Brown 1999) and as an articulation of the felt experience of 'post-industrial economic desperation' (Monk 2000).

Significantly, it is the same melancholic song that frames the romantic closure of the film: no words are exchanged when M. proposes to Irma, and a fantasy of uncomplicated courtship and unconditional love beyond politics of gender, so typical of Kaurismäki's films, is enacted. In the final frame of the film, the couple leave the communal *soirée*, but – unlike in Kaurismäki films of the late 1980s – they do not escape in a rowing boat to Estonia. M. and Irma just disappear into the darkness. Ignoring the political concerns and sentiments of anger voiced by the film and the utopia of communality suggested by the container village, heterosexual couplehood is in itself the closure and the suggested futurity of 'the man with a past'. For some viewers, this ending reads as an allegorical new beginning; for others it suggests a further confirmation of social exclusion of those not empowered by romance and compulsory intimacy. As Lauren Berlant argues in the recent anthology on *Compassion* (2004), some people and some desires must always remain invisible and veiled 'in order that a scene of social belonging may still be experienced as such' (2004:8).

Emotion Trouble

Since the early days of his career, Kaurismäki's public persona has been one of an auteur with 'the educated eye of a cinéphile' (cf. Eleftheriotis 2001:204). At the same time, Kaurismäki has often provided his films with outspokenly sentimental framings. *Ariel* (1988) was dedicated 'to the memory of Finnish reality', and *Pidä huivista kiinni, Tatjana/Take Care of Your Scarf, Tatjana* (1994) was described as his 'henkilökohtainen hyväksijättöni' (personal farewell) to that Finland in which he grew up and which 'surukseni tiedän iäksi menneen' (regretfully is known to have vanished forever) (Toiviainen 2002:91). While *The Man without a Past* takes place in a setting that evokes both a sense of pastness and contemporaneity, both period objects as well as the soundtrack may effect an authentication, an experience of 'the real Finland'. 'Low', popular music (*schlagers*, tango) and *milieux* (bars, restaurants) are coded as signs of authenticity in Kaurismäki's narration (cf. Skeggs 2004:106-107). As for music, such authentication may invoke an emotional, if not psychological, realism:

> Aki Kaurismäen ihmiset ymmärtävät toisiaan ilman turhia sanoja, ruumiin, katseiden, eleiden tai sydämen kielellä, tai sitten puhuvat toivottomasti toistensa ohi. Tärkeintä on joka tapauksessa se mitä ei voida sanoin ilmaista, se mikä näkyy kuvassa tai kuuluu musiikissa, mistä voi saada aavistuksen kuuntelemalla suomalaisten tangojen sanoja: oi jospa kerran sinne satumaahan päästä vois, ennen kuolemaa, kohtalon tuulet, pois kauas pilvet karkaavat. (Toiviainen 2002:97)

> (Aki Kaurismäki's characters understand each other without unnecessary words through the language of body, gazes, gestures or heart, or else they talk past each other. In any case, the most important is that which cannot be expressed in words, that which is to be seen in the images or heard in the music, that which is foreshadowed in the lyrics of Finnish tangos: Oh if once I could go to that fairytale land, Before dying, The winds of fate, The clouds drift away.)

In this reading seeking to pin down the affective appeal of the film, it is the Finnish songs in the soundtrack that 'antavat pelkistetylle ja viitteelliselle kerronnalle sen emotionaalisen latauksen ja kokemuksellisen kaikupohjan', 'muistojen ja tunteiden tulvana' (Toiviainen 2002:82) (charge the reduced and elliptical narration emotionally, and provide it with the sounding board of experiences, a flood of memories and emotions).

On the other hand, as Tarja Laine (2004:93-94) has recently argued, Kaurismäki's aesthetics work through 'emotional detachment'. A sense of artifice is evoked as the protagonists articulate in a formal and mannered way and the screen is filled with Technicolor-inspired, carefully planned frames. The camera is most often immobile, but lighting and setting produce elaborated compositions for the spectator's pleasure. In this sense, *The Man without a Past*, as well as earlier Kaurismäki films, fits Fredric Jameson's (1984) description of 'nostalgia film'. While retro cultural objects (such as jukeboxes, guitars, radios, and cars) as well as an eclectic soundtrack that mixes American rhythm and blues with Finnish tangos have been defining stylistic features of Kaurismäki's narration since the mid-1980s, the feeling of pastness is also in the image-track itself. As Vera Dika argues, pushing Jameson's analysis further, 'nostalgia film' or the aesthetic of recycling involves not only the period objects, but also the 'sensual surface of the images themselves' (Dika 2003:10). Rather than nostalgic, the soundtrack of *The Man without a Past* produces comic effects by bringing together dissonant elements: Irma, the Salvation Army Officer falls asleep listening to 'Do the Shake', the jukebox that M. saves from the garbage and takes home plays Blind Lemon Jefferson, blues music accompanies the scene where M. plants a potato garden outside his container, and the Salvation Army Band entertains container villagers performing both 1960s rockabilly and 1950s Finnish schlagers. In this way, the aural register is vital for the emotional cartography of the film. Through the music, too, the film moves its viewers between different modes, moods and sentiments, between places, times, and affects.

While operating with communitarian rhetoric and via tropes of nostalgia, *The Man without a Past* does not partake in the production of national sentimentality: the rhetoric of *ressentiment* as well the theme of revenge underline that there is no sense of promise as to the nation's possibility of overcoming social differences through channels of affective identification and empathy (cf. Berlant 2002). Furthermore, any singular moment of sentimentality in Kaurismäki films is haunted by the aesthetics of artifice and the sense of pastiche. But, as Linda Hutcheon (1995:91-92) and Margaret Cohen (2002:115) have argued, irony is as deeply engaged with the production of community as sentimentality. Irony requires a shared understanding of a text's different levels, of what it says and what it means. Furthermore, through irony a community can problematise itself. The co-presence of proximity and distance characterises *The Man without a Past*.

The film manifests the duplicity analysed by Richard Dyer as inherent to the aesthetics of pastiche. In his words, pastiche evades 'the two great modes of modern political art', naturalism and distanciation (Dyer 2001:78-79). On the one hand, pastiche is deeply involved in its object; on the other, an awareness of artifice and imitation haunt all claims of certainty.

The co-presence of sentimentality and irony, political agitation and artifice, melancholia and romance is, in my understanding, vital to the late-modern cinematic vernacular as developed by Aki Kaurismäki. The particular narrative ambivalence and the fluctuating affective transport between proximity and distance that characterises *The Man without a Past* is, indeed, a transnational feature of recent European cinema (see Iordanova 2001). While Peter Cowie (1992:76) maintained in 1992 that in order to fulfil the promises of an international breakthrough and to become true 'giants' of Finnish cinema, the Kaurismäki brothers 'must relinquish their childish jocularity and improve on their comic-book characterisation', I am certain that the Finnish, Nordic and European funders of Aki Kaurismäki's films feel great relief that he did not take Cowie's advice. Even if it may have been at the cost of being a 'giant' abroad, but only a cult director at home.

References

A-Talk 29.5.2002.: 'Aki Kaurismäen kurjalistotaru niitti mainetta Cannesissa'. Discussants: Markku Soikkeli, Hannu Salmi, Helena Ylänen, & Matti Heikkilä. YLE TV 1. (Actualities TV Show discussing *The Man Without a Past* and its success at Cannes Film Festival.)

Bagh, Peter von (2000): *Drifting Shadows. A Guide to the Finnish Cinema.* Translated from the Finnish by Sue de Nîmes. Helsinki: Otava.

Bagh, Peter von (2002): 'Ankaran arjen ja ihmisarvon kuvaaja'. *Turun Sanomat* 23.5.2002.

Berlant, Lauren (1997): *The Queen of America Goes to Washington.* Durham: Duke University Press.

Berlant, Lauren (2002) 'Capitalism, Compassion, and the Children: *Rosetta* and *La Promesse*'. Keynote lecture, Lancaster University, Re-Imagining Communities conference, May 23-25 2002.

Berlant, Lauren (2004): 'Compassion (and Withholding)'. In Berlant, Lauren (ed.): *Compassion. The Culture and Politics of Emotion.* New York: Routledge.

Brown, Wendy (1995): *States of Injury. Power and Freedom in Late Modernity.* Princeton: Princeton University Press.

Brown, Wendy (1999): 'Resisting Left Melancholia'. *Boundary 2* 25:3, 19-27.

Bruno, Giuliana (2002): *Atlas of Emotion. Journeys in Art, Architecture, and Film.* New York: Verso.

Cohen, Margaret (2002): 'Sentimental Communities'. In Cohen, Margaret & Carolyn Dever (eds): *The Literary Channel. The Inter-National Invention of the Novel.* Princeton: Princeton University Press.

Collins, Jim (1993): 'Genericity in the Nineties: Eclectic Irony and the New Sincerity'. In

Collins, Jim, Hilary Radner & Ava Preacher Collins (eds): *Film Theory Goes to the Movies*. New York: Routledge.

Cowie, Peter (1992): *Scandinavian Cinema. A Survey of Films and Film-makers in Denmark, Finland, Iceland, Norway and Sweden*. London: The Tantivy Press.

Dika, Vera (2003): *Recycled Culture in Contemporary Art and Film. The Uses of Nostalgia*. Cambridge: Cambridge University Press.

Dyer, Richard (2001): 'The Notion of Pastiche'. In Gripsrud, Jostein (ed.): *The Aesthetics of Popular Art*. Kulturstudier nr 19. Program for Kulturstudier, Oslo: Norwegian Academic Press.

Ehrnrooth, Jari (1996): 'Heijastuksia kansallisesta minästä'. In Apo, Satu & Jari Ehrnrooth: *Millaisia olemme. Puheenvuoroja suomalaisesta mentaliteetista*. Kunnallisalan kehittämissäätiön Polemia-sarjan julkaisuja nro 17. Helsinki: Vammala.

Ehrnrooth, Jari (2002): *Kaksi syntymää ja yksi kuolema*. Helsinki: WSOY.

Eleftheriotis, Dimitris (2001): *Popular Cinemas of Europe. Studies of Texts, Contexts and Frameworks*. New York: Continuum.

Eng, David L. (2000): 'Melancholia in the Late Twentieth Century'. *Signs* 25:4, 1275-1281.

Eng, David L. & David Kazanjian (2003): 'Introduction: Mourning Remains'. In Eng, David L. & David Kazanjian (eds): *Loss. The Politics of Mourning*. Berkeley: University of California Press.

F & L Research 1999: *Suomalaisen elokuvan markkinat ja kilpailukyky*. Suomen Elokuvasäätiön ja Kauppa- ja teollisuusministeriön Sisältötuotantoprojektin toimeksiannosta: www.flms.com/elokuva.html

Filmzeitung.de 13.11.2002. 'Der Mann ohne Vergangenheit' (a film review). Available at www.filmzeitung.de/article.php?article_file=1037228113.txt

Freud, Sigmund (1957; 1917): 'Mourning and Melancholia'. *The Standard Edition of the Complete Psychological Works of Sigmund Freud*. Translated from the German under the General Editorship of James Strachey. London: The Hogarth Press.

Grainge, Paul (2000): 'Nostalgia and Style in Retro America: Moods, Modes, and Media Recycling'. *The Journal of American and Contemporary Cultures* 23:1, 200, 27-34.

Hansen, Miriam Bratu (2000): 'Fallen Women, Rising Stars, New Horizons. Shanghai Silent Film as Vernacular Modernism'. *Film Quarterly* 54:1 (Fall), 10-22.

Helén, Ilpo (1991): 'Ajan läpi?'. *Filmihullu* 5/1991, 12-18.

Hill, John (2000): 'Failure and Utopianism: Representations of the Working Class in British Cinema of the 1990s'. In Murphy, Robert (ed.): *British cinema of the 90s*. London: BFI.

Hutcheon, Linda (1995): *Irony's Edge*. New York: Routledge.

Iordanova, Dina (2001): 'Displaced? Shifting Politics Of Place And Itinerary In International Cinema', *Senses of Cinema*: www.sensesofcinema.com/contents/01/14/displaced.html

Jameson, Fredric (1984): 'Postmodernism, or The Cultural Logic of Late Capitalism'. *New Left Review* 146 (July-August), 53-92.

Kaplan, Cora (2003): 'The Death of the Working-Class Hero'. *Social & Cultural Review*. The Pavis Centre Newsletter 4, 1-8.

Koivunen, Anu & Kimmo Laine (1993): 'Metsästä pellon kautta kaupunkiin (ja takaisin) – jätkyys suomalaisessa elokuvassa'. In Ahokas, Pirjo, Martti Lahti & Jukka Sihvonen (eds): *Mieheyden tiellä*. Nykykulttuurin tutkimusyksikkö, Jyväskylä: Jyväskylän yliopisto.

Koivunen, Anu (2003): *Performative Histories, Foundational Fictions. Gender and Sexuality in Niskavuori Films*. Studia Fennica Historica 7. Helsinki: Finnish Literature Society.

Lahti, Martti (2001): 'Powerful Innocents: The "Victimization" of White Men in *Regarding Henry* and *Forrest Gump*'. In Pomerance, Murray & John Sakeris (eds): *Closely Watched Brains*. Boston: Pearson Education.

Laine, Tarja (2004): *Shame and Desire. Intersubjectivity in Finnish Visual Culture*. Amsterdam:

ASCA.

Monk, Claire (2000): 'Men in the 90s'. In Murphy, Robert (ed.): *British cinema of the 90s*. London: BFI.

Nestingen, Andrew (2003): 'Nostalgias and Their Publics: The Finnish Film Boom, 1999-2001'. *Scandinavian Studies* 75:4 (Winter), 539-566.

Nestingen, Andrew (2005): 'Aki Kaurismäki's Crossroads: National Cinema and the Road Movie'. In Nestingen, Andrew & Trevor G. Elkington (eds): *Transnational Cinema in a Global North. Nordic Cinema in Transition*. Detroit: Wayne State University Press.

Peltonen, Matti (1996): 'Matala viisikymmenluku'. In Peltonen, Matti (ed.): *Rillumarei ja valistus. Kulttuurikahakoita 1950-luvun Suomessa*. Helsinki: Finnish Historical Society.

Raeste, Juha-Pekka (2003): 'Kunniallisen köyhyyden kaipuu'. *Helsingin Sanomat* 19.4.2003.

Roos, J.P. (2002): 'Suomalaisen miehen oivaltava havainnoitsija'. *Helsingin Sanomat* 23.8.2002.

Sennett, Richard (2003): *Respect in a World of Inequality*. New York: W.W. Norton.

Skeggs, Beverley (2004): *Class, Self, Culture*. London: Routledge.

Timonen, Lauri (2002a): *Mies vailla menneisyyttä. Filmihullu* 2/2002, 32-34.

Timonen, Lauri (2002b): *Mies vailla menneisyyttä*. Sodankylä Film Festival catalogue.

Toiviainen, Sakari (2002): *Levottomat sukupolvet. Uusin suomalainen elokuva*. Helsinki, SKS.

Notes

1. Most of his films have attracted only 20,000-40,000 viewers, whereas domestic box office hits in Finland usually make 200,000, sometimes up to 600,000 viewers. Of the earlier films, *Leningrad Cowboys go America* (1989) had 26,000 viewers in Finland, about 600,000 viewers abroad; *I hired a Contract Killer* (1991) was seen by 40,000 viewers in Finland and 560,000 abroad. In 1996, *Drifting Clouds* had the attendance rate of 50,000 viewers in Finland, whereas elsewhere in Europe it was seen by 400,000 viewers. (F&L Research 1999, 28.) *The Man without a Past* (2002) achieved 160,000 viewers in Finland, but two million viewers abroad, and a million dollar profit in the US.

2. See, for example, von Bagh 2000; Toiviainen 2002; Ehrnrooth 1996, 2002; Laine 2004. For a summary of readings which frame Kaurismäki's films as essentially Finnish, see Nestingen 2005:284.

3. For example, von Bagh 2002; A-Talk 29.5.2002; Timonen 2002a.

4. For a discussion of nostalgia in Finnish films of the 1990s, see Nestingen 2003.

5. For an analysis of Kaurismäki's style as a combination of nostalgia and irony, see Helén 1991:12-14.

6. 'Juna hiljaista miestä kuljettaa / Kuka onkaan tuo mies ja mihin matkustaa' ('Laulu siirtotyöläisestä' ('Song about a migrant worker'), lyrics Aulikki Oksanen, music Kaj Chydenius).

7. Throughout this essay, extracts from the film's dialogue are given in my own English translation.

8. Quoted at www.cinematheque.bc.ca/archives/clouds_jf99.html

9. Aki Kaurismäki entered the national public sphere in 1981 as his short film, *Liar*, was screened at the Tampere film festival. As for the film business, he was an outsider as he has not been trained at the Helsinki Film School. First, he was best known as a member of the post-seventies Finnish new wave generation rock music, thanks to the documentary *Saimaa-ilmiö* he shot with his brother Mika in 1981. From the beginning, his public persona was one of few words and lots of drink. While his twisting on the red carpet

leading to the 2002 Cannes prize gala provoked some, including the Minister of Cultural Affairs, today he is also known for many political statements. In 2000, he refused an honorary doctorate at the Helsinki University of Art and Design in protest at the promotion of Marimekko CEO Kirsti Paakkanen who had connections to the fur industry. In 2002, he boycotted the New York Film Festival to express his support for Abbas Kiarostami who was not allowed to enter the USA in 2002; and in 2003, he protested against the US war against Iraq by not attending the Academy Awards at the Oscar Gala.

10. Among the many international prizes *The Man without a Past* was awarded, at least two came from church organisations praising the humanist message of the film: one from the Danish Church, the other, the John Templeton Award, from the ecumenical Conference of European Churches. A former winner of the European Templeton Award is Ken Loach's *My Name is Joe*.

11. In this respect, Kaurismäki is a representative of this time: in the early 1980s, the Finnish art world discussed postmodernism, the first Seinäjoki Tango Festival was arranged in 1984, and in 1986, Peter von Bagh and Ilpo Hakasalo published *The Golden Book of Finnish Schlagers (Iskelmän kultainen kirja)* which initiated a revival of old schlagers. The same year, an anthology presenting postmodern theorisation in Finnish, *Moderni/Postmoderni*, was published.

Incense in the Snow: Topologies of Intimacy and Interculturality in Friðriksson's *Cold Fever* and Gondry's *Jóga*[1]

C. Claire Thomson

> What does not register in the orders of the seeable and
> sayable may resonate in the order of the sensible
> (Marks 2000:111)

> 'Just stupid people believes [sic] in what they can see
> and touch' (Siggi, in *Cold Fever*)

In Friðrik Þór Friðriksson's Icelandic-Japanese road movie, *Á köldum klaka/Cold Fever* (1994), one of the first natives encountered by the jetlagged hero Hirata is a patriotic taxi driver. His monologue is a statistical litany of Icelandic culture re-packaged for a transnational age:

> How do you like Iceland? You know, we have the most writers per capita of any
> country in the world. And the most Nobel Prize winners per capita. And we got
> the most beautiful women in the world. Two of the last six Miss Worlds. Would
> you like some *lakrids* – liquorice? We make the best in the world [...] We got
> more sheep than people in Iceland. And the best, purest land in the world. And
> we are very proud of it.

In his random bragging, the taxi driver hits on the topological approach to mapping the concrete and imaginative world which contemporary social science is beginning to call 'hybrid geography'. His snapshot of all that Iceland produces, consumes, and *is*, echoes Sarah Whatmore's account of interactions by multiple actors in complex global spacetime: 'the intimate, sensible and hectic bonds through which people and plants; devices and creatures; documents and elements take and hold their shape in relation to each other in the fabrications of everyday life' (Whatmore 2002:3). In mapping out the relations, boundaries and overlappings between human bodies, non-human bodies, texts and environment, hybrid geographies begin to displace the human as privileged, rational, thinking subject, and move towards an emphasis on 'knowing and doing' as corporeal. A space then opens up in which relationality, rather than individuality, is seen as 'the axiom of social life' (ibid.:118).

Cold Fever's portrayal of Hirata's encounters during his trip were met with derision and annoyance amongst some Icelandic audiences, who feared that the film, with its 'catalogue of Icelandic curiosities and clichés' (Møller 2005:322), exoticised national culture for the global gaze as innately quirky and consumable. While *Cold Fever* does luxuriate in the global flux of images and bodies in which many of its protagonists participate with alacrity, it is also, I want to argue, deeply concerned with the intercultural encounters that such circulations engender: encounters of bodies, practices, and memories. A hybrid geography of relationality becomes the axiom of the filmic narrative, so that Hirata encounters the 'foreign' though his bodily meeting with the texts, humans, foodstuffs, animals and, above all, the landscape of Iceland that the taxi driver eulogises.

Before moving on the discuss how *Cold Fever* negotiates the intercultural encounter with a strange land and its human and non-human inhabitants, I want to try to flesh out the relations between landscape, body and the contemporary visual arts by turning to a multimodal text released just a couple of years after Friðriksson's film: Michel Gondry's collaboration with Björk on the pop music video *Jóga* (1997).

'Emotional landscapes'

The musician, singer, lyricist and actor Björk is arguably Iceland's best-known contemporary export. She recounts the genesis of her third solo album, *Homogenic* (1997), thus:

> I'd never been so long away from Iceland, so when I started preparing for *Homogenic*, it was very obviously supposed to be a love album to Iceland nature [...] It isn't Icelandic music trying to be English or American [...] With this song ['Jóga'], I really had a sort of National Anthem in mind. Not the National Anthem, but certain classic Icelandic songs – very romantic, very proud. (Bjork.com 2002: Björk interviewed by David Hemingway.)

Neo-romantic nationalism or postnational irony? As Birgir Thor Møller comments, both Björk herself and Icelandic culture in general are invariably framed in cultural journalism as products of 'the country's larger-than-life landscape, history, or folklore' – or simply as downright odd (Møller 2005:307). Björk's siting of her own work firmly within a domestic musical tradition and a national territory is a prime example of the contemporary cosmopolitan's simultaneously affective and self-reflexive discourse of belonging (Hedetoft & Hjort 2002:xv-xx). But the means by which Björk roots the *Homogenic* project in the Icelandic landscape goes beyond the discourse of romanticism; it re-configures the relationship between technology, culture and the material world, feeling towards 'a direct fusion of her creative vision with the forces of Icelandic nature' (Sullivan 2003:121). Digital recording technology enables the incorporation of the landscape's auditory output into the music. For example, volcanic activity was sampled and used as the basis of the songs' 'deep, rumbling, hard-edged beats' (Sullivan 2003:121).

The video which accompanied the track 'Jóga' was directed by Michel Gondry, one of music video's few auteurs, and it redoubles this play across the boundary of the earthy (or indexical) and the æsthetic (or digital). The finished video merges film of the natural landscape, shot from the air and in close-up on 16mm film, with digital morphs of dancing stones and gaping chasms of molten rock, created in post-production. The camera swoops over coastline, mountain and river delta, and zooms in on patterns at ground level: mineral formations, lichen on rocks, ice on slate, grasses. These two perspectives correspond, more or less, to the two key lyrical concepts of the song: 'emotional landscapes' and 'state of emergency' (Björk 1997). The singing subject's professed puzzlement and confusion at life's coincidences and her emotional response to them (emotional landscapes) is accompanied by the complex rhythm of those sampled volcanoes and by the camera's slow, intermittent trawl across the surface texture of the land. The chorus's expression of thankfulness to the friend who lifts the singer to a state of insightfulness (state of emergency), meanwhile, is signaled by the dominance of strings and the 'eye' of the camera taking to the air.

The conflation of emotional and filmic perspective becomes more complex when the landscape itself comes to life after the second verse. Vast vistas are made to crack open and slide against each other, revealing the lava and tectonic shifts which characterise this island on the cusp of two plates on the earth's crust. These panoramic shots are intercut with close-ups of single, palm-sized elements on the surface of the land – rocks, crystals, clumps of grass – which are made to swell, or jump. This landscape is living and moving both at the macro-level (Iceland at the meeting of tectonic plates) and at the micro-level (local varieties of minerals and flora). *Jóga*'s panoramic view is both of the time of deep ecology – the interconnectedness of life-forms on different scales – and a glimpse of what Manuel de Landa calls 'non-linear history', the 'rocks and winds, germs and words [that] are all different manifestations of this dynamic material reality' (2000:21). But these visions of vistas of non-human time are shot through with the insistent rhythm of the time of the body, the heartbeat.

That the human is inextricably embedded both in the ecosystem and in ecological history is suggested by Björk's periodic appearance in the video: with the last chorus, the camera circles in towards a (clearly digitised) singer standing on a hilltop. She opens her jacket and beckons the camera into her chest cavity, which resembles a rocky cavern, eventually opening out onto an aerial view of a green island vaguely reminiscent of the shape of Iceland. The suture between the volcanic samples used as beat and the heartbeat of a human body is complex: it is affective, conjuring up memories and imaginaries of the national landscape; it is ecological, in that body and landscape can be understood as part of the same natural system, and it is metaphorical, suggesting that the landscape is – a metaphor rendered literal in the world of the video – 'in' Björk's heart. At high volume, the connection is visceral for the listener, too, via the thud of the bass in the breast. Indeed, this complex of physical and affective interpenetrations between the 'bodies' of listener, landscape and music is echoed by Jenny Edbauer (whose work we will return to later), who describes the work of music on the body as one example of artistic 'impact' that is more than merely metaphorical:

> During the event of hearing a song that jives with your body, you enter into a zone of permeability with other elements that are 'properly' outside your own sense [...] Commonly perceived delimitations – proper borders of identity and substance – break down in these instances, disclosing the affective sensation of peripheral relations at work. (Edbauer 2004:23)

The very notion of an affective relationship between art and the human subject is at the core of theories of national imagining (see Anderson 1991; Culler 2003), but this relationship is rarely theorised as involving an explicitly *embodied* national 'subject'; rather, it tends to rest on the correspondence between spatio-temporal figurations in the narrative structure of novel and national(ist) historiography. Giving the body its place in the process of imaginative involvement in a national community opens up a space in which to undertake the first sketchy mappings of a more holistic understanding of the nexus of culture, material world and affective belonging. After all, national histories are among the master narratives whose foundering leaves affect as one key to understanding our postmodern culture, saturated with images and information, in which 'belief has waned for many, but not affect' (Massumi 2002:27).

What I am trying to feel my way towards here is the possibility of a national narrative that *resists* narrative; a telling of the nation that roots itself in the landscape without romanticising Nature or the Human. As we shall see, one approach to art that sidesteps narrative is to trace the reception of an image as multilevel, involving, firstly, its 'indexing to conventional meanings in an intersubjective context' (Massumi 2002:24) – that is, the cognitive processing and narrativisation of images – and, secondly, the intensity of its bodily impact, which is 'not semantically or semiotically ordered' (ibid.). This is not the same as the convention that music videos, for example, are inherently multimodal, and tend to subsume narrative and performance into spectacle (Mundy 1999:239). It is to recognise that we react autonomically to visual stimuli, especially at the level of the skin, in ways that are measurable but scarcely theorised; a response that is 'outside expectation and adaptation, as disconnected from meaningful sequencing, from narration, as it is from vital function' (Massumi 2002:25). For Massumi, the Icelandic heartbeat – human and geological – would perhaps trope the interface between consciousness and 'the autonomic depths'. A quickening heartbeat, for example, indicates involvement in narrative expectation: 'Modulations of heartbeat and breathing mark a reflux of consciousness into the autonomic depths, coterminous with a rise of the autonomic into consciousness' (ibid.). Björk's and Gondry's heartbeats are the interface between the metronomic rhythms of national narrative and the affective collision of the nation's bodies: the land, and the creatures who live on it.

Jóga is blessed with a particular characteristic that tends to unearth the embodied dimension of response to images – outside and alongside their contextualisation and narrativisation as 'images of the nation'. This characteristic is its recourse to the haptic, a strategy it shares with *Cold Fever*, but one which the music video, as a more inherently 'spectacular' medium, can tap more fruitfully than the commercial feature film. In *The Skin of the Film*, Laura U. Marks shows how the camera can bring the eyes to 'function like organs of touch' (2000:162) (a phenomenon which Bodil Marie Thomsen also explores in her chapter in this book). A haptic work might cause the eye to linger on the surface plane of the screen before resolving into a recognisable image, or might privilege the texture of the object shown; in any case, it is the material presence of the object, rather than its representation as such, that is key (Marks 2000:163). The effect might be achieved by material intervention on the film (scratching, solarisation, incidental decomposition), a play with scale, focus or resolution. Whatever the technical means, Marks' point is that haptic visuality staves off narrativity: 'at the point where the image becomes recognizable [...] narrative

Stills from Gondry's *Jóga*, by kind permission of Kevin Holy

rushes in' (2000:187). Engaging haptically with the image evokes responses that are rooted in individual and collective sense memory, rather than national narrative or historical pedagogy. In *Jóga*, I would argue, the contrast between bird's eye and snail's eye views of the Icelandic landscape plunges the viewer into haptic visuality in the close-up shots. Dancing stones differentiate themselves from their background of smaller rocks in their movement and therefore their outline; they are all pattern – each shot has its own texture, jagged, striated, glossy, bulbous – and invite the viewer to touch, feel the stone in the palm of the hand, the burn of ice on rock, smell the soil and grass. The ambiguity of scale, the pulsing of the objects, and the intermittent gliding motions of the camera, invite a recourse to touch as well as sight.

'State of Emergency'

The transitions between points of view in the video, together with these writhings of the landscape itself, and the flagrantly digital quality of the images, compel us to hear the echo of the word 'emergence' in 'emergency', so that the sense of bodying forth – rising from or emerging from the earth – coalesces with the lyric's insistence on urgency or panic. Homi Bhabha also plays with this echo when he declares: 'the state of emergency is also always a state of emergence'. Bhabha is writing here of the postcolonial emergence/y of the oppressed that erupts into the 'progressive, ordered whole' of Western history (Bhabha 1994:41). To be sure, he does not have in mind the postcolonial travails of a wealthy European nation that peacefully gained its statehood sixty years ago; I am not implying, here, a straightforward analogy with the political struggles of minority cultures whose filmmaking feels its way towards expression through the gaps and silences engendered by long-term suffering and repression (see Marks 2000:55ff).

Nevertheless, there is something to be learnt from letting Bhabha harmonise with Björk: that the emergence/y of their visions is an eruption of new temporalities and identities into History, into, indeed, the story of the human subject, which, in such circumstances, 'emerges not as an assertion of will nor an evocation of freedom, but as an enigmatic questioning' (Bhabha 1994:42). In other words: what does it mean to be human? I venture to suggest that in pausing and probing at this conceit of historical 'emergence/y' in the Icelandic context, we can flesh out the potential of film to visualise the emergence of a hybrid geography at a time of posthuman panic, a topological geography that draws (on) the fleshy, the affective, and the technological as well as the spatial.

Popular anxieties about Iceland's rapid transition to self-determination and prosperous modernity seem to have found their expression in film in the 1980s, whereupon, as Møller (2005:322) shows, the films of the 1990s began to represent the national dichotomy as negotiating between present and past, not city and country.[2] In Møller's reading, the foreign protagonist turns his or her gaze on the national community, and also acts as 'the international audience's proxy to Icelandic magic and lunacy'; the presence of the Other 'delineates difference' (2005:325). It may be, however, that it is the very transformation of 'Icelandic' sites and sights into experiences for consumption by the tourist that is discombobulating; the transmutation of daily practices and places of memory into 'image commodities' or simulacra (Harvey 1990:289). As I will argue later, one of the concerns of *Cold Fever* is to enmesh the intimacy of sense memories with supermodern mnemotechnics. The visceral shocks of intercultural encounter – the inappropriate interaction with the familiar – open up fissures between cultures and temporalities akin to the digital chasms of deep time in *Jóga*.

The state of emergence/y, then, that Icelandic film feels its way towards in the 1990s has much to do with vision, imagination, and memory. For Marks, the recourse to senses other than visual – or, at least, other kinds of visuality – is most often the response of intercultural cinema to the inadequacy of western cinematic practices to represent living between cultures and narrative traditions (Marks 2000:1). The propensity of intercultural cinema to evoke nonvisual sense experience and invite embodied responses to the film text is relevant to contemporary Icelandic visual culture, not just because of the complex socio-historical and natural world that film needs to engage with, but also because of the historical dominance of saga-culture. This impacts on Icelandic cinema in terms of the canonical status of the one medium relative to the other, and, crucially, in the very ability of the national audience to become spectators rather than readers (or listeners). It is sometimes observed that contemporary Icelanders are relatively visually illiterate; the school system's emphasis on the continuity of the native literary heritage, and the late arrival of most of the visual arts in Icelandic culture, claims Gísli Pálsson (1995:21), have resulted in a lack of sensitivity to the visual arts, and, paradoxically, an intensification of the debate about an alleged dwindling in knowledge of the national heritage.

But a lack of visual literacy should not be regarded exclusively as an Icelandic malady. Gondry's *Jóga*, I think, actually thematises the 'state of emergence' of digital special effects – and our learning to 'see' them – back in the mid-nineties. The distinctive sliding, or stop-start, motion of the morphs between still frames functions both to suture the rhythm of the camerawork to the beat of the music, and to emphasise the mediated, digitally-manipulated nature of the images. This film wants, all at once, to posit its relationship to the landscape as indexical and symbolic: the oscillation between – and fusion of – the real and the unreal itself becomes the spectacle, the emergence of a terrain that is visibly both imaginative and geophysical. New technologies of vision and recording are here staking their claim to *tell* national time and place as an affective, hybrid geography, without always letting narrative 'flood in'.

In this wider context, a cinema trying to gain a foothold in national culture could usefully exploit the potential of film to convey experience through an appeal to embodied and nonvisual cultural knowledge and memory. *Cold Fever* does just this, not by mapping tradition and modernity onto country and city, but asking its audience about the meeting of visual, inscribed and incorporated cultural practices (Connerton 1989): what do we become when we are recorded and encoded, and our culture sanitised, synthesised and packaged?

Cold Fever's original tagline was 'The best Icelandic/Japanese road movie you'll see all year' (Møller 2005:324). True to the genre, Hirata has a car, a trajectory, a mission, and a landscape to drive through. It may seem perverse, if not impossible, to try to arrest the forward momentum of his journey in order to linger on his embodied meeting with the local culture. What interests me, though, is not so much the teleological trajectory of the road movie, more the scope for intercultural encounters that it generates. With Hirata, our own non-linear trajectory is the following: we explore the Icelandic 'wilderness' as a topological mapping of transnational spacetimes of intimacy and distance; we return to Japan to trace the film's incorporation of visual and mnemonic technologies into an ultimately unsatisfactory battery of tools of memory; we zoom in on the time-image (Deleuze 1986, 1989) to approach the temporality of intercultural encounter; and then we join Hirata on his trek through the snow to witness his body's accommodation to the physical and cultural landscape.

Hybrid mappings: wilderness, graveyard and Blue Lagoon

Cold Fever's producer, Jim Stark, is said to have called the Icelandic landscape 'a billion dollars of free production design' (Berardinelli 1996), a chance remark that belies the film's engagement with the landscape as multisensory, dynamic and imbued with memory and history. It is in and by the landscape that Hirata's intercultural encounter is engendered. The Icelandic landscape is not the 'theatrical flat' of history, the 'empirical, rational space perceived as a void to be filled up', and neither is it merely representational space, 'charged with emotional and mythical meanings, community symbolism and historical significances' (Middleton & Woods 2000:284). But a humanist attitude to the land as a passive backdrop to social and cultural activity is hard to unlearn. Even in his protest against the 'production design' approach to landscape, the Icelandic actor and director Baltasar Kormákur betrays a concern for nature as ripe for exploitation in the wrong directorial hands: 'For me, landscape in a film is fine if it has a special meaning. If it's the same as sex, if it's only for exploitation, then it's not interesting' (Kaufman 2001).

The Iceland which Hirata encounters is a hybrid cartography of intercultural and more-than-human space, which bodies forth to meet his body. *Cold Fever* moves to sketch the kind of map that Sarah Whatmore envisions as 'attending simultaneously to the inter-corporeal conduct of human knowing and doing and to the affects of a multitude of other "message-bearers" that make their presence felt in the fabric of social life'. Appropriately for our road movie, she goes on to write that 'to map the lively commotion of these worldly associations is to *travel* in them' (Whatmore 2002:3, my emphasis). Whatmore, like Marks, insists that intercultural relations are dynamic, 'implying diachrony and the possibility of transformation' (Marks 2000:6), and both theorists are alive to the involvement, if not actually the agency, of non-human actors in these encounters.

Whatmore warns against the ingrained western tendency to construct certain spaces as 'wilderness'. The binary 'syntax of distance and proximity; inside and outside; then and now' and defiled and pristine (2002:11), trope the tundra (and other wild spaces) as a land of innocence, a timeless *tabula rasa* awaiting destruction or conservation through human intervention. Writing in a specifically Icelandic context, the anthropologist Gísli Pálsson also cautions against the reproduction of patterns of them-and-us, pseudo-colonialist or paternalistic protection of nature. 'One avenue out of the modernist project and current environmental dilemmas,' he argues, 'is to reject the radical separation of nature and society, object and subject, and the notions of certainty and monologue' (Pálsson 1995:165). This is also a principle that lies at the heart of Massumi's project to bring affect into cultural studies: positing the posthuman as the 'end of Man', he points out, succeeds only in re-stating human culture as 'the meaning and measure of all things', not least as the author and Other of an inert Nature. 'The concepts of nature and culture,' he insists,

> need serious reworking, in a way that expresses the irreducible *alterity* of the nonhuman in and through its active *connection* to the human and vice versa. Let matter be matter, brains be brains, jellyfish be jellyfish, and culture be nature, in irreducible alterity and infinite connection. (Massumi 2002:39, emphasis in original)

As Whatmore (2002:6) would have it, holistic mappings that show these alterities and connections actually depend on abandoning 'scientific' cartography in favour of a more affective and relational appreciation of space and time: 'The spatial vernacular of such geographies is fluid, not flat, unsettling the coordinates of distance and proximity; local and global; inside and outside'. Accordingly, *Cold Fever* begins to give voice to the sense that distance in space and time does not correspond to relative intimacy or independence, not least through its attraction to sites which can be described as heterotopic – as Foucauldian spaces both inside and outside society, both concrete and abstract. Wilderness is one such space – we must, argues Whatmore (2002:12ff.), learn to read wilderness as heterotopia – but more generally they are 'other places' such as museums, gardens and cemeteries, spaces where sites co-exist and relations come into being, which 'silently question the space in which we live' (Flynn 1991:167).

The relationality of memory and the heterogeneity of contemporary spacetime are suggested in *Cold Fever* in that the supermodern spaces of the tourist infrastructure coincide with and question the 'authentic' spaces of wilderness and memory. The distinction I am making here is of course a problematic one, but it is based on Marc Augé's idea of the difference between anthropological place, which is an ongoing negotiation of place as relational, historical, and concerned with identity (Augé 1995:77), and the 'non-place', which is peculiar to supermodernity and is characterised by the absence of these criteria, either because it is inherently transitory (the airport, the hotel) or is circumscribed and categorised as a 'place of memory' without actually incorporating memory (tourist attractions). The overlaps or points of encounter between the supermodern and historical versions of Iceland often have to do with the senses.

Hirata's trajectory from home through the non-places of transit lounge, aeroplane and transfer coach are relatively uneventful, but by boarding the wrong coach in pursuit of his mistakenly stowed suitcase, he ends up in the famous Blue Lagoon, a hot pool complex between Keflavík airport and Reykjavík. Hustled into the shower rooms, he is bewildered to encounter a multilingual sign indicating the parts of the anatomy that have to be washed before bathing, and walks along the boardwalk to ask the guide if this is really the capital city. The jobsworth guide is busy entreating his charges to avoid the sharp stones on the bottom, and the scalding water from the power station nearby marks out this space as a liminal one – one of Iceland's natural geothermic wonders, and nevertheless an extension of the 'non-place' of the airport, somewhere to kill a few hours during a stop-over. When Hirata later experiences total immersion in a hot pool out in the wilderness, alongside the eggs his friend Siggi is hard-boiling for lunch, the one place is inevitably mapped on to the other, this time without the sanitised tourist and civic infrastructure, but with the sensory experience effectively submerging Hirata in 'nature'; he scoffs the eggs that have just been cooked in his 'bath'.

Another heterotopic space featured in the film is the cemetery, in its Japanese and Icelandic manifestations.[3] Conversations in these cemeteries allow for explorations of human relations and social memory at the interstices of society. In a Tokyo graveyard, for example, Hirata's grandfather tries to persuade him to travel to Iceland and perform the memorial rites for his parents. Just as this cemetery and its encounter has its counterpart in the churchyards Hirata visits in Iceland, so too does its stonescape of graves parallel the city of the living. Through temporal suture, the cemetery links the space of the living to the space of the dead: it is an '"other city", where each family possessed its dark dwelling' (Foucault 1998:181). In Iceland, Hirata is taken to a local graveyard by a hitchhiker, Laura, the 'funeral collector'. One local woman, the gravedigger tells Hirata as he emerges from the gloom of a half-dug grave, is so impatient to join her husband in eternity that she has had the putative year of her own death carved on the family's headstone. The film also introduces the strange temporality of the photograph into the cemetery, as we shall see.

However, it is the most intimate site imaginable, that of Hirata's parents' death, where he performs a memorial ritual, that most unsettles the coordinates of distance and proximity. A corner of the wilderness becomes a site of memory; the temporal connections and disjunctures embodied by the cemetery also obtain here, at the specific site of a tragedy seven years before. The ceremony fulfils what the event prefigured, hinting at a quasi-medieval sacred understanding of time which is supposed to have been superseded by the linear history of the nation-state (Anderson 1991:24). Instead, it is the spacetime of the transnational that is evoked, by the things Hirata brings with him. Marks contextualises intercultural æsthetics in a globalising culture by tracing the cinematic conveyance of cultural memory in the 'transnational object'. Such objects 'travel along paths of human diaspora and international trade [and] encode cultural displacement'. And intercultural cinema fleshes out these objects, saves them from the status of commodities or fetishes, often by inviting the viewer to experience the object bodily (Marks 2000:78-9). Hirata must carry with him certain objects for use in the funerary rite: a memorial tablet, candles, sake, and incense. We do not see these objects until he is ready to embark on the final leg of the journey – they have been squirrelled away, first in his suitcase and then in a back-pack – but now he struggles to 'translate' their significance into English for Siggi. Hirata does not know the English word for one item, which is hard to perceive in the dim light of the bothy, and we must live with the suspense of the failure of translation until he reaches the right spot and unpacks the objects in the evening light – it is a bundle of incense. Appropriately for a memorial ritual – and for the climax of the film and of the journey – the camera lingers in close-up on the objects as Hirata's hands shape them into useable form as memorial tools: lighting the incense, embedding the candles in blocks of snow to float downstream. A long shot shows him in silhouette against the sunset, pouring the sake into the river, so that the writhing stream of liquid is perceived through the glints of light it reflects – an intersensory transmutation of sound into light.

The objects are thus transformed from inert signifiers of Japanese exoticism to sensual material imbued with the intimate relations between Hirata and his parents, largely through the sense memories they evoke in us: the scent of incense, the sharp, delicate heat of small candle-flames against the ice, the plash of liquor on water. It is this movement between the transnational and the personal that produces the intercultural moment in this case. On our behalf, Siggi stands and watches the ceremony, corroborating Marks' claim that '[t]he transnational object is a transitional object not only for the person in transition from one cultural reality to another, but also for the one whose cultural reality is entered and changed' (2000:123).

The transnational objects are filips to sense memory, but they also embody the fluid spacetimes of Whatmore's cartography, where the organic, the technological and memory come together. The candles, tablet and incense, after all, have probably been industrially-produced, and have certainly been transported via aeroplane, automobile and on horseback to their destination, whereupon they float downstream into the oblivion of wilderness. The wilderness as timeless *tabula rasa* is besmirched by our knowledge of Hirata's family's presence there – as tourists, as scientists? – years before.[4] Links to the past, the family, and the community are transformed and re-wired by intercultural encounters; new technologies, languages, temporalities and knowledges provide fruitful ways to visualise and narrate emerging forms of belonging.

Techno-orientalism: envisioning technologies of memory

Jack the hitchhiker remarks on his chauffeur's country of origin, and what he says is worth dwelling on, for it alerts us to the entanglement of Japan with technology in the film's global imaginary. This has implications for the weaving together of time, technology, wilderness, nation and memory in *Cold Fever*. Frustrated by the incessant Icelandic folk-pop music on the broken car radio, Jack throws away the volume knob and observes, 'I bet this would have never happened if this thing was Japanese, huh?' It comes naturally even – or especially – to a redneck like Jack to invest Japanese recording technologies with late-twentieth-century imaginings about the direction of global society and science.

Morley and Robins (1995:147-73) detect a brand of 'techno-orientalism' in contemporary relations between the West and Japan, a particularly potent brew in which Western fears of Japanese technological and economic supremacy swirl around with imaginings of that part of the East as the embodiment of post- or supermodernity. In the Western imagination, Japan became synonymous in the 1990s with 'technologies of the future – with screens, networks, cybernetics, robotics, artificial intelligence, simulation [...] the techno-mythology is centred around the idea of some kind of postmodern mutation of human experience' (ibid.:168). In particular, the suspicion is that Japanese innovation is taking us all into a world where the relation between the real and the simulated is not as it was before. Again, the narrative of emergence segues into a historical emergency.

Cold Fever's opening scenes are in Tokyo: a sequence establishing Hirata's environment and workaday life. From the first panoramic establishing shot, the minimalist lines of Mount Fuji lurk behind the cityscape, and crane shots of ant-like commuters scurrying through stations are replaced at sunset with neon-lit streets and fast-food vendors. The trees of a quiet cemetery and the volcanic national topography hint that the flux of the city hides the material continuity of earth and of history. But, overwhelmingly, this is a city of screens. Hirata is seen for the first time slurping noodles in front of a television game show; neon messages roll across electronic billboards, and Hirata's deceased parents speak to him from the past via video playback. Forced by his colleagues to sing karaoke, Hirata stoops on a darkened stage bisected by green neon stripes; behind him, two pop video screens show disembodied hands typing on a computer keyboard, and he reads the lyric of his song from a monitor. The built environment, his soft furnishings, the nets of the executive golf driving range, even the glass bricks behind his parents in the video, are all edges and corners and frames. This impression is intensified by the motionless camera in most shots, and especially by the most distinctive characteristic of this sequence: the use of the television-like aspect ratio of 1:66. We are constantly aware of looking at a screen – arguably a miniaturised screen – for the image is surrounded by a black band, and what we see within the frame echoes its edges and limits.

The æsthetics of this opening sequence contrast in quite complex ways with the undulating lines and much wider dimensions (2:35) of the cinematography when the film reaches Iceland. The shift from one aspect ratio to another makes the first explosion of Icelandic whiteness onto the screen, in the form of an aerial view of snow-covered mountains, a visual and visceral jolt for the viewer, a transmutation of the shock of cultural dislocation into light and height. Arguably, the change in aspect ratio codes the Icelandic landscape as mediated through the screen, such that myths of 'Japanese' technology and simulation – representation as a hall of mirrors, all surface and image – have always already infected the putative authenticity and materiality of Icelandic soil. The shift in scale is also suggestive of the disorientation involved in negotiating an unfamiliar space, which obeys the same geometrical or topological rules as the known space, but is qualitatively different due to a lack of personal historical investment in it. In any case, anxieties about the circulation of images and the alleged incompatibility of technology and authentic identity continue to haunt the film once it reaches Iceland.

During his road trip, Hirata twice meets a Funeral Collector, an American photographer called Laura, who reminds us that technology is not the sworn enemy of cultural memory. As she sees it, photographing and recording funeral services (making written notes and taping the singing) is a form of prosthetic memory (Lury 1998; Middleton & Woods 2000) which enhances the 'wonderful memories' she stores in her own mind and body. Indeed, far from etiolating the aura of the funerary event, Laura's recording of an Icelandic hymn serves as the soundtrack to the observation she makes to Hirata: rituals are beautiful because they are obligations that allow people to learn to grieve. The moment in time captured on tape, the unique event of one deceased individual's mourners singing in unisonance, is a poignant counterpoint to the incessant pop that takes over the space of the car when the radio breaks.

But the one-off recording also stands in for the photographs taken in the film that we do not see. Hirata is photographed twice: the first time by Laura as he wanders past a burial in Reykjavík, and the second time by a mourner at the funeral he attends with Laura. Hirata is an unwilling subject. On the first occasion, as Laura turns to snap Hirata, her camera points straight out of the film towards Hirata's point of view, implicating the audience in the action, whereupon Hirata is shown turning round, puzzled, to see what it is she is aiming her camera at. On the second occasion, a young mourner seems to want a picture of the exotic Japanese visitor standing behind the coffin. Sullying the solemnity of funerals with snap-happy abandon is thus experienced by Hirata and the audience as a moment of cultural dislocation, the re-jigging of elements of acceptable cultural practice – in other words, the jolt of an intercultural encounter. But why should it be shocking that a memorial service is punctuated by the use of a technology of memory? After all, as Barthes (2000:14) muses, to regard a photograph is to be reminded of the continuum of life and death, that s/he who is photographed fast becomes an object, one that *has been there*, but who will be outlived by the photograph. Conventional wisdom has it that digital technology removes even the mystically material connection between object and photograph that Barthes thinks makes the print 'literally an emanation of the referent [...] [which] will touch me like the delayed rays of a star' (2000:80-1).[5] This strange temporality of the image is borne out by the video greeting sent round the world by Hirata's parents, and remote-controlled into action seven years later when an errant golf ball knocks against the play button. This is a nice example of Whatmore's decoupling of proximity from intimacy, both in time and space.

It is, then, technological advances in recording and transportation that inspire and enable Hirata to commune with his deceased parents. Technology is a helpmeet of both 'inscribing' and 'incorporating' practices of memory (Connerton 1989), providing an invaluable but unsatisfying record of the presence of the loved ones – unsatisfying because it is only visual and auditory. As Marks admits, images can only ever imitate the other senses, though by flirting with them – touch, smell, taste – 'the image points to its own asymptotic, caressing relation to the real, and to the same relation between perception and the image' (2000:192). Similarly, the grizzled Icelander Siggi is sceptical as to the ability of both vision and touch fully to grasp the world: 'just stupid people believes [sic] in what they can see and touch'.

Snow and any-space-whatever

The Iceland that Hirata drives across is such a busy, peopled, hectic space of histories, memories, texts and the paraphernalia of modernity. And yet, there is all that white – a landscape of black and white, of rock formations, flurries and white-outs. The landscape is filmed in multiple guises. It is the mountainous whiteness, shot from a plane, for tourist consumption and as establishing shot; it is the interchangeably exotic vista of the road movie genre, through which the impossibly small red car moves in the distance; it is a hostile environment through which Hirata must learn to move. Here, I need to admit a tension between, on the one hand, the landscape as living culture, and, on the other, the landscape as a kind of cinematic space which Deleuze describes as characteristic of post-war cinema: the 'any-space whatever'. These filmic spaces have their roots in the socio-cultural conditions of post-war Europe, but their artistic symptom in the cinema is an occasional dwindling of time and break with narrative action. 'Any spaces whatever' are 'deserted but inhabited, disused warehouses, waste ground, cities in the course of demolition or reconstruction' in which new kinds of characters begin to see, rather than act. And in such moments, time

> rises up to the surface. Time ceases to be derived from the movement, it appears in itself and itself gives rise to *false movements*. Hence the importance of *false continuity* in modern cinema: the images are no longer linked by rational cuts and continuity, but are relinked by means of false continuity and irrational cuts. Even the body is no longer exactly what moves; subject of movement or the instrument of action, it becomes rather the developer [*révélateur*] of time, it shows time through its tiredness and waiting (Deleuze 1989:xi-xii)

I quote this passage directly to show how entangled are social space, cinematic time, and the body, for Deleuze. Discussing the any-space-whatever, Marks (2000:27) argues that it is also a postcolonial space of migration, exile and hybridity, one where cultural memories and (post)national histories meet, clash and coalesce. As such, the time- or affection-image that grows from these spaces also implies a 'disengagement of affective response from action' (ibid.:28). The cinematic time out-of-time with which Deleuze and Marks work, then, is a filmic spacetime in which the unsayable, unseeable, or incomprehensible can be sensed, can work as affect, in a time disjointed from the narrative flow.

In *Cold Fever*, the Icelandic landscape is Whatmore's heterotopic wilderness and Deleuze's any-space-whatever, and so can intermittently host the intercultural time-image which Marks seeks out.

The textural, tactile images of pulsing stones in Gondry's *Jóga* have their counterpart in Friðriksson's harnessing of the phenomenon of *skafrenningur*, the drift of powdery snow across the ground or surface. This is in evidence in many scenes, but in a sequence shortly before Hirata and Siggi reach their destination, it seems to embody the play of time across the surface of the image. Hirata slips outside the bothy to escape Siggi's snoring, and for around ten seconds the camera lingers on an expanse of snow and rock bathed in moonlight, *skafrenningur* skimming over the surface. The scale of this snowscape is indeterminate – the rocks and snow mount towards the moon, but spatial coordinates are veiled in the texture of smoothness and striation – until Hirata, surprisingly, wanders in from stage right some distance away to smoke a cigarette and, for the first time during his stay, simply contemplate his surroundings. We then cut to the sleeping Siggi, and back to the *skafrenningur*, whose scale is again immediately disturbed by the superimposition of Siggi's dream of a tiny Hirata walking to meet a flock of white-clad spirits. The curious, continuous movement of the surface layer of snow, paradoxically, arrests the forward motion of the road movie here. The haptic image is replete with the timeless flux of nature, so that the approach to the sacred place seems, for the moment, asymptotic; a quirk of imaginative geometry that is also *performed* by the snowdust skimming the surface.

The most striking use of a natural 'white-out' in *Cold Fever* is during Hirata's long walk to Reykjavík. Abandoned by the taxi driver, he has set off alone and is now stumbling through the snow, dragging his wheeled suitcase behind him. Clad entirely in black except for his red scarf, Hirata cuts an abstract figure on the far right of a screen which is otherwise more or less entirely white and devoid of perspective. The line of the ground is suggested by his feet, and the passage of time by their rhythm, but all other co-ordinates and even the type of terrain are obscured by faintly textured whiteness; the eye ceases to search for perspective and starts to enjoy the spectacle of oblivion. This space is a variation on Deleuze's any-space-whatever of temporal detachment and emptiness; the time of the long haul in a strange and hostile terrain. With heart-stopping suddenness, an enormous white truck emerges from below what we now understand as the brow of a hill, dwarfing Hirata, and emitting not only the squeaks, gasps and roar of a juggernaut, but also the ethereal boom of a male voice choir. Dwarfed by the singing Icelanders in the back, Hirata must then spend the journey to the capital – a constellation of points of light bathed in the velvet blue of a winter night – politely answering the standard-issue, self-reflexive enquiry: 'So, how do you like Iceland?' This is the practical reality of the intercultural encounter, but the affective spacetime in which it occurs has already been limned in the any-space-whatever just before the truck's arrival.

We can also explore the idea of the affection-image as intercultural encounter in Hirata's encounter with one of the *huldufólk*, Iceland's 'hidden people'. The car has shuddered to a halt on a hill, and Hirata – freezing and hungry – beds down for the night. The camera watches the sky lighten around the car, and we are suddenly back inside with Hirata, as a single thud is heard. As the camera's perspective shifts with the agonising unfurling of his stiff body, a figure comes into view outside, framed in the car window – a young girl with matted hair and a patchwork jacket, looking at him with apparent disdain. She emits a long, high-pitched scream, and a nearby ice-floe cracks and splashes into the water; turning back to a nonplussed Hirata, she screams again, and the engine starts up, which always entails this car seeming to rise off its haunches. Then the girl turns to go, and disappears in a quick dissolve – which resembles a jump cut – to an erupting geyser.

This scene exploits the folk belief that the 'hidden people' can show themselves, and indeed intervene in our material world. But the æsthetic strategy of showing the girl as a surly teenager – she could be the little sister of the tousle-haired woman who sold Hirata her car – constructs a continuum of anthropomorphic form between the human and hidden residents of Iceland. The alternate close-ups of the girl and Hirata during her visit brings him literally face to face with a representative of a (usually) invisible community. Enveloped in the ear-ringing soundwaves from the girl's scream, the two faces embody the binary typologies of east/west, man/woman, human/non-human, but the scream also embeds them, and the ice-floe – and the viewer – in a common soundscape. It is not so much that the film invites an analogy here between the human and the natural, for that would imply that the two categories were distinct; rather, it embodies the human man, the nonhuman girl, the ('natural') ice floe and the (technological) car in a space demarcated by sound. For Deleuze, the close-up extracts the face from spacetime, but can carry with it its own – 'a scrap of vision, sky, countryside or background'; the important point for him is that the face – in a similar but not identical way to the any-space-whatever – has the quality or power of 'compound and mixed affections', can extract 'the birth, the advance and the spread of the affect' (1986:113). I would argue that in the space of this resolutely embodied encounter, the otherworldly scream renders the scene an affection-image, a viscerally-experienced moment where all bets are off as to the line between natural and supernatural time and place.

The outcome, of course, is that Hirata can get in the car and continue his journey in his mechanical capsule, the use of which necessitates not straying too far from the infrastructure of modernity: petrol stations, transport cafés, rest stops. The logic of the road movie is to map out this infrastructure as it overlays, or intertwines with, the wilderness. One final scene which approaches the condition of the intercultural time-image, but in a resolutely scatological (and therefore corporeal) spirit, is an enforced toilet stop before the hitchhikers hijack the car. As Hirata and Jack wait for Jill to finish, they stand side by side, urinating beside the road. The screen fills up with a virgin white bank of snow, which is gradually besmirched by two yellow trickles, one a random scattering of droplets, the other a purposeful, targeted stream. The connection of human body to the cycles of the earth could hardly be more eloquently expressed, but this is also an instance of intercultural bonding which calls on universal bodily knowledge to paint in the snow the samenesses and differences of bodily practice and training across cultures. The wilderness, here, is a happy substitute for the modern facilities they would have reached, given enough time in the car.

The Skin of the Stranger

Poor Hirata just wants to be warm. In the graveyards and fish markets of Tokyo, he repeatedly declares how much he hates the cold; a week or two in Hawaii, he says, will keep him going for a while. Instead, his familial duty leads him to Iceland, where his visceral reaction to the chill winds of Tokyo achieves a new intensity.

The apparent oxymoron of the film's international title describes the universal experience of feeling hot and cold simultaneously when in the grip of the common cold: the sensation of being at once feverishly hot inside and shivering with cold at the skin. However, the Icelandic title of the film – *Á köldum klaka* – connotes the sense of the English expression 'to be on thin ice',[6] shifting the imagery from a hyper-awareness of the surface of the body to the perilous membrane that makes 'dry land' out of watery depths. The idea contained in both these images – that of a plane joining and separating two conditions or entities – is echoed in the complex of connotations of the title of Marks' book, *The Skin of the Film* (2000). Like the intercultural works of which Marks writes, *Cold Fever* 'pollute[s]' viewers' ideas of cultural distinction', not least via its 'tactile and contagious quality' which we 'brush up against like another body' (Marks 2000:xii). That is, the potential of the medium of film to approach the multisensory and affective nature of the intercultural encounter lends itself to negotiating the plane of difference via cultural collision, immersion and permeation, rather than translation *per se*.

The one culture is not forced to speak in the language of the other, which Marks sees as 'the tokenism of multicultural cinema'; intercultural cinema begins with the recognition that one cultural regime of knowledge cannot be expressed in the terms of another (2000:24). When an Icelandic woman in the SAS jet asks whether Hirata speaks English, the asymptotic approach of thumb and forefinger that accompanies his mumbled 'a little' speaks volumes. The international English spoken throughout much of *Cold Fever* is only a blunt tool – the real meeting comes with living through the flesh.

Anthropology, too, has been re-thinking its foundational concepts of 'cultural translation, the ideas of bridges and boundaries' in a supermodern world shaped by migration and 'a transnational public sphere' (Pálsson 1995:175). The intercultural encounter in anthropology, suggests Pálsson, could usefully be couched in terms of what the Icelanders call *sjóast* (getting one's sea legs): 'For them, enskilment is not only a physical exercise, it is a process involving *both* sociality and bodily dispositions' (ibid.:173). Pálsson advocates an anthropology based on dialogue and corporeal involvement in daily life, rather than a 'translation' of an exotic island culture into an authoritative language. Accordingly, we watch Hirata undergoing *sjóast* in the snow.

Hirata's facility with the range of practices of supermodern city life is established in the opening scenes. His body is involved in a range of orthodox and quirky practices around the screens of Tokyo: singing karaoke, eating a tv-dinner, practising his putt in the lounge. His body is schooled in the motions of domestic and public urban life, an experienced user of the prostheses of golf club and microphone alike. The narrative emphasis on the need to practice one's golf swing, be it at home or at the driving range, drives home not only the occasional incommensurabilities of available space and bodily movement, but also the daily involvement of our bodies in 'habitual skilled remembering', such that memory is 'sedimented in the body' (Connerton 1989:72).

In Iceland, however, Hirata's body is an *event*. The interaction of his body with the landscape and environment warrants consideration as what Jenny Edbauer (2004:9), following Massumi (2002), calls an 'affectively generative event'. Before and beyond our registration of the meanings of his body and its place in the narrative, Hirata's encounter with the temperature and terrain of Iceland furnishes our (viewing) bodies with 'the pleasure of intensity' – 'a jump cut, a jolt, a shock that exists on the surface of signification' (Edbauer 2004:4). Thinking about the irruption of Hirata's body into the snow-world, into relations with other human, animal and environmental bodies, alerts us to how '[i]ntensity disrupts the linear narrative' (ibid.), in this case of the road movie, and of the national narrative.

Hirata has particular difficulty gaining *sjóast* on the snowy terrain. He is forced to walk at intervals – due to the vagaries of taxi drivers' family commitments, the lack of spare tyres, or car-jacking by hitchhikers – and his well-cut wool coat and smart brogues are far from suitable trekking gear. On packed-down snow, he slips and slides, and his wheeled flight-case teeters and topples behind him. In deeper drifts, he must lift his knees ridiculously high, and has to shift his body weight back and forth. Clambering over rocks on the way to seek shelter for the night, he ends up on all-fours, falls in the dim light, flails and slides up to the farmhouse door. This 'failing, falling, flubbing body' (Edbauer 2004:31) of the apprentice hiker is, to be sure, a stage in Hirata's journey towards gaining his cultural and bodily 'snow legs'. But while it is on screen, we are struck by his body's '[e]xcessive intensity', its affective impact, which 'hits our body before we have the chance to contain it safely within a story' (ibid.). Snow gives Hirata more than goosebumps – it throws him literally off-kilter, and the encounter is an 'event' for us, both narratively and affectively speaking.

Hirata's body also needs to learn how to consume the foodstuffs of his new environment; liquorice and sheep's heads turn out to be not only an acquired taste, but also to entail the acquisition of skills. The local liquorice proffered by the patriotic taxi driver as the best in the world is, it seems, a salty *vade mecum* in all Icelandic glove compartments, for when Hirata's jalopy breaks down and he is stranded overnight in the freezing vehicle, the sweet is on hand as nourishment. Unfortunately, the effort required to tear off a length with his teeth, and the initial hit of ageing saltiness, prompts an instinctive gagging and spitting from Hirata's uninitiated mouth. The delicacy of boiled sheep's heads involves a shallower learning curve. The knack of teasing the meat from various nooks and crannies – the cheekbones, the eye socket – is first revealed to Hirata by the old couple who take him in for the night and give him dinner. By the time he encounters the dish again at the Icelandic Cowboys' buffet, he is sufficiently *au fait* with this foodstuff to incorporate it into the film's narrative watershed. After a bottle or two of 'Black Death' liquor with Siggi, Hirata lurches back to his room and pulls a sheep's head out of his pocket. Face to face with the boiled head, in a pose reminiscent of Hamlet's examination of the skull of 'Poor Yorick', Hirata (fluent now, if slurred, in his native tongue) ponders his neglect of his parents when they were alive, and recognises the meaning of his mission: atonement. He then takes a lusty chomp out of the sheep's cheek, in a move that subverts Hamlet's revulsion at his memories of bodily horseplay with Yorick, when he was more flesh than skull: 'My gorge rises at it [...] Here hung those lips that I have kissed I know not how oft' (*Hamlet* Act V, scene I, l.195-6).

While national delicacies can be counted among the indigenous practices most prone to commodification and synthesis for the tourist trade – not to mention their potential as signifiers of cultural quirkiness in a transnational context – it is important not to disregard the more workaday functioning of foodstuffs in networks of cultivation, production and consumption on local, national and international scales. Gustatory regimes of knowledge – how to cook, consume and taste particular ingredients – are networks of memory, practice and history (Marks 2000:226). These networks do not exclude the spectator by virtue of the unfamiliarity of the food shown on-screen; images of tasting and eating 'evoke sense experience through intersensory links' (ibid.:213), and trigger 'sensuous geographies' of novel combination (ibid.:246-7) that co-exist with and travel through the more sanitised sensoria of supermodern non-places.

Hirata's enskilment in eating strange dishes is therefore an integral part of his journey in space and time. For Whatmore, the sheer density of trajectories on local and global scales of food, in consort with its centrality to everyday practices of production and consumption, make it 'a ready messenger of connectedness and considerability that is fleshing out the spaces and practices of a relational ethics' (2002:119). *Cold Fever* tends to present the local nodes of international trade networks as relations between bodies, working against the notion that global currents constitute simply a human-controlled 'traffic in things'. This is not to posit an animist investment in the non-human, but to recognise that human flesh and intentions are entangled with the vagaries of other bodies, be they animal, mineral, meterological or technological (ibid.:118-9). The fish laid out on ice in the Tokyo markets are, like Hirata, destined for export, but, as his colleague remarks, being dead, they do not feel the cold like Hirata does. However, this allusion to the erstwhile livingness of the fish, now unprocessed raw material for sale, resounds in the haunting physiognomy of the boiled sheep heads, and even in the liquorice and liquor that Hirata consumes: the simulacra of national speciality become imbued with the 'geographies of intimacy' (ibid.:118) of field or sea to mouth. And in relating and consuming, the human body is witnessed as enmeshed in the same geographies. After all, as Massumi comments with relish, the internal branches and networks of the human body are enfolded into a membrane of skin, not a box. The integrity of the human body is 'all an act, a complex nutritive, excretive act' (2002:203). Is this not why patrons of the Blue Lagoon must thoroughly cleanse their bodies, lest they besmirch the unsullied waters of Icelandic nature? In consistently lingering on the encounter of the body with the unfamiliar culture, *Cold Fever* both punctuates the narrative trajectory of the road-movie with the intensity of the affectively generative event (Edbauer 2004), and embeds the body in relational geographies of 'people and animals, plants and soils, documents and devices' (Whatmore 2002:14). The skin of the stranger is not an impermeable barrier; it only 'twistedly envelopes' (Massumi 2002:203) an Other within.

Conclusion: horse sense

If *Cold Fever* explores the potential and the shortcomings of mnemotechnics to maintain bonds in a world in motion, it also has much to say about local and national place, and about the dimensions of space that have to do with community and memory. In Hirata's case, the ultimate intimate space – the site of his parents' death – is on the other side of the world, in a 'very strange country'. But it is the resulting intercultural exchange and getting of new knowledge that galvanises him fully to experience his participation in his own familial and cultural history.

By the time we are witness to the facility of Hirata's hands with the ritual objects, he has been 'enskilled' in the snow, largely by the provision of practical clothing and a horse, via Siggi's contacts. The fluidity of his movement on horseback belies the bumbling of his earlier encounters with 'nature', and links him through bodily practice to local, historical imaginative investment. For the Icelandic landscape, perhaps more than any other, is also an achievement of literary documents, amongst them the sagas. *Hrafnkel's Saga* has been singled out as a uniquely detailed, 'visual and tactile' image of the landscape of Iceland (Hermann Pálsson 1971:9). The saga peppers its precise description of the terrain with advice on how best to navigate it on horseback:

> Þar er svarðlaus mýri, og er sem ríði í efju eina fram, og tók jafnan í kné eða miðjan legg, stundum í kvið; þá er undir svo hart sem hölkn [...] Þeir ríða nú vestur af hrauninu. Þá er fyrir þeim önnur mýri, er heitir Oxamýri. Hún er grösug mjög. Þar eru bleytur, svo að nálega er ófært yfir. (Halldórsson 1965:50-2)

> There is a swamp there, and one has to ride through watery slush, with the mud reaching up to the horse's knee or mid-leg, sometimes even up to its belly; but underneath the mud the rock is very firm so there's no risk of sinking any deeper [...] They rode on west across the rocky ground, and then they came to another swamp which is called Oxmire. It's very grassy and has a good many soft patches which make it almost impassable. This bog is about as wide as the previous one but much softer, so that travellers have to dismount. (Pálsson 1971: 9-10)[7]

There is a tactility to this imagery which resides in the functional relationship between landscape, horse and rider; not only is the topography familiar to generations of Icelandic readers, but the bodily experience of riding through bog, the repeated dismounting, the sounds and scents of different types of grass and mud, and the feeling of the wind on one's face, all contribute to a multisensory engagement with the text as an account of local, lived experience. In shifting to a more organic kind of horsepower to complete the last leg of his quest, Hirata is thus participating bodily in historical continuity of practice. The vision of a Japanese tourist on horseback demonstrates, of course, that continuity of practice is also transformation of practice; Björk's, Gondry's and Friðriksson's lyrical, digital and cinematic interventions in the landscape tap into histories of national place, all the better to visualise the relational and affective dynamic of community.

Developing a vocabulary of affect within cultural studies necessarily requires a turn to the event of the encounter. Catching a glint of the autonomic impact of images entails a recognition that it is collisions, immersions and permeations that get the attention of the body, on-screen and off. The metanarratives by which national identities are traced are, then, only sustainable insofar as they saddle up with the intercultural:

> Rather than acting as the emotive means by which to solidify one's individuality, affect is the sensation of being affected by another body. It is the experience that we are not *a/lone(ly)*, but that we exist in relations beyond what we may recognize or even wish. (Edbauer 2004:15)

References

Anderson, Benedict (1991): *Imagined Communities: Reflections on the Origins and Spread of Nationalism*. London: Verso.

Augé, Marc (1995): *Non-places: An Introduction to the Anthropology of Supermodernity*. London: Verso.

Barthes, Roland (2000; 1980): *Camera Lucida*. London: Verso.

Berardinelli, James (1996): 'Cold Fever: A Film Review'. http://movie-reviews.colossus.net/movies/c/cold_fever.html.

Bhabha, Homi K. (1994): *The Location of Culture*. London & New York: Routledge.

Björk (Guðmundsdóttir) (1997): 'Jóga', from the album *Homogenic*. One Little Indian.

Björk.com (2002): 'Greatest Hits and Family Tree Special: Jóga'. Available at http://unit.bjork.com/specials/gh/SUB-04/index.htm.

Connerton, Paul (1989): *How Societies Remember*. Cambridge: Cambridge University Press.

Culler, Jonathan (2003): 'Anderson and the Novel' in Culler, Jonathan & Pheng Cheah (eds): *Grounds of Comparison: Around the Work of Benedict Anderson*. London: Verso.

Deleuze, Gilles (2005; 1986): *Cinema 1: The Movement-Image*. London: Continuum.

Deleuze, Gilles (2005; 1989): *Cinema 2: The Time-Image*. London: Continuum.

Edbauer, Jenny (2004): 'Executive Overspill: Affective Bodies, Intensity, and Bush-in-Relation' in *Postmodern Culture* 15:1. Available at: www3.iath.virginia.edu/pmc/

Flynn, Thomas R. (1991): 'Foucault and the Spaces of History' in *Monist* 74:2, 165-186

Foucault, Michel (1998): 'Different Spaces' in *Essential Works of Foucault 1954-1984. Volume 2: Aesthetics*. Edited by James D. Faubion. London: Penguin.

Halldórsson, Óscar (ed.) (1965): *Hrafnkels Saga Freysgoða*. Íslenzk úrvalsrit:1. Reykjavík, Skálholt.

Harvey, David (1990): *The Condition of Postmodernity. An Enquiry into the Origins of Cultural Change*. Cambridge, MA & Oxford, UK: Blackwell.

Hastrup, Kirsten (1992): 'Uchronia and the Two Histories of Iceland' in Hastrup, Kirsten (ed.): *Other Histories*. London: Routledge.

Hedetoft, Ulf and Mette Hjort (2002): 'Introduction' in Hedetoft, Ulf and Mette Hjort (eds): *The Postnational Self: Belonging and Identity*. Public Worlds, vol. 10. Minneapolis: University of Minnesota Press.

Kaufman, Anthony (2001): 'Interview: *Cold Fever*; Baltasar Kormákur Ushers in Icelandic New Wave with *101 Reykjavik*', 25.7.01. Available at: www.indiewire.com/people/int_Baltasar_Kormak_010725.html.

Landa, Manuel de (2000): *A Thousand Years of Nonlinear History*. New York: Swerve Editions.

Lury, Celia (1998): *Prosthetic Culture: Photography, Memory and Identity*. London: Routledge.

Marks, Laura U. (2000): *The Skin of the Film: Intercultural Cinema, Embodiment, and the Senses*. Durham & London: Duke University Press.

Marks, Laura U. (2002): *Touch: Sensuous Theory and Multisensory Media*. Minneapolis: University of Minnesota Press.

Massumi, Brian (2002): *Parables for the Virtual: Movement, Affect, Sensation*. Durham & London: Duke University Press.

Middleton, Peter & Tim Woods (2000): *Literatures of Memory: History, Time and Space in Postwar Writing*. Manchester: Manchester University Press.

Morley, David & Kevin Robins (1995): *Spaces of Identity: Global Media, Electronic Landscapes and Cultural Boundaries*. London: Routledge.

Mundy, John (1999): *Popular Music on Screen: From the Hollywood Musical to Music Video*. Manchester: Manchester University Press.

Møller, Birgir Thor (2005): 'In and Out of Reykjavik: Framing Iceland in the Global Daze' in Nestingen, Andrew & Trevor G. Elkington (eds): *Transnational Cinema in a Global North: Nordic Cinema in Transition*. Detroit: Wayne State University Press.

Pálsson, Hermann (1971): *Hrafnkel's Saga and Other Stories*. London: Penguin.

Pálsson, Gísli (1995): *The Textual Life of Savants: Ethnography, Iceland and the Linguistic Turn*. Chur, Switzerland: Harwood.

Shakespeare, William: *Hamlet*.

Sullivan, Paul (2003): *Waking Up in Iceland: Sights and Sounds From Europe's Coolest Hotspot*. Bodmin: Sanctuary Books.

Whatmore, Sarah (2002): *Hybrid Geographies: Natures, Cultures, Spaces*. London: Sage.

Notes

1. I am very grateful to David Martin-Jones for his encouraging and helpful comments on this essay, to Merek Cooper and Alex Mason for first bringing Gondry's video to my attention, and to Kevin Holy of www.director-file.com for advice on Gondry's work.
2. The Danish anthropologist Kirsten Hastrup (1992) has argued that the medieval Icelandic historical imaginary delayed the coming of modernity and its historical structures, so that the eventual meeting with modernity was especially traumatic in Iceland.
3. Friðriksson's films all feature a funeral (Møller 2005:324).
4. Møller (2005:324) tells us that the film was inspired by an article about a group of Japanese geologists who had drowned, and whose families had travelled to Iceland to mourn them.
5. It is worth noting, though, that Marks playfully employs the principle of wave-particle duality to argue that electrons have a form of memory, and that the 'indexical link' or 'existential connection' between image and object is therefore not necessarily severed in digital media (Marks 2002:161-75).
6. I am very grateful to Thuridur Águstsdóttir and to Guðrun Dröfn Whitehead for helpful advice on this expression.
7. The Icelandic text given here is from the 1965 edition edited by Óskar Halldórsson. The English translation is Hermann Pálsson's, as cited in his own introduction to the volume (Pálsson 1971).

The Old Wave: Material History in *Cool and Crazy* and the New Norwegian Documentary

Gunnar Iversen

In January 2001, the documentary *Heftig og begeistret/Cool and Crazy* was released for theatrical distribution in Norway. The film was directed by the veteran filmmaker Knut Erik Jensen, and financed by the state-owned production company Norsk Film A/S (Norwegian Film Ltd). *Cool and Crazy* premiered at the Tromsø International Film Festival, and became an immediate success with the critics as well as with audiences all over Norway. The production company and the distributor originally estimated that between 10,000 and 15,000 Norwegians would want to see this film, about the Berlevåg Male Choir in a tiny fishing village near the North Cape, but six months after the premiere more than 600,000 Norwegians – out of a population of 4.5 million – had seen the film.

In terms of attendance Jensen's film became one of the biggest box office successes ever in the history of Norwegian cinema. *Cool and Crazy* became the must-see for Norwegian audiences, even attracting a young audience, and became a fixture in Norway's cinemas. Everybody praised the film; in Oslo the film was shown for more than a year. In April 2001, even the Norwegian King and Queen saw the film, in an ordinary screening in Oslo, and they both announced to the newspapers after the screening that the film was wonderful. The national newspaper *Dagbladet* summed up the year 2001 by noting that it had printed one article mentioning the film or the choir every third day.

The film also made national stars of the singers, whose ages ranged from twenty-nine to ninety-six. The Minister for Cultural Affairs invited the choir to Oslo, and they also went on tour in the US as well as in Norway. They appeared at the Roskilde Rock Music Festival in Denmark in the summer of 2001, opening the final concert with Scottish band Travis to an enthusiastic audience of more than 40,000. Their CD also sold well, and the tabloid press was full of stories about the men, especially about the offers of marriage they had received from groupies.

Cool and Crazy not only became a national event, earning the Berlevåg Choir something of a cult status, but the film also became a modest international success on the film festival circuit, winning prizes at several festivals. It was later sold to several countries, among them the UK. In a review for *The Guardian*, in a special report from the Edinburgh Film Festival, Bob Flynn wrote: 'You know that you haven't seen anything quite like this.' He compared the film favourably to Wim Wenders' *Buena Vista Social Club* (1999), and wrote: 'Very cool and not a little crazy, the film brims with affection for the cantankerous, romantic community of men, capturing their lives and the extraordinarily emotive impact of their songs of faith and hope in the face of blacked-out winters and nightless summers.'

In this chapter, I will focus on *Cool and Crazy* in the context of the 'New Norwegian Documentary', which brought documentary back to the cinemas in the 1990s. I will also briefly present the work of the director Knut Erik Jensen, and discuss history and nostalgia in *Cool and Crazy*, moving towards the film's role as an inspiration for the Norwegian reality-tv series *Super Senior*, which was a huge success in 2002.

The New Norwegian Documentary

The 1970s was a good decade for the Norwegian documentary. A new form of politically radical and rhetorically aggressive documentary was produced, earning an audience in the cinemas. By 1981 this wave of political pamphlet-documentaries, angrily criticising the new, affluent Oil Nation, was nearly over, and in the 1980s only three feature-length Norwegian documentaries were produced and shown in the cinemas. The documentary genre survived on television, but seemed unable to return to the cinema as something more than an odd exception.

In the 1990s this changed drastically, and in 1995 alone, five feature-length documentaries were shown in the Norwegian cinemas. Seventeen documentaries altogether were shown in the course of the decade, and this trend continues today. In 2002 alone seven Norwegian documentaries were released, and in the period from 1991 to the summer of 2004 the number of Norwegian documentaries shown in cinemas reached thirty-one. The only really new 'trend' in Norwegian film history, quantitatively speaking, is this return of the documentary to the cinemas.

The documentaries that have been produced since the early 1990s are very diverse, from portraits of artists and travelogues to critical documentaries exposing ill-treatment of psychiatric patients or the elderly in institutions, police brutality, or the secret organisations within the army during the Cold War. Most of these new Norwegian documentaries combine the sober discussion of a topic or theme with intimate close-up portraits of ordinary men or women, giving the audience a chance to see the topic through an individual or collective, giving voice and body to the topic being described or discussed.

The explanation as to why so many documentaries have been made, and why they have been so popular in Norway in recent years, is complex and multidimensional, but one obvious and important part of the explanation has to do with the state support for Norwegian films.

Today, two basic types of public support for the production of Norwegian films are in operation: production support and box-office bonus. Production support is awarded selectively by the newly established Norwegian Film Fund, an organisation created in 2001 as part of the 'New Norwegian Film Policy' intended by the Norwegian Ministry of Cultural Affairs to renew and modernise the film sector, combining the three national institutions – the Norwegian Film Institute Production Support, the Audiovisual Production Fund, and Norwegian Film Ltd – that previously distributed production support to Norwegian film producers. Production support was principally intended to provide a source of funding for films with artistic aspirations, although not exclusively art cinema productions, but the New Norwegian Film Policy also added a '50/50 scheme', modelled on the Danish system, with automatic advance support for feature films in which producers have managed to raise a minimum of fifty per cent of the capital.

The other form of state support for Norwegian films is a box-office bonus, which is based on the ability of the individual film to attract an audience, awarded as a general measure. Thus all Norwegian feature films, documentaries as well as feature films, are entitled to a ticket subsidy of fifty-five per cent of box office gross. Films for children are entitled to one hundred per cent. Box-office bonus has an upper limit, calculated for each individual film, and is based on the amount of financial risk taken by the producer's financial share in the production.

These two types of public support, plus various funds for project development for feature films, guarantee a continuous film production in Norway. Very few Norwegian films cover their production costs or make substantial profits at the box office. The explicit aim of the old as well as the new policy of state support was to guarantee that a wide range of films was produced, and in recent years another explicit aim has been to boost output, so that the state would get more films for its support.

Documentaries turned out to be a perfect vehicle for these aims, being sober and artistic, dealing with important topics, but in a new and more audience-friendly way, and at the same time being cheaper than most fiction films. The use of new light-weight digital cameras in recent years has made it possible to make documentaries even cheaper, and, at the same time, more intimate and close-up than earlier documentaries. By awarding documentary filmmakers state support more films could be produced, and many of the documentaries produced in the 1990s combined box-office appeal with the discussion of important topics in Norwegian society. These topics were, as mentioned above, tackled via intimate protraits, as in Margreth Olin's important film *Kroppen min/My Body* (2002), about how women's bodies are disciplined in modern society through specific ideals as to how a woman should look and be.

The success of documentary filmmaker Sigve Endresen, and especially his socially-concerned documentaries about young drug addicts, may also be an important part of the explanation as to why so many documentaries have been produced in Norway since the early 1990s. Endresen's feature *For harde livet/For Your Life* was a modest box-office success in 1989, showing not only that it was possible to get theatrical distribution with a documentary about an important topic, but also combining a socially-aware approach with observational and interactive techniques, giving unforgettable portraits of several young drug addicts. Endresen's counter-strategy, refusing to make simple and one-dimensional victims of the drug-addicts, became typical not only of his later documentaries, among them the feature *Leve blant løver/Living Amongst Lions* (1998), about young people with terminal cancer, but also typical of most of the new Norwegian documentaries.

The socially-concerned documentaries of Sigve Endresen, and, later, filmmakers such as Margreth Olin, Trond Kvist and Øyvind Sandberg, were engaged, intimate, direct and close-up, often with humour as well as pathos and anger, and managed to get decent box-office results.

The tremendous success of *Cool and Crazy* in 2001 made it more fashionable to produce and direct documentaries in Norway, and the changes in the state support system made it even easier to get public funding for documentaries. These elements, the state support system and the example of Sigve Endresen, as well as a boom in television documentaries and reality-tv, help explain why documentaries returned to the cinemas. Norwegians had an appetite for authentic stories from 'real life', a general interest in human life as well as an urge to map the contemporary nation in a time of change, and the cinemas, in Norway mostly owned by the municipalities, supposedly operating for the common good of the local community, and thus being a cultural service institution as well as a commercial enterprise, followed up by showing the popular state-funded documentaries.

The favourable situation for documentaries in the Norwegian cinemas inspired veteran filmmaker Knut Erik Jensen. After directing fiction films for nearly a decade, Jensen turned to feature-length documentaries with *Cool and Crazy* in 2001.

History written from below

The director Knut Erik Jensen was born in 1940 in Honningsvåg, in the far north of Norway. At the age of four he experienced the Nazi strategy of scorched earth and total war, when every house, bridge or industrial building was burnt down or blown up by the departing German troops at the end of the Occupation. His mother had to leave in a hurry with four children, for an unknown destination, and Jensen's family could not return to his village until 1951, after years of moving between German and Russian prison camps. Until he was fourteen, he lived in barracks which the Germans had built. In Honningsvåg everything was gone, the village had to be reconstructed from scratch, and the only remembrances of the old days were the things people could carry when they were evacuated. Not surprisingly, then, memory and war have played important roles in Jensen's films. His own personal history also could explain why he is so interested in the material/concrete objects that surround us in our lives.

After studying in Norway, France and Russia, he attended the London International Film School, and returned to Norway to make 'films about my homeland from an outsider's perspective.' (Flynn 2001) However, most of all he has worked from an engaged *insider's* perspective, making films about his beloved northern Norway. From his first short films in the early 1970s to his feature-length documentary *På hau i havet/Arctic Cabaret* (2004), Jensen has made tributes to the people and nature of his region.

His first important short documentary was *Farvel, da, gamle Kjelvikfjell/Goodbye, Old Kjelvik Mountain* (1974), a portrait of three old bachelors on a remote island in the far north of Norway. The three old men are the only remaining inhabitants of what was once a thriving fishing village. Jensen's camera follows them in their daily chores: fishing, mending nets, cooking and telling each other stories or singing old songs. The film is an observational documentary, giving a warm and nostalgic, but distanced, view of the old men and their quiet lives. As viewers, we are watching them in their life-world, but Jensen never comments directly on their lives or include interviews. The old men become symbols of a disappearing world, a way of life that was simple, friendly, close to nature, warm and inclusive. At the same time, Jensen's fascination with ruins, overgrown churchyards and neglected houses reveals an almost surrealist interest in misplaced or old objects. Most of all, the objects stand for the effect of time on the material and immaterial aspects of life, and the objects become material forms of memory, but the objects could also be seen as emblems of the people, who are also 'misplaced'. *Goodbye, Old Kjelvik Mountain* was an original and important documentary, and the combination of individualism and a collective, keeping old ways and old songs alive, became an important motif in Jensen's many short documentaries in the 1970s and 1980s; a motif to which he returned in *Cool and Crazy*.

In 1978, Knut Erik Jensen joined the staff of the Norwegian Broadcasting Company (NRK Television), and has since made documentaries and short films at NRK as well as independently. In the 1980s, Jensen made three short films about life in the Svalbard archipelago that became important in Norway. The first two films, *Svalbard i Verden/Svalbard in the World* (1983) and *Kald Verden/Cold World* (1986) depicted the Svalbard archipelago through silent impressionistic collages. Cultivating the odd detail, he obtained a surrealist and powerful evocation of the arctic landscape. In the third film in this 'Svalbard Trilogy', *Min Verden/My World* (1987), Jensen portrays a fur trapper who has chosen a rough and lonely life in the arctic wilderness as a conscious alternative to modern city life. The trapper fights against the 'southern' bureaucracy with the same fervour with which he hunts foxes and other animals.

At the same time, in the mid-1980s, Jensen made his most important work as a television producer and director, the documentary series *Finnmark mellom øst og vest/Finnmark Between East and West* (1986). This six-part, eight-hour series was an audiovisual history lesson about the war in Finnmark, and the slow reconstruction of this part of Norway in the post-war years, based on archived material and interviews. The series is an example of 'history written from below', history written by the people themselves and not by professional historians. The many small participants in history, each with a story to tell, are documented in Jensen's series and saved for posterity. These stories are at once a corrective from below and a complement to other sources and historical discourses. The experience of the people is placed at the centre, and the rhythm is slow and elaborate, giving the audience time to reflect on the stories and images. Jensen himself commented upon his artistic choices and the use of archive film in the series:

> In the television series I usually left the scenes the way they were made, instead of killing them with my own interpretive narrative. I preferred to let them stand in surprising contrast to other scenes in order to cast doubt on the truthfulness of preceding or succeeding scenes. I also tried to eliminate the span of the years that had passed since the film was shot by letting people who had experienced these events comment on the scenes or record their reactions. In this way I attempted to eliminate time and somehow show that 40-50 years of history can be travelled in a film montage. I thus tried to avoid giving the audience the possibility of distancing themselves from what happened and from what I wanted to tell them by saying 'this was only a long time ago and not now'. (Jensen 1996:82)

The series criticised the political establishment in southern Norway, and its plans for the rebuilding of the burnt down areas, arguing that the people of Finnmark had to rely on their own strength, struggling not only with harsh nature, but also with the intervention of bureaucracy from the South. This has been an important theme in many of Jensen's documentaries, especially in short films like *My World* or *Natur-Barn-Natur/Nature-Children-Nature* (1987). The latter film was made for a planning department in the capital city Oslo, and was supposed to argue for the need to secure children's playgrounds in the North against harsh climatic conditions, but Jensen turned the tables on his mandate and on the bureaucrats, making a film that ridiculed the task and the deskbound bureaucrats who launched mindless campaigns, and in the end argued that it was southern bureaucracy that really needed shelter.

In 1993, Jensen's first feature, *Stella Polaris*, premiered, a fragmented modernist story about a woman and her life, from wartime childhood to life and love as a mature woman. *Stella Polaris* is an ambitious and experimental work, without any dialogue or voiceover, but a fascinating and beautiful movie. The camerawork and the editing in this film echoes the documentaries, and emphasises the materiality of a life history. Stimulated by the artistic success of this innovative film, he then directed two other features: *Brent av Frost/Burnt by Frost* (1997), and *Når mørket er forbi/Passing Darkness* (2000). After these three fiction films, Jensen returned to documentary, and turned to the Berlevåg Male Choir in *Cool and Crazy*.

A musical about men, landscape and politics

In the autumn of 1998, Knut Erik Jensen visited the village Berlevåg while looking for locations for the feature *Passing Darkness*, and, hearing the choir singing in a snowstorm, he was amazed. He went to their concert the same night: 'I was so emotionally affected by the amazing sound and the way they performed that I wanted to make a film to explain why, even to myself. It's about collective memory, a nostalgia for an old reality that we are losing very quickly. The basis of their songs and the way they sing is a culture that lives with the sea; the future is about living on natural resources, if the politicians will allow it.' (Flynn 2001)

Cool and Crazy is a musical about men, landscape and politics. The director called it a 'feel-good docu-musical', and this characterisation sums up the film's attraction. A literal English translation of the film's Norwegian title – *Heftig og begeistret* – would be something like 'Wild and Enthusiastic', and the film is an enthusiast's hymn to faith and hope. *Cool and Crazy* combines a playful formal experimentation with an affectionate portrait of the members of the choir. The film is, most of all, about the dignity of ordinary lives lived under extreme circumstances.

The film opens with images of the stormy sea, and closes with images of a street in a snowstorm, and between these images the Berlevåg male choir is portrayed with warmth and humour. The first part of the film is a presentation of some of the members of the choir, and interviews with the men are intertwined with musical numbers when the choir sings their old songs in different, often striking, places, such as the street, a lighthouse, and on the shore beside the monumental concrete groynes. In the second part of the film, after about one hour, we follow the choir when they travel by bus to the Russian coastal town of Murmansk, where they hold concerts.

Jensen's film is in many ways a typical example of the New Norwegian Documentary; combining a discussion of issues of globalisation and individualism, which have sparked debate in Norway, with intimate portraits of men who give body and voice to the topics being discussed. The choir is a microcosmos, a small community that resembles or mirrors the larger Norwegian society, but at the same time the film describes an older and disappearing world and way of life. The film shows that when changes in the international fishing industry turn a thriving fishing village into a shadow of its former self, not much is left. As the second tenor, eighty-seven year old Reidar Strand, says during rehearsals with his ninety-six year old brother Einar: 'In Berlevåg, if it wasn't for the choir and breakwater, we couldn't exist.'

Cool and Crazy is, like the songs sung by the choir in the film, a sweet hymn to the simple life and the homeland. In spite of people leaving the village, because there are no jobs left in the disappearing fishing industry, the men are optimistic, warm, humorous and inclusive. The members of the choir are, as Jensen loves to call it, 'people without clothes on their faces'. In their own homes, the men are often filmed very close up, even in the collective choir scenes, the camera pans slowly over the individuals' frozen faces, showing their bodily traits, such as dripping noses, so that the men become both unique individuals, but part of a community of flesh singing as one voice. One of the main attractions of the film, and one reason why it was such a huge national and international success, probably has to do with the men themselves: funny, odd, friendly and passionate. Jensen and his female photographer Aslaug Holm, who photographed all the interviews and followed the men on their trip to Murmansk, come very close to the men, and present them as personalities as well as types.

The film combines warm nostalgia with a series of fascinating portraits of individuals that are special, but at the same time the men are mostly without names: the communist satyr singing Elvis songs in the bathtub, the ex-drug addict returning to life in his home village after a harsh existence elsewhere, the fisherman who could have had a different career, but chose the simple life. The portraits of the men also represent a nostalgia for an older – and simpler – masculinity, and a longing for an older male community. The film has a male perspective, and Jensen himself sees this as the heart of the film: 'I wanted to show how charming and clever, but stupid and childish men can be. They think they have the same charm at ninety-six as they did when they were nineteen, and the only things that most of them are interested in is how to get women.' (Flynn 2001)

Jensen playfully uses the stereotypes of the typically northern Norwegian: extremely open and outgoing, slightly promiscuous, with a vocabulary of swearwords, and extremely robust; thus able to survive harsh climatic conditions. He plays up to many of the expectations and prejudices that Norwegian 'southerners' have about the northerners, thus combining authentic-feeling close-up portraits and a serious comment upon the vanishing village culture with making fun of cultural stereotypes in contemporary Norwegian society. These cultural stereotypes have specific Norwegian elements, but are also to some extent universal, making it possible for international audiences to identify with or recognise the playful juxtapositions of north/south, or equivalent divisions of a nation.

The individual portraits of the men are warm and funny, presenting the men as both individuals and members of the choir, thus giving the film the opportunity to discuss the role of the individual in the collective. Film historian Bjørn Sørenssen has noted that '[t]he strength of the northern individualists in Jensen's portrayal is that, however individualistic and egregious they may appear, they always have the strength of the *collective* with them.' (Sørenssen 2003). The relationship between the individual and the collective is emphasised in various ways in the film. The choir is filmed alternately as a group in the distance, and as a series of individuals in close proximity. Thus, the film charts a disappearing way of life, but also shows that despite great changes in the village and in Norway the spirit of the collective still lives on.

These aspects of the film – a warm nostalgia for a simple life, an older and simpler masculinity, a collective that gives room for individualists, and a playful discussion of the uniqueness of the cultural expression of the northern Norwegian – make the film pleasant and moving, and at the same time they bring important themes in several debates in Norway to life through a series of heartwarming portraits of older men. The film has all the qualities of a feel-good film, and a box office success, but no-one could have foreseen the enormous commercial success of the film. The success of *Cool and Crazy*, though, shows how Jensen managed to tell a story that also discussed underlying streams of anguish and hope within Norwegian society today.

Cool and Crazy on the Road

The success of *Cool and Crazy* inevitably brought on the idea of a sequel, and when the choir was invited on a tour of Norwegian-American audiences in New York and the Midwest in autumn 2001, Jensen and his crew followed the choir on the road. Many warning voices were raised about this project, and these voices were more or less proven right by a lukewarm critical reception and dismal audience figures in Norway, and none of the international acclaim of the first movie.

The hostile reception of *På sangens vinger/Cool and Crazy on the Road* (2002) helps pin down what was unique about *Cool and Crazy*, as well as seeing which elements were necessary to tell a story that resonated through a national or international audience. *Cool and Crazy on the Road* starts much like the first film. We hear the majestic song of the Berlevåg Male Choir over images of a wild mountainside. The camera pans over rocks and snow, until we see the choir standing high on the mountainside singing about how they want to travel, and get away from the tiny community. Then we see the choir members sleeping on the airplane on their way to New York, and the first musical number ends with images of the twin towers of the World Trade Centre collapsing.

Cool and Crazy on the Road is a much more sombre, bleak and odd film than its predecessor, and nearly totally lacks its wit and charm. The sequel does not add much to the portraits in *Cool and Crazy*, and catches the old men as fish out of water. They obviously do not belong in any of the places where they are filmed – New York, Memphis or Hollywood – and the film becomes a combination of a holiday travelogue and a sad comment about the events in New York of September 2001. Most of all, the choir members are seen only as sad old men, given nothing of their majestic 'larger than life' quality from the first film. The Norwegian title of the film – literally 'On the Wings of Song' – surely feels ironic, when the film itself shows an environment where the songs do not work. Singing does not provide an 'uplift', but seems more out of place than a comment on or a solution to the recent events in the US.

Without the nostalgia and the reassuring vision of good masculinity and inclusive collective spirit, the film turns the tables on the themes in the first film. *Cool and Crazy on the Road* gives an interesting representation of a country in shock and grief, but this underlines the feeling that the choir is an anachronism. In one scene in the film, one of the older men listens to a young woman telling him about the loss of her husband in the terrorist attack, but he is unable to help or comfort her, and the audience feels that they are intruding on a private scene. Thus the old way of life represented by the men is shown to be unable to mend what has been broken, or comfort in this time of grief.

Jensen's sequel not only lacks the hope, wit and warmth of the first film, but it also exposes the work of *Cool and Crazy* as nostalgia for a time and a way of life that already has been lost to us. A nostalgia that does not mend the fragmentation of modern life. The sadness of the men, and of the country through which they travel, gives the film the aura of a 'feel-bad' movie, which, for obvious reasons, does not have the same box-office appeal. *Cool and Crazy on the Road* is an interesting film, and the hostile reception from the critics was not completely deserved, but to some degree it strips the old men of charm and personality, and it is not possible for the audience to participate in the same naïvité and hopefulness after seeing the sequel. The second film even reveals the rhetorical and ideological work behind *Cool and Crazy*, and casts doubt on many of the solutions offered implicitly in the first film.

Super Senior

One of the reasons why Knut Erik Jensen's film made such an impact in 2001 was that the premiere coincided with the first real wave of reality television in Norway. The debilitating effects of these reality-tv series, both on the documentary genre itself and on young viewers, was a favourite topic of discussion in all media in early 2001.

Since the mid-1990s, there had been some Norwegian documentary series on television that could be seen as forerunners of reality television, for example, some youth programmes that imitated MTV's *The Real World*, but in the year 2000 the first version of the series *Robinson-ekspedisjonen*, the Norwegian *Survivors*, were broadcast, as well as other Norwegian reality-tv series, and most of the Norwegian television channels started producing this type of television. Discussion raged about 'bully-tv', which was said to communicate, especially to children and young people, all the 'wrong' attitudes to life. For many viewers of *Cool and Crazy*, Jensen's film obviously also worked as a nostalgic example of an older documentary form, that communicated all the 'right' attitudes to life and community.

In the late autumn of 2000, the commercial television channel TvNorge ('TV Norway') decided to broadcast a version of *Big Brother*, and, until the premiere on February 2001, this was the most discussed topic in the media. The public service channel NRK, which had had a monopoly on television broadcasting from 1960 to the mid-1980s, was the slowest to participate in the new wave of reality-tv shows. NRK had produced some of the early *Real World* imitations, and series about life in various institutions in Norway, such as schools and the Police Academy, but NRK needed to find an idea that could be used in their strategy of counter-programming, presenting an alternative to

Big Brother or *Survivor*. The success of *Cool and Crazy* became an example for NRK, and they decided to make a reality-tv series about senior citizens. All the participants in the numerous reality-tv series made by the commercial channels were young, sexy and urban, so NRK responded with the concept of *Eldrebølgen/Super Senior* (2003), involving older people who were not sexy and not even very urban.

Super Senior became one of the most successful television programmes in Norway in 2003, and just like *Cool and Crazy* it made stars of the participants. The series premiered in January and was broadcast four days a week, with a total of forty-two episodes, and attracting an average of 751,000 viewers. The concept was sold to several countries in Europe as well as to Australia, New Zealand and the US. RAI3 in Italy made its own version in the autumn of 2003. In Norway, no sequel was produced, but the series was repeated in the spring of 2004.

In the series, twelve senior citizens, whose ages ranged from sixty to seventy-four, were placed in an old school in Tromsø in the north of Norway. The participants did not know each other beforehand, and for ten weeks they lived together and collaborated on writing and performing in a cabaret. The end result, presented in the final episode, was the cabaret, and just like the Berlevåg Male Choir, the twelve participants embarked on a short tour around Norway with their performance.

Super Senior was created and advertised as an explicit alternative to 'bully-tv', and the counter-strategies of the programme – contrasting in content and declared ethos with other reality-tv shows – were crucial. In *Super Senior* there were no competitions where the participants voted for or against each other, and no interactive elements where the viewers voted for the participants; none of the twelve was forced to leave the programme. Competition was replaced by collaboration, and the excitement the show generated was not linked to animosity and fights, but on how the diverse, strong personalities could learn to co-operate in reaching a common goal. The makers of the programme thus managed to keep many of the conventions of reality shows, such as the focus on people's reactions to living with strangers, but at the same time all the competitive and sensational aspects of shows like *Big Brother* and *Survivor* were rendered superfluous. In *Super Senior*, as in *Cool and Crazy*, we witness the building and negotiating of bonds that hold a community together.

Super Senior was inspired by the success of *Cool and Crazy*, but Knut Erik Jensen did not like the comparison, and he was involved in several heated discussions about the film and television series in 2003. To Jensen, *Super Senior* was still 'trash tv'; a cheap and false alternative to real documentaries. He criticised *Super Senior* for not depicting real people in real places, but creating a sort of media-driven laboratory situation where people were observed like rats. In his opinion, the series lacked all the qualities of a serious and authentic documentary, and he castigated NRK for choosing to make this and other series, instead of concentrating on socially-concerned or artistic documentaries.

Although both *Cool and Crazy* and *Super Senior* are about old people, share a nostalgia for old times, and deliver counter-images in a culture fixated on youth, competition, sex and the latest fashions, the big difference between the film and the television series is, as Jensen suggests, in the siting of the protagonists in a naturally-occurring or manufactured community. In Jensen's films – at least, in *Cool and Crazy* – the choir is depicted in its natural surroundings. Jensen sometimes positions the choir in odd places, but the men are filmed in Berlevåg where they have lived all their lives, and they are filmed doing what they probably would have been doing even if Jensen's camera crew was not present. *Super Senior* is different, and the participants are doing things they never would have had the opportunity to do without the television series. To Jensen, this is a falsehood, but his verdict is probably coloured by his situation in NRK, and the diminishing resources allocated to the production of 'serious' documentaries. One might add, however, that Jensen's critique also could be applied to *Cool and Crazy on the Road*, which shows artificially-manufactured situations.

Both *Cool and Crazy* and *Super Senior* are very interesting examples of counter-programming; making a film or television series that deals with sectors of society or topics which no-one would expect to have broad popular appeal. In different ways, they represent a nostalgia for old days and old ways, and communicates all the 'right' attitudes to life – collaboration, toleration of difference, co-existence with nature – in a media climate of aggressive and consumerist 'bully-tv'.

The Old Wave

On November 23, 2002, the Norwegian television news programme *Dagsrevyen* ('Daily News') sadly announced that the ninety-seven year old singer Einar Strand, the oldest of the stars of *Cool and Crazy*, had died. NRK's *Dagsrevyen* remains the dominant source of television news in Norway, with around a million Norwegians watching the news programme each evening. The report on the death of Einar Strand was accompanied not only by a clip from the film, but also by a short collage of moments from his life after the film had made him famous; receiving a medal from the King, meeting the Minister of Cultural Affairs, and the old singer Erik Bye, a most cherished national icon. The news item demonstrated the cultural importance of the Berlevåg Male Choir, their stardom and status as celebrities in Norway, and how deeply the film and personae of the choir members had penetrated the Norwegian consciousness.

Cool and Crazy is a unique documentary, full of humour, wit and affection. It definitely is a 'feel-good' film, a hymn to faith and hope, and the dignity of ordinary life. The film is the work of an enthusiast and an insider, portraying an older and disappearing world and way of life, representing a nostalgia for an older and simpler masculinity and inclusive collective. Balancing the warm nostalgia with an almost surrealist vein, especially in the musical numbers, and with an ironic play on stereotypes about men from the north of Norway, *Cool and Crazy* is a complex and multidimensional documentary. It is also a documentary focusing on the materiality of daily life and landscape.

Together with the reality-television series *Super Senior* – whose Norwegian title, *Eldrebølgen*, literally means 'The Old Wave' – Jensen's film represents an interesting moment in Norwegian cultural life. Indeed, an old wave, and a reaction to the increasingly youth-centred media and film culture. In a climate where youth, the latest fashions and sexiness dominates, *Cool and Crazy* was a history lesson, but a history lesson told indirectly and without overt didacticism. The telling of this history reminds us that the disappearing world is not completely lost.

References

Berg, Kjell (ed.) & Knut Erik Jensen (2001): *Heftig og begeistret*. Tromsø: Polar forlag.

Birkvad, Søren & Jan Anders Diesen (1994): *Autentiske Inntryk*. Oslo: Det norske samlaget.

Brinch, Sara & Gunnar Iversen (2001): *Virkelighetsbilder – Norsk dokumentarfilm gjennom hundre år*. Oslo: Universitetsforlaget.

Flynn, Bob (2001): 'Freeze Frame'. *The Guardian*, August 7.

Iversen, Gunnar (1998): 'Norway'. In Soila, Tytti, Astrid Söderbergh Widding & Gunnar Iversen: *Nordic National Cinemas*. London: Routledge.

Jensen, Knut Erik (1996): 'A Filmmaker's View of Archive Films' in Smither, Roger & Wolfgang Klaue (eds): *Newsreels in Film Archives – A Survey Based on the FIAF Newsreel Symposium*. London: Flicks Books / Fairleigh Dickinson University Press.

Sørenssen, Bjørn (2003): 'Persistency Pays Off: Knut Erik Jensen from *Farewell Old Kjelvik Mountain* to *Cool and Crazy*. Paper presented at the Fourth Popular European Cinema Conference: Methods and Stars, Stockholm, July 11-13, 2003.

Auteur • Authority • Subjectivity

Ibsen, Lagerlöf, Sjöström and *Terje Vigen*: (Inter)nationalism, (Inter)subjectivity and the Interface between Swedish Silent Cinema and Scandinavian Literature

Bjarne Thorup Thomsen

Connecting low and high cultures

When, in 1909, Swedish novelist and soon-to-be Nobel Prize winner Selma Lagerlöf (1858-1940) was approached by a teacher in Malmö, F. Hallgren, with a proposal to film her recent and highly acclaimed adventure novel, national travelogue and textbook for Swedish schools *Nils Holgerssons underbara resa genom Sverige* (*Nils Holgersson's Wonderful Journey Through Sweden*, 1906-07), the author's reaction typified the schism between the high culture of literature and the low culture of cinema that obtained at the time. In a letter to Alfred Dalin, editor of the ambitious textbook series of which *Nils Holgersson* formed the first volume, Lagerlöf expressed her reservation about the proposed project and conveyed a general scepticism towards the new medium: 'Han [Hallgren] förefaller ju så entusiastisk för sin plan att göra biografen gagnelig i stället för skadlig, men jag tycker att detta inte kan genomföras' (Sahlberg 1960:191) ('He [Hallgren] does appear to be very enthusiastic about his plan to make the cinema useful rather than harmful, but I do not believe this can be achieved'[1]). In his reply Dalin was distinctly dismissive of the 'mechanical images' which he identified as the enemy of imagination: 'De mekaniska bilderna av olika slag befordra icke barnfantasins sunda växt, utan hindra och förslöa den, helst om de i större antal ställas inför barnens ögon' (Sahlberg 1960:191) ('The mechanical pictures of various kinds do not promote the healthy growth of a child's imagination: indeed, they rather hinder and discourage it – particularly if the child is exposed to them in large numbers'[2]). However, only twelve years later, in February 1921, Lagerlöf's appreciation of the cultural potency and prestige of cinema had developed dramatically when she wrote to congratulate director Victor Sjöström on the artistic success of his adaptation of her 1912 novel *Körkarlen* (*The Phantom Carriage*), acknowledging that Sjöström's work not only paved the way for Swedish film abroad but could be instrumental in the international dissemination of her books:

> Nu är nog den filmen lyckligt i hamn, och det utmärkta arbete, som Ni har nedlagt på filmen både som filmförfattare, regissör och aktör blir denna gång till fullo uppskattat ... Nu tycks det emellertid, som om Ni skulle ha brutit väg inte bara för svensk film, utan också för mina böcker ... Jag tänker, att det roar Er att höra, att filmer också hjälpa fram böckerna. (Sahlberg 1960:199; Forslund 1980:137)[3]

> (Now this film has safely reached port, and this time the excellent work you put into it as author, director and actor will be fully appreciated ... And it does seem as if you have not only paved the way for Swedish films but also for my books ... I think you'll be amused to hear that films can also boost books.)[4]

The u-turn in the evaluation of cinema that Lagerlöf's letters communicate reads as a reflection of the artistic and commercial rise of Swedish silent film that is traditionally termed its Golden Age. This is normally periodised as inaugurated by Sjöström's adaptation of Henrik Ibsen's 'Terje Vigen' in 1917, reaching its high-water mark, in terms of thematic, stylistic and technical complexity, with *Körkarlen/The Phantom Carriage* (1921), and concluding in 1924 with *The Atonement of Gösta Berling*, Mauritz Stiller's adaptation of Lagerlöf's breakthrough novel *Gösta Berlings saga* (published 1891). In 1925, Stiller followed the example Sjöström had set two years before by electing to continue his directorial career in Hollywood, the two leading directors thus moving away from the national cinema they had helped set in motion.

While the work of Selma Lagerlöf[5] and Henrik Ibsen (1828-1906) made essential contributions to the development of Golden Age cinema by supplying plots, thematic concerns and cultural prestige to landmark films, the two national icons were by no means the only prominent Scandinavian writers embraced by the industry. In his comprehensive study *Den nationella stilen. Studier i den svenska filmens guldålder* Bo Florin stresses the significance of a wider alliance between Golden Age cinema and canonical Nordic writers, Nobel Prize winners in particular: works by Bjørnstjerne Bjørnson (Nobel Prize 1903), Knut Hamsun (Nobel Prize 1920), Henrik Pontoppidan, Karl Gjellerup (shared Nobel Prize 1917), August Strindberg and Hjalmar Bergman were all transferred to the screen between 1917 and 1924 (Florin 1997:186f). In Florin's analysis this alliance between literature and film is of a dialogic or reciprocal nature and is characterised by both continuities and discontinuities. Florin notes that as many as eight of the literary sources of the Golden Age films were reprinted in editions illustrated with film images (Florin 1997:188f), instances in other words of the imitated art form copying its imitator and, like Lagerlöf's letters, indicative of a shift in the relative cultural 'strength' of the two media. Following Henry Bacon, Florin proposes to view Golden Age adaptation of literature as a process of *re-telling* that serves to retain and disseminate a cultural heritage while also reexamining and reinterpreting this (Florin 1997:187).

In accordance with the tenets of this argument I aim to offer in the following some reflections on both the faithfulness and flexibility with which the film that is credited with marking the beginning of the Golden Age relates to its textual precursor. While there is a tradition in film scholarship for emphasising the agreement between film and text versions of *Terje Vigen* and the indisputable accuracy and care with which Sjöström adapts Ibsen's epic poem,[6] the dialogues the film enters into with its own medium and with the ideological issues of its own day should not be overlooked. Thus, it may be proposed that Sjöström's *Terje Vigen* bridges the gap between the cinema of attractions that went before it and the art cinema it contributed to institutionalising by intensifying the role of spectacle and suspense in the storyline without, however, losing sight of the illumination of international and interpersonal conflict and reconciliation that lies at the heart of Ibsen's poem. It will likewise be argued that the film foregrounds the role of seeing – particularly appropriate in the age of silent cinema – and the representation of audience. Finally, it will be suggested that the film adaptation, while thorough in its treatment of the theme of violation of national sovereignty, realises some subtle shifts from a Norwegian to a pan-Scandinavian focus.

Appeal and adaptability

In his recent study of Henrik Ibsen's life and work, *Ibsen. Kunstnerens vei*, Bjørn Hemmer stresses the connections between Ibsen's early epic poetry and his subsequent dramatic work. In his two major poems from around 1860, 'Paa Vidderne' ('On the Moors', 1860) and 'Terje Vigen' (1862), Ibsen succeeds in dramatising human development through stages of crisis, choice and clarification and achieves, by means of intricate scenic interrelationships connecting past and present, the cohesion, firm structure and 'logical' development that were to become hallmarks of his main plays (of which both *Brand* (1866) and *Peer Gynt* (1867) were in verse and characterised by Ibsen as dramatic poems) (Hemmer 2003:44ff). The compositional and scenic qualities Hemmer identifies would have contributed to the appeal of 'Terje Vigen' to silent cinema as the new medium sought to approach issues connected with subjectivity, society, nature and nation in structured and subtle ways and develop complex methods to represent time, place and mind. Bengt Forslund (1980:83f, 1988:55) documents in his seminal study of Victor Sjöström's life and work how, as early as 1913, the main Swedish film production and distribution company Svenska Biografteatern had shown an awareness of the cinematic potential of Ibsen's work by signing a contract with the author's son, the then Norwegian prime minister Sigurd Ibsen, for the rights to film three of Ibsen's earliest, historical plays – *Fru Inger til Østeraad* (*Lady Inger of Østeraad*, 1854), *Gildet paa Solhoug* (*The Feast at Solhoug*, 1856) and *Hærmændene paa Helgeland* (*The Vikings at Helgeland*, 1858) – plus *Peer Gynt*. Interestingly, however, in December 1915 the four stipulated plays were replaced, in an amendment to the original contract, by *Brand* and 'Terje Vigen' whose attractiveness to the film industry was thus underscored.[7]

In addition to its careful composition, 'Terje Vigen' provided silent cinema with an adaptable thematics. While 'Terje Vigen' is centred on events caused by the British naval blockade of Norway during the Napoleonic Wars, its treatment of war, international relations and (lack of) self-determination – both for the protagonist and his nation – acquired renewed topicality in subsequent periods: first in connection with Norway's late-nineteenth-century struggle for independence, resulting in the dissolution of the Swedish-Norwegian union in 1905, around which time the poem experienced a surge in popularity, and then in the context of World War I during which the film version was produced and premiered. Adapting 'Terje Vigen' in the silent film era thus offered the possibility of combining the weightiness of a cultural and historical heritage with resonances of more contemporary conflicts and concerns, thereby echoing the central focus of the plot on the protagonist's rootedness in and eventual *reworking* of the past.

The dominant environment in which the film's demonstration of the connectedness of present and past takes place is the sea. Alongside its compositional, thematic and temporal complexity, 'Terje Vigen' offered silent cinema the visual impact and symbolism that the element of water could supply. Hemmer sees a further significance of Ibsen's epic poems in the fact that they shaped the author's symbolic landscapes of mountains ('Paa Vidderne') and sea ('Terje Vigen') (just as his naturalistic dramas would fill the bourgeois drawing room with significance). In an illuminating study of Romantic travel, Roger Cardinal stresses the importance of both peak experiences and turbulent waters to the Romantic sensibility (Cardinal 1997:141). Following Hemmer and Cardinal, Sjöström's *Terje Vigen* may be understood as connecting with Romantic notions of place by using the Skagerrak sea as a trope for the protagonist's turbulent and traumatised soul and as a site in which his heroism and lonely struggle is performed, while also imbuing the sea with (inter)national and collective history. The composition of marine and other images in Sjöström's film seems, moreover, to have been informed by Christian Krohg's naturalistic illustrations that accompanied editions of Ibsen's text from 1892 onwards (Florin 2003:64, Hemmer 2003:59), the film thus linking Romantic and post-Romantic approaches to the representation of landscape. Bengt Forslund (1980:90, 1988:60) goes as far as to suggest that the sea is the real main 'character' in Sjöström's film (in parallel with the role of the arctic mountainscape in *Berg-Ejvind och hans hustru/The Outlaw and His Wife* (1918) and the sandstorm in his last major work, *The Wind* (1928)). It is indisputable that the representation of awesome or sublime geographies is central to the appeal of Golden Age cinema, in Sjöström's films frequently feeding into a dramatic dialectic between exteriors and interiors.

Sea, subjectivity, suspense, spectacle

A covert reference to Ibsen the dramatist may be found in the fact that Sjöström's adaptation of 'Terje Vigen' is divided into three 'acts', a literary and theatrical device that, ironically, is absent from the source text.[8] This expresses a striving for structure and form in a film that flourishes in repetitions, parallels, complementarities and contrasts. At times it modifies or develops the patterns present in the source text, as a closer consideration of some aspects of the compositional strategy that underlies act 1 of Sjöström's film will demonstrate. It will show, moreover, that the natural environment is central to the film not only as a correlate of the protagonist's subjectivity but also as a sphere of spectacle and suspense.

The film opens with an elegant tripartite sequence that presents soul, sea and their interconnection in an economical and very visual way while also stressing the act of seeing: an interior frontal shot of a troubled, elderly and isolated Terje, demonised by his 'mad' gaze and the surrounding smoke (from the fireplace, presumably), is followed first by a long shot of violent waves and then by a combining shot that shows Terje from behind and framed by the doorway looking restlessly at the relentless sea. Interestingly, in Ibsen's text a similar foregrounding of trauma and threatening landscape is, in a very filmic 'flashforward' fashion, juxtaposed with another 'take' of Terje Vigen which functions as a flagging up of the final rejuvenation of the protagonist, his marginalisation and apparent madness as represented in the initial scene replaced by mobility, agility and positive social contacts made possible by the connecting sea and the benevolent weather:

> Siden jeg så ham en enkelt gang,
> han lå ved bryggen med fisk;
> hans hår var hvidt, men han lo og sang

og var som en ungdom frisk.
Til pigerne havde han skemtsomme ord,
han spøgte med byens børn,
han svinged sydvesten og sprang ombord;
så hejste han fokken, og hjem han foer
i solskin, den gamle ørn.
(Ibsen 1917:stanza 2)

(Distant the day, and that only day
I saw him with fish by the quay;
his hair was white, but he sang as gay
and blithe as a boy might be.
The lasses he used a light banter toward,
he joined in the town-lads' talk,
he waved his sou-wester, and leaped aboard;
then homeward he sailed with the jib set broad
in sunshine, the agèd hawk.)
(Ibsen 1986:63)[9]

In Sjöström's film, however, this second scene and the clues it provides are
omitted in order, it would seem, to keep the audience in suspense about the fate
of the hero and create the conditions for a stronger happy ending effect. After
its mysterious opening the film embarks instead on a linear narrative of the
hero's life drama by adding a spectacular sequence that demonstrates notions
of agility and merriment not dissimilar to those found in the omitted scene but
now realised in the context of carefree youth. The sequence seems to reveal
some of the film's visual goals and salient stylistic features. It contains a
prolonged, fascinated and visually inventive depiction of the young Terje's
acrobatic achievement as he is commanded to climb the sails of a large ship,
balances on a rope, hangs on a crossbar... Interestingly, these physical feats
appear to be copied by the camera as extreme long shots of the climbing
seaman captured in a low camera angle from the level of the ship's deck are
followed by a dizzying straight-on medium shot of the hero among the sails
with the glittering waves deep below him. Thus the camera refuses to be
outdone by the main character, its capability not realised in mobile frames,
though, but in the creative cutting between static shots from very varied camera
positions which typifies Sjöström's style in *Terje Vigen* and elsewhere. In
addition, a visual dynamic is achieved by characters or objects entering and
exiting individual static frames or appearing to be moving 'between' different
frames. In the sequence in question the ascending hero climbs through the
bottom line of one frame and disappears through its top line only to make his
re-entry through the lower edge of the subsequent frame that captures a higher
segment of the ship. Thus co-ordination and rhythm are features of both action

and image composition/combination, with subject matter and filming style working in unison. Overall, the spectacle of the sequence could be seen as, on the one hand, echoing the acrobatic bravura performances in circus milieux that were so popular in the cinema of attractions and, on the other hand, prefiguring the famous surreal scene in Sjöström's *Ingmarssönerna/The Sons of Ingmar* (released two years after *Terje Vigen*) where the troubled protagonist accesses his forefathers' world and consequently their wisdom by climbing a giant ladder that connects his home soil and heaven. The sequence may thus be read as reaching out to both simpler and more sophisticated stages in the history of silent cinema.

The other main addition to act 1 of *Terje Vigen* is the concluding scene that shows Terje successfully hiding when seeing that he has been spotted by the blockading British fleet at the beginning of his bold boat trip to Denmark to obtain food for his starving family. Thus, notions of hiding, seeking and restricting are introduced and a cliffhanger effect is achieved. The addition leads Bengt Forslund to comment that 'when Sjöström freely composed what the action entailed, so he also demonstrated what he had learnt from the simpler type of film drama – and was not afraid of exploiting this' (Forslund 1988:60). It should not be overlooked, though, that the concluding scene works as a premonition of and counterpoint to the climactic boat chase and capture scene in act 2, with the filmic inventiveness in this and other instances thus remaining true to the general idea of inter-scenic illumination that governs the composition of Ibsen's text.

The significance of seeing

As the cliffhanging scene exemplifies, the motif of seeing that informs Ibsen's 'Terje Vigen' is reinforced by Sjöström. True to the concerns of silent cinema, his work displays a recurring, sometimes self-referential interest in the phenomenon of visual perception, with the formally experimental *Dödskyssen/The Kiss of Death* (1916) and *Körkarlen* particular cases in point. While the latter celebrates the existential implications of showing and seeing and could be understood as a tribute to cinema itself, the former interestingly contains, as Bo Florin documents, a copyright frame picture featuring an extreme close-up of the director's eye peering through a keyhole. Florin observes that '[k]eyhole scenes were common in early films, but generally from the perspective of the peeker' (Florin 2003:62). In *Terje Vigen* seeing is significant in several senses: as surveillance and control, as witnessing, and as insight into common ground between self and other.

The sinister aspects of this *leitmotif* are, as suggested above, mainly manifested in the sphere of international conflict. They are introduced in act

1 in a depiction of people in Terje's community discovering a blockading British cruiser which, in a brief arresting shot, is shown, motionless and reminiscent of a pirate ship, in the distance of a still seascape. The sequence cross-cuts between images of the watching crowd and the surveying ship, the latter represented by means of what may be termed an intersubjective shot. The implications of the notion of negative seeing that this scene signals are then explored in the hide-and-seek sequence discussed above and, most compellingly, in the climax of act 2. This shows the true power of the 'ørneøjne' ('eagle-eyed gleam') of the English "'Man of war'" (stanza 12; p.66). While images of soldiers using telescopes figure in the conclusion of act 1, it is only in act 2 that we encounter what may be termed telescopic images, i.e. images made out to be shot through a telescope by the use of a mask technique. As an ingenious illustration of how the gaze of the enemy closes in on the hero after his illicit journey to Denmark, Terje is 'caught' in three telescopic images, the second shot closer to him than the first and with cannon balls splashing into the sea around him in the third. Then follows a sequence, informed by complex choreography, camera work and cross-cutting, that displays how the defiant individual is overpowered by the collective might and unstoppable momentum of the military. Particularly poignant is the alternation between extreme close-ups of Terje's hands, desperately working the oars, and richly patterned pictures of the co-ordinated machine-like movements of the many uniformed bodies propelling the pursuing boat. Taken together the images read as a stylisation of the power imbalance of the conflict that is being played out. As this suspense-fuelled section of the film nears its disastrous denouement, the sophistication of cutting and the intensity of the illumination of the idea of viewing reach a high point: approaching a montage technique, the film now alternates not just between shots of the two boats connected through mutual seeing but between two additional scenes both set on land, one capturing the wife waiting in vain at home, cut off from seeing and hence knowing the fate of her huband, and the other showing the local people gathered on the shore witnessing the unfolding drama as a viewing audience.

Not all acts of seeing in *Terje Vigen* are tied to conflict, however. Seeing as understanding and insight comes to the fore in act 1 in a sequence that visualises the first in the series of turning points that structure Terje's life story, just as it introduces the film's recurring technique of focusing on the onlooker. The sequence centres on the protagonist seeing his newborn girl for the first time through the window of his cottage having arrived home from his early easy-going existence at sea. It cross-cuts between depictions of exterior and interior aspects of the scene, but instead of representing what is seen inside by means of point-of-view shots the sequence uses reverse shots to combine in the same image a foregrounding of wife and child in a domestic setting with a continued representation of the observing husband, now shown *en face* and framed by the window in the top section of the background. Thus the scene never loses sight of the man whose mind it investigates while also visualising the coming-together of the family and the turn towards interpersonal commitment that occurs in the protagonist at that point, summed up in the poem in these lines: 'Der sagdes, at Terjes sind med et / fik alvor fra denne stund' (stanza 9; 'That instant, and Terje's mind, men say, / turned sober upon the spot' (p.65)). The full potential reach of this commitment is not demonstrated, however, until deep into the film's third act in a climactic and cathartic sequence that, typical of the composition of both film and text, echoes earlier turns, including the one considered here, as the effect of seeing a baby girl is duplicated: revenge is replaced by reconciliation and the affinity between antagonists recognised when Terje takes in through emphatic seeing that the English lord and naval commander who occasioned the death of his wife and child years earlier himself has a daughter (who shares the name of Anna with Terje's child). Narratively, the scene is noteworthy in its complementary distribution of memory shots as images of the fateful earlier encounter between the men are evoked twice, first tied to Terje's consciousness and then to the mind of the lord. Thus, the sequence expresses, thematically as well as formally, the emergence of an intersubjectivity that transcends national and class boundaries.

Connecting countries

Just like Sjöström's reworking of Ibsen, the premiere of *Terje Vigen* was an inter-Scandinavian phenomenon. The film was released simultaneously in Sweden (Stockholm, Gothenburg, Malmö) and Denmark (Copenhagen) on 29 January 1917, and the Norwegian premiere (Kristiania and Bergen) followed a few days later (Sjöström 1980:87, 1988:58). In terms of filmic content Sjöström's adaptation likewise promotes connections, or downplays tensions, between the Scandinavian countries. His version thus makes a good deal more of Terje's visit to the Danish shores than Ibsen's text does. Whereas the poem's treatment of the topic consists of the cursory lines 'Til Fladstand kom han i god behold / og hented sin dyre last' (stanza 13; 'At Fladstrand, reaching there safe and sound, / he gathered his precious stores' (p.66)), the film opens act 2 with a prolonged scene that is set in a Danish harbour and suggests a Scandinavian continuum of solidarity with the hero's symbolic struggle by focusing on his local helpers and an 'audience' of supportive bystanders, thereby echoing the depiction of Terje's departure from Norway. Conversely, the film chooses to ignore the text's far from unambiguous reference to Sweden's and Norway's post-Napoleonic union relationship. In Ibsen's poem the description of the protagonist's release from British prison is combined with an indirect and very economical summing-up of the ties that came into existence between the two Scandinavian nations after the conclusion of peace: 'Så kom attenhundred og fjorten med fred; / de norske fanger, og Terje med, / førtes hjem på en svensk fregat' (stanza 23; 'Then eighteen-fourteen came and with it accord; / a Swedish frigate brought home onboard / Norway's prisoners, and Terje too' (p.68)). The tension that may be identifiable in this statement between the simultaneous emergences of freedom and dependency could explain why the film, which is otherwise, as shown, drawn to the sights of sea and vessels, refrains from realising this scene. In contrast, Sjöström invests clear cross-national values in the film's penultimate scene, its real conclusion in many ways. It is a harmonising ending in the form of striking visual 'palimpsest' that combines maritime motifs, main characters and national emblems. As the English lord's departing yacht enters the frame from one side and Terje, bidding farewell on the cliffs in the foreground, enters from the other side, a Norwegian flag is projected on to the image at the very moment the protagonist and the waving English family overlap. The following images then focus on the flag which, interestingly, is the Norwegian version of the union marked flag that was in official use 1844-1905 and featured a cross combining the colours of Sweden and Norway in one of its upper quarters. While this emblem is not without its own ambiguities (not paralleled, in this instance, by the text version[10]), the main idea informing the interweaving of the national signs in this scene seems to be the stressing of commonality between countries rather than dependency or dominance. The emblem could additionally read as a reflection of the dual Norwegian-Swedish origins of the film. Overall, the inclusion of the 'inter-Scandinavian' flag, the overlapping former foes and the British vessel in a unifying image work as a summing-up of the film's desire to promote cross-national, cross-class and interhuman connections. Although the film was marketed in Germany as anti-British and criticised by a Danish commentator for being 'un-neutral' (Forslund 1980:89, 1988:59), it could more appropriately be classed as anti-war and as influenced by an ideological turn away from nineteenth- and early-twentieth-century nationalism.

References

Cardinal, Roger (1997): 'Romantic Travel', in Porter, Roy (ed.): *Rewriting the Self. Histories from the Renaissance to the Present.* London & New York: Routledge.

Florin, Bo (1997): *Den nationella stilen. Studier i den svenska filmens guldålder.* Stockholm: Aura förlag.

Florin, Bo (2003): *Regi: Victor Sjöström/Directed by Victor Seastrom.* Stockholm: Cinemateket, Svenska Filminstitutet.

Forslund, Bengt (1980): *Victor Sjöström. Hans liv och verk.* Stockholm: Bonniers.

Forslund, Bengt (1988): *Victor Sjöström. His Life and His Work*, translated from the Swedish by Peter Cowie. New York: New York Zoetrope.

Hemmer, Bjørn (2003): *Ibsen. Kunstnerens vei.* Bergen: Vigmostad & Bjørke.

Ibsen, Henrik (1917; 1862): 'Terje Vigen'. Illustrated by Christian Krohg. Kristiania & Copenhagen: Gyldendalske Boghandel.

Ibsen, Henrik (1986): 'Terje Vigen'. In *Ibsen's Poems in versions by John Northam.* Oslo, Bergen, Stavanger & Tromsø: Norwegian University Press.

Lagerlöf, Selma (1919): *Ingmarssönerna. Berättelse. Illustrerad med filmbilder.* Stockholm: Albert Bonniers förlag.

Sahlberg, Gardar (1960): 'Selma Lagerlöf och filmen'. In Afzelius, Nils, Gunnar Ahlström & Bengt Ek (eds): *Lagerlöfstudier*, vol. 2. Malmö: Allhems förlag.

Sjöström, Victor (1917) (director): *Terje Vigen.* Statens ljud- och bildarkiv, Stockholm, tape number B18323.

Notes

1. Translated by Peter Graves.
2. Translated by Peter Graves.
3. Lagerlöf's letter refers specifically to the reception of her work in Britain where her writing had not had the same impact as in continental Europe. The first screening abroad of *Körkarlen* took place in London 4 February 1921, only one month after the film's Scandinavian premiere (1 January), and led *The Bioscope* magazine to conclude its review with the assessment that '[w]herever it is shown it will help to add dignity and importance to the art of cinema' (Forslund 1988:90f).
4. Translated by Peter Graves.
5. Between 1917 and 1924 no fewer than eight of Lagerlöf's works were adapted to films, four of these directed by Sjöström: *Tösen fra Stormyrtorpet/The Girl from the Marsh Croft* (1917), *Ingmarssönerna, I & II/The Sons of Ingmar, I & II* (1919), *Karin Ingmarsdotter/Karin Daughter of Ingmar* (1920) and *Körkarlen* (1921) (Florin 1997:186f).
6. Cf. Florin: 'In retrospect, the most striking thing about *Terje Vigen* is the extent to which Sjöström adapted it to Ibsen's poem' (2003:64).
7. This followed Svenska Bio's acquisition a couple of months earlier of a screenplay by Gustaf Molander based on 'Terje Vigen'. Molander's script was subsequently used for Sjöström's film. (Forslund 1980:83f, 1988:55)
8. A similar tendency to subdivide the filmic work is in evidence in Sjöström's *Ingmarssönerna* which was narrated and released in two parts (further subdivided into eight acts in all) although both parts were based on the opening chapter of Lagerlöf's novel *Jerusalem* (1901-02). In a letter (20 January 1919) to the director, the author,

while complimentary about the film in general, disputed the wisdom of the two-part structure (Sahlberg 1960:195). *Karin Ingmarsdotter*, also based on *Jerusalem*, was subtitled 'en berättelse för film i fem avdelningar' (a narrative for film in five parts).

9. In Ibsen's text the scene is duplicated, almost word for word, in the penultimate stanza, its portrayal of a liberated state thus forming an overarching vision in the poem.

    In what follows, quotations from the 1917 edition of the Norwegian text are indicated by stanza number, and the subsequent English translations by their page number in the 1986 edition.

10. The text simply states: 'Da yachten drejed for Hesnæs-sund, / den hejste det norske flag' (stanza 41; 'The yacht then headed for Hesnes-sound, / with Norway's own flag for wear' (p.73)).

The Passions of Lars von Trier: Madness, Femininity, Film

Emma Bell

> We want to see mistresses of the screen vibrant with life: unreasonable, stupid, stubborn, ecstatic, repulsive, wonderful, not tamed and made sexless by a moralizing, grumpy filmmaker, a stinking puritan cultivating the moronic virtues of the nice façade. (von Trier 1984)

We can't approach Lars von Trier's work without encountering images of madness. One of Europe's foremost auteur directors, von Trier's name is synonymous with originality, controversy and provocation; his public image is of a maverick-eccentric, nobly blasting the 'nice façade' of decadent culture. Despite such radicalism, von Trier has a disturbing tendency to use women, the mentally ill and disabled as ciphers of a marginalised, innocently-maudlin force of goodness which he fatefully pits against a duplicitous, unjust world. In von Trier films, women, the mad, and the disabled are uncorrupted by the vicissitudes of artifice or social self-censorship because he freely associates them with a morally charged notion of integrity. That few directors consistently focus on female protagonists might incline some to commend him on this account. But his preoccupations with feminine suffering and sexual violence provoke accusations of misogyny and sadism that are hard to deflect, perhaps because his conflation of femininity, madness, and disability is equivalent with moral passion and aesthetic purity. And this equivalence is crucial to our understanding of his innovations in cinematic form because they consistently mimic 'abnormal' states of mind and identities.

Von Trier works from the deeply held conviction that self-imposed rules and constraints revolutionise and intensify creativity, an idiosyncrasy which echoes the social rules and constraints his films expose: 'I have always been crazy about manifestos. I read the Surrealist Manifesto as a young man and was impressed by it. I have also been a communist and, as far as I believe, there was also a manifesto there. Manifestos are a good thing.' (Cit. Schepelern 2003:58). By adhering to their rules or manifesto, the production processes of his films are as significant and as managed as the text. His rules increasingly promise a 'purer', more socially engaged cinema, toward the sardonic ascetism of Dogme'95. Simultaneously, his preoccupation with female suffering, madness and disability intensifies. The question is, 'how do these blood-stained women fit in with his rallying of the avant-garde?' (Kavenna 2004:34) Do they transcend the ethical wilderness of relativism? Or do they only tenant the wasteland of von Trier's cynical contempt? By framing his preoccupations with femininity, mental illness and disability as co-extensive with his dogmatic experimentation with cinema form, we can make sense of his saintly *ingénues* in terms other than those of an *entirely* disillusioned feminism.

In the cult of personality surrounding von Trier, his brilliance is correlated with his own mental ill-health – his depression, agoraphobia, hypochondria and control-freakery. Critics enliven their reviews with scandalised anecdotes of madness, like the 'all nude' filming days, therapy and hypnotism sessions he puts actors through. A veteran of psychotherapy, he maintains that sublimation of one's psychological complexes is 'the driving force' of creativity (Björkman 2003:16). In interviews that read like therapy sessions, von Trier aligns his creative processes with his psychopathology. For instance, as the child of radical socialists, he was burdened with the freedom of imposing on himself his own rules and decisions: 'Having that sort of trust can be a positive thing, but there were also a lot of negative side effects from having to take that kind of responsibility. I was clinically anxious, and still am [...] tormented by childish fantasies and feelings of guilt' (ibid:7). He attributes his fanatical dependency on creative restrictions and mental ill-health to these childhood insecurities: 'I'm a neurotic person and my biggest problem in life is lack of control. The greatest form of happiness for me would be to accept a lack of control, but that's an almost masochistic thought [...] As a child you create all sorts of rituals to maintain control. To prevent everything reverting back to chaos' (cit. Lumholdt 2003:109). Accordingly, there is a temptation to read his films from a psychoanalytic position, and critics routinely construe his work as symptomatic. Jack Stevenson typifies this attitude when he describes Dogme'95 as a therapeutic self-overcoming of the desire for control that marked von Trier's early work: '[von Trier] naturally wanted to continue his craft and maintain his mental health at the same time, and this is what gave rise to the invention of Dogme' (Stevenson 2002:52).

Such straightforwardly auteurist psycho-biography crudely rationalises as 'the return of the repressed' von Trier's transition from the slick, unemotional, and self conscious Europe trilogy – *Forbrydelsens element/The Element of Crime* (1984), *Epidemic* (1987), *Europa* (1991) – to the spare, emotionally indulgent and self-reflexive Golden Heart trilogy – *Breaking the Waves* (1996), *Idioterne/The Idiots* (1998), *Dancer in the Dark* (2000). But the first trilogy very consciously engages with such psychoanalytic mechanisms, and 'aims straight for the unconscious' (von Trier, cit. Lumholdt 2003:85) with hypnotic devices and hysterical structures. The trilogy's use of mind-as-form has more in common with surrealism's anarchistic psycho-activism than with, say, postmodernism's discontinuous pastiche. *Europa* uses to great effect classic stylistics from art and noir cinema, but also surrealist dream imagery – evident in the film's oneiric sepia and absurdist juxtapositions. The saturated landscapes that run throughout the trilogy symbolise the historical unconscious, and von Trier compels his audience to repeat the traumas that blackly dog European history. And the trilogy's constant theme of hypnosis is a crude metaphor for cinema spectatorship as a kind of somnambulism – passive immersion into dimly lit dreams of an inescapable history: 'You want to wake up, to free yourself of the image of Europe', drones Max von Sydow at the end of *Europa*, 'but it is impossible...'

Detached and somewhat passé, these imitative psychological devices slowly gave way to more affectingly literal representations of mental illness. Von Trier's madwoman first appears in his realisation of Dreyer's adaptation of Medea, Euripides' tragedy of an abandoned wife's vengeful degeneration into madness and infanticide. *Medea* (1988) is shot on video transferred to celluloid, a technique chosen for its murky dream-like feel, and to emphasise form as integral to content. Von Trier skilfully enhances the corrupted footage with theatrical silhouettes, superimpositions and back-projections, creating a psycho-active mise-en-scène that reflects and intensifies Medea's emotional state. All other characters are reduced to mere avatars in her psycho-drama. Both form and mise-en-scène reproduce her disintegrating psychological state, eschewing realism for Dreyer-esque symbolism. And this amalgamation of form and content foreshadows his treatment of madness in the Golden Heart trilogy.

Breaking the Waves entered production just after von Trier released the Dogme'95 manifesto, and set the terms of engagement for the subsequent Golden Heart films by exploring female suffering and idealism within the radical hyper-realist form that defines the trilogy. 'Passion' can mean religious suffering or martyrdom, desire or eroticism, as well as the madness of base desires and sensations that 'Reason' need restrain. *Breaking the Waves* is a sensual melodrama and passion play about Bess, a disturbed young woman whose overwhelming faith in both divine and physical love tragically exposes the hypocrisy and heartlessness of her patriarchal Calvinist community. An accident leaves Bess' new husband Jan paralysed. Increasingly unstable, he tricks her into taking other lovers, convincing her that this act of love will save his life. Bess is driven to devastating sexual encounters and prostitution before sacrificing herself to a sadist. Miraculously, Jan does recover, and buries Bess to the sound of heavenly bells. The film is inspired by De Sade's *Justine*

(1791) as much as by the films of Sirk, Bergman and especially Dreyer's *La Passion de Jeanne d'Arc* (1928), *Ordet/The Word* (1954) and *Gertrud* (1964).[1] Bess, Gertrud, St Joan, and Justine are fantasies of the idealistic purity and goodness that might reside in womanly passions, and their forbearance of suffering is all the more horrifying given their compulsion to martyr themselves for an ideal. At stake is the madness of woman's morally transcendent complicity with the retribution that such goodness might provoke.

In terms of psychopathology, Bess's case is complicated. Seemingly learning-disabled, over-emotional, and obsessive, her *idée fixe* is her paradoxically rebellious submissiveness. Her irrationality has an inner logic: Bess is obeying the dogma to be a 'good girl', even though that means breaking rules, to reinforce her faith in the redemptive power of love and sexuality. Psychoanalytic readings usually diagnose Bess as a figurative archetype of 'hysteria' by which to discuss the more urgent matter of *jouissance* or transgression of the phallic order.[2] To assert the truth-claims of a given theory, the film is reduced to a merely demonstrative function at the expense of engaging with it on its own terms. Bess becomes a pin-up girl for theories of madness as a libidinal force or subversion of repression. Anyway, the usually dextrous work of a psychoanalytic critic is, in this context, effortlessly tautological because von Trier consciously worked madness into both the film's form and content. Such resistance to psychoanalytic theory is defensible because, as Freud said of surrealism, it is more meaningful to look for the conscious than the unconscious. Might not a shrewder critique explain as symptomatic von Trier's own schizophilia – his attraction to madness and his repetitive urge to extol its virtues?

Von Trier is accused of misogyny because his films naturalise and deify feminine sexuality as masochistic, and pathologise resistance to patriarchal power (Faber, 2003). With Marianist sacrifice and maudlin sensuality, Bess challenges the patriarchal, socially dictatorial Calvinist culture. Her passion conflates mythically 'feminine' archetypes of love – the Virgin Mary, the Magdelene, the martyr, the mystic, the hysteric – which some feminists see fit to salvage as icons of radical feminism. In much in the same way that Cixous and Irigaray glorified the hysteric and the mystic as resisting patriarchal subjugation,[3] Bess' madness has been interpreted as a similar kind of radical feminism (Restuccia, 2001). Compelling though these ideas are, is it not the case that they are recuperated by and reinforce patriarchy precisely because they collaborate to conceal the political and the social forces that shape and put such archetypes to work? By conforming to the myth that the feminine speaks and acts as the body itself, consolatory images of woman's 'mad' and numinous essence reinforce patriarchal notions of femininity as wholly somatic and affect-driven, as the Other of masculine Reason. Femininity and madness are re-established as irrational, bodily, silent, and of Nature, by way of pathologies intrinsic to them. In this way, Bess becomes synonymous with the supposed general condition of femininity and its passions. As André Breton put it, 'veritable *tableaux vivants* of a woman in love' (cit. Lomas 2001:73).

To understand Bess, we need to look closely at the film's radical aesthetic because her 'madness' constitutes its form. *Breaking the Waves* crashes ultra-realism up against the imaginary to signify Bess's 'intense sense of self (subjective camera)' (Schepelern 2003:66) and its wilfully incompatible fusion of romantic melodrama and hyper-realism represents her state of mind. Melodrama involves suffering which its stereotypically 'feminine' (because tragic, masochistic, yet morally righteous) characters work through with self-abnegation and a martyr's nerve, soliciting for melodrama's predominantly female audiences the vicarious pleasures of identification and heightened emotional response. Hyper-realism has an ethical function: to disallow the passive spectatorship and emotional cliché of classical cinema, normalising drama by encouraging a sense of immediacy and witness. *Breaking the Waves'* degraded images, shot on hand-held 35mm Cinemascope, transferred to video then back to 35mm, ensure this impression of authenticity, as well as a grainy urgency appropriate to its naïvely impulsive protagonist. The narrative is divided into literary chapters divided by hand-coloured romantic-kitsch landscapes that intensify Bess' emotional state. The landscapes effect quixotic ruptures into the otherwise staunchly realist piece, and bring to mind innumerable romantic images of madwomen like Crazy Kate, Cowper's love-mad inamorata (Cowper, 1785). The musical accompaniment of indulgently morose power-ballads updates Bess' romanticist passion for the outsider and his music. Even the audacious editing form follows only Bess' moods and emotional states, as 'hysterical' jump-cuts and whip-pans follow and strengthen the rapid movement of her emotional life, with no consideration given to best-take, proper framing, or continuity conventions.

Although no formal manifesto exists for *Breaking the Waves*, the correlation of Bess' madness with the film's form is unambiguous in the script's only and manifesto-like direction: 'Bess will, as the only person, look directly into camera. She will look without leaving her mood or motivation' (von Trier, 1995:23). A scene where Jan watches Bess watch the movie *Lassie* with a childlike suspension of disbelief farcically underscores her relationship to the medium itself and to the male gaze. Bess' gaze might subvert the female character's conventional mode of 'being-looked-at' rather than 'looking at' the camera. Offering the madwoman's gaze as a transcendental function linked to passion – love, madness and sacrifice – exposes the cathartic, redemptive function of suffering. To appreciate what was required of Bess,

Emily Watson was ordered to study Renée Falconetti's ecstatic presence in Dreyer's *La Passion de Jeanne d'Arc* – of which poor Bess' bovine gawp could only ever be a travesty. But Bess' gaze also makes her complicit in her fate while transforming the audience into powerless witnesses. For psychoanalysts, this might bring to light the erotic nature of the gaze which is always, in the end, 'for death'. Consciously, at least, von Trier uses Bess' gaze to augment his vision of her mental state as the simultaneous presence of the real and the imaginary. *Breaking the Waves'* innovative form *is* Bess' point of view, and represents her mental state as simultaneously realist and imaginary: the film itself is crazy.

The ultimate magical shot of ringing bells is generally interpreted as a 'God's Eye' shot that assures narrative closure. But couldn't it also be the point toward which Bess was gazing herself, the object cause of her madness? When those bloody bells, the ones Bess and Jan pledged to make ring again, toll exultant at her funeral, they capsize the absurdity of her passion to salvage the miraculous, the supernatural, the irrational: the 'feminine'. But her agonistic sacrifice was no more beautiful or saintly for her endurance of its passion. *Breaking the Waves* reduces Bess' madness to symbolic transcendence, to social and aesthetic dissent. Bess is no feminist: she is a catalyst for change and, like all catalysts, she is burnt up and spent in the process. Bess' madness reflects the cinema that von Trier pits against both decadent art-house and contrived Hollywood film-making: raw, faithful, naïve, good, a 'mistress of the screen, not tamed and made sexless...'

Breaking the Waves' vision of madness as eroticism and rebellion prefigures the avant-gardist antics of the Dogme'95 movement and von Trier's Dogme film; rooted in his own directorial obsessions, Dogme'95 is a meta-cinematic vehicle for *The Idiots*, in which von Trier confronts his own passions. All four signatorial Dogme films (and a number of others besides) have at their moral centre characters with a mental illness or disability. This could be a consequence of von Trier's dictatorial influence, or a means of by-passing the manifesto's injunctions against technical effects and dramaturgy while satisfying its demand that 'the characters' inner lives justify the plot'. With his television ghost story, *Riget/The Kingdom* (1994-7), von Trier began to 'purify' his filmmaking style, reducing technological effects to the bare minimum in anticipation of Dogme'95's austerity. *Riget* featured as a dramatic chorus two actors with Down's Syndrome playing manual workers. The unifying function of the chorus could be seen as subverting the naïveté stereotypically allocated to this disability. Yet, as an interchangeable homophonic voice, they become merely ingenuous equivalents lacking individuality. 'Mental illness' and 'mental disability' are not secure scientific categories, essential political identities, or moral equivalents. In *The Idiots*, however, von Trier's confusion of imaginary forms of mental illness and disability are represented as essential modes of authenticity and affirmation which expose one's interdependency with the Other. 'Idio' is, after all, the prefix that assures individualism.

The Idiots sustains von Trier's idiosyncratic paradigms of madness and disability to expose uncomfortable 'truths' about erstwhile socialist ideals. The idiots operate a simulated radical collective evocative of Denmark's Christiania Free State, R.D. Laing's therapeutic communities, or even von Trier's Film-Town in Avedøre. The ersatz-communards search for their 'inner idiot' by 'spassing' – invoking a romanticised idea of mental disabilities which promises freedom and authenticity – to unburden themselves of false consciousness and 'bourgeois' self-censorship. Like Bess in *Breaking the Waves*, they express forbidden passions – the censor-testing 'gang-bang' scene, in particular, correlates mental disability with sexual and moral deviancy. Wilfully marginal, the idiots appear to transcend the vulgar aspiration and self-interest of the local bourgeoisie they gleefully provoke. Karen, a severely depressed woman, has inadvertently joined the commune and become their moral barometer and arbiter of truth. 'Spassing' unites the group, allowing them to connect with one another and unreservedly express emotions, but also to control and exploit one another.

Karen's melancholic virtuousness reveals less revolutionary motives behind the desire to confront society with idiots. She exposes 'spassing' for what it is: bad faith. Solidarity fractures when the idiots encounter these real truths about themselves. Axel is an idiot to escape the responsibilities of family and corporate work; Katrine, his spurned mistress, 'spasses' to expose him. Stoffer 'spasses' to control his friends, and to emit his seething resentment of bourgeois and corporate power. An art teacher and a psychologist hope to profit by intellectualising 'spassing' as a social experiment. Jeppe and Josephine fuck like idiots, but cannot even mention their feelings when they are not 'spassing'. Crisis occurs when the idiots encounter people with Down's Syndrome and simulated 'spassing' is demystified only to be rapidly replaced with what seems like real madness. The merry pranksters' mental health is genuinely put to question as they flit between 'authentic state[s] of nervous breakdown' and mere 'surrealist *amour fou.*'(Smith 2003:118). Jeppe intensely acts on his feelings after discovering that Josephine actually has mental health problems and is forcibly removed by her dictatorial father. Stoffer has a hysterical breakdown when the local council – 'Sollerød Fascists!' – bribe him to relocate his 'home for the disabled' to a less wealthy neighbourhood. Von Trier's insistence on madness as morally transcendent has replaced mere 'spassing', revealing madness to be redeemable as truly revolutionary.

Habitually leftist, the avant-garde has practised active rejection of social, political, and aesthetic norms, and of 'normalised' modes of identity and consciousness. Madness has been especially useful to the avant-garde as an un-recuperable symbol of alienation and creative dissent - expressionists, surrealists, and dadaists, in particular, assumed a solidarity of alienation with the mentally ill. While the idiots certainly revive 'the project of wilful surrealist dementia' (Smith 2003:116), the ethics of this avant-gardist project are also on trial. Because the group's survival is dependent upon an unjustifiably indignant identity (the 'inner-idiot' which assumes equality with mental disability), the film 'is not a critique of the oppressive structure of the collective', but rather of 'the fantasy of emancipation through [marginalised] identity [due to] a shared political desperation and impotence' (Roberts 1999:147). The 'inner idiot' – an attempt to return to some supposed origin – is also analogous to the pure and anarchic cinema that Dogme'95 pursues. The manifesto's aesthetics, methodology, and avant-gardist format is reflected in the idiots' search for authenticity and liberty whilst violating so-called 'bourgeois norms': *The Idiots* is the superlative Dogme'95 film. Taken in its avant-gardist context, *The Idiots* is simultaneously the deconstruction of the Dogme manifesto's ironic claims to purity, truth, coalition, and political significance, and the paradigm of von Trier's search for moral purity in madness, disability, and avant-gardism. Together with its meta-cinematic framework, *The Idiots* confronts and undermines the very idea of an avant-garde movement as a still-viable campaign.

If the retreat into idiocy was symptomatic of anything meaningful it would be 'left-wing melancholy' (Benjamin 1994:305), Walter Benjamin's term for the embittered ex-radical who is so attached to a defeated and obsolete political ideal, to mourning its loss, that s/he fails to struggle for real change in the present. '"Left melancholy" indicates not only a refusal to come to terms with the particular character of the present. It signifies, as well, a certain narcissism with regard to one's past political attachments and identity that exceeds any contemporary investment in political mobilization, alliance, or transformation' (Brown 1999:20). The film mourns as obsolete core socialist tactics of protest, collectivisation, and communalism. Antagonistic separatism and avant-gardism may have promised a kind of freedom, but they are here sorrowfully mocked as no longer having integrity or efficacy given the contemporary political scene. *The Idiots* suggests that leftist experiments with communalism, and with self and Other (of which spassing is a wonderful parody), can be thinly-veiled strategies for self-interested and indignant retreat. The film's 'soixante-retards' are pathetic symbols of the modish tendency to believe that the left is resentfully reluctant to modernise its arsenal of activism, negation, and protest. That von Trier chose to criticise avant-gardism and radicalism by mimicking an avant-gardist and leftist mode of cultural change suggests that his satire on contemporary political resistance is the mourning of its own abandoned ideal. That said, Dogme'95 did effect radical change in the contemporary film scene. But if avant-gardism is anti-traditional and rebukes conventions (even avant-gardist conventions) then the self-reproachful *The Idiots* may be the quintessential avant-gardist gesture of instantaneous self-annihilation.

Avant-gardist idiocy is only a mournful retreat from the crisis of contemporary political agency, yet von Trier consoles himself by maintaining that his notion of madness is a more authentic and active expression of negation than merely reactive change. In this militantly satirical Dogme film, we might expect von Trier's mad Mariah to renounce her usual talent for securing change, but his cynical affection for romanticised madness prohibits such optimism. Karen is the only idiot to face the ultimate challenge. The final scene of her 'spassing' to defy her (in any case obnoxious) family is excruciating, but fulfils the experiment's more sincere aims. Karen willingly sacrifices her chance of returning home to venerate the idiot project. The bathos of madness ought to insure that psychic and spiritual injuries are atoned for, but films like *The Idiots*, which parody society's injurious effects on the mind, only deflect responsibility back onto individual pathology, such that, in the final analysis, any political or social critique is effectively neutralised.

Dancer in the Dark, von Trier's musical melodrama, delivers another innovative and psychologically expressive hybrid of hyper-realism and cinematic fantasy that revisits the aesthetic potential of disability. *Dancer in the Dark* is an oxymoron: an 'anti-musical'. Its unique form utilised 100 digital cameras capturing panoramically fantastic yet realist action. Von Trier's now signature hyper-realistic style was secured by transferring the grainy DV images to video and then 35mm. The opening scene of rehearsals for a musical appears as a sort of documentary introduction to the film, rather like the documentary sequences in *The Idiots*. These neo-Brechtian devices suggest a 'making of' documentary about the ongoing film, and show the audience (as if we need to be shown) how ridiculously unrealistic even such social-surrealist films are. *Dancer in the Dark*'s emotional and psychological momentum is foregrounded because characters in musicals generally collectively burst into song to express strong emotions or denote pivotal narrative developments, while melodrama (as in *Breaking the Waves*), habitually navigates repressed, forbidden emotions and individual crises. *Dancer in the Dark* combines these generic conventions to allow Selma's inner life to merge with the realist mise-en-scène.

Von Trier's 'Selma Manifesto' describes a spirited blind immigrant struggling as part of the American underclass. Because Selma is going blind the film is a complex amalgamation of her real and imaginative states. But her secret ability to bring together reality with fantasy enables her to survive hardship as well as compensate for her disability: 'When things get too much to bear she can pretend she is in a musical ... All the joy that life can't give her is there.' (Björkman 2003:237-40) There is, again, a neo-Brechtian hyper-reflexivity at work that underscores that this is only a film. Throughout the manifesto's philosophical exposition of spectatorship, cinema comes to represent and be a substitute for the imagination, which is given sovereignty over reality. *Dancer in the Dark*'s amalgamated form allows us to see simultaneously both Selma's inner and outer worlds. Her ability to integrate fantasy/cinema into reality is a psychological stratagem directly reflected in the film's form. As in *Breaking the Waves*, meta-cinematic scenes in which Selma 'watches' a musical movie signify her disability (because Selma is too weak-sighted now to actually see much of the film, Kathy signs the dance sequences onto Selma's open palm and she fills in the gaps with her imagination), but also her relationship to the medium and, hence, to the very film we are watching. Selma is a filmmaker who creates musical films out of her own imagination: 'This isn't escapism! It's much, much more... it's art!' (ibid.) The film-makers, both Selma and von Trier, construct from this mental smashing together of imagination and reality a sort of neo-Brechtian alienation of cinematic spectacle. But Selma's ability to sublimate in this way is celebrated as a creative enhancement of experience and an escape from alienation. Immigrant Selma is alienated in the classically Marxist sense, and her 'goodness' and her imaginary musicals alienate her from reality. Selma's sacrifice of her life for her son's is an idealistic expression of her fateful 'goodness'. Idealistic Selma's policy is of always avoiding the final number in a musical because it's a sign the film is about to end. She prefers to believe that films go on without their audiences, that they are real.

Von Trier's novelty in the Golden Heart films, his avant-gardism, if you will, is to employ hyper-realist aesthetics to integrate, indeed privilege, inner psychological and expressionist experience over exterior and documentary realism. This novelty, which his radical forms impose on hypothetically mad and disabled female martyrs, might better substantiate those accusations of misogyny than critiques that diagnose his films as symptomatic of psychoanalytic theories. Despite connections made between von Trier's mental health and his film-making, the strategies and techniques described above are no straightforward case of film as symptom or sublimation. There is a need to move beyond the routinely romanticised image of von Trier as mad genius, especially when approaching the images of madness in his films. As an alternative, it is possible to think about him as a militantly self-reflexive filmmaker who strategically puts to use his insights into and beliefs about mental illnesses and disabilities in creating truly innovative if fantastically problematic films.

By exploiting the romanticised notion that the mentally ill and disabled have a special perspective and power, von Trier's politically controversial films reinforce the aura of uncanniness that continues to stigmatise mental illness and disability. The Golden Heart women are abused, beaten, raped, cast out and executed, yet they willingly sacrifice themselves because they are outsiders and, thus, morally and intrinsically 'good'. His visions of feminine morality are radicalised, being entwined within ethically charged notions of madness and disability as synthetic prospects of a sanctified release from moral resentment. For von Trier, to be feminine or feminised is to liberate the passions – madness, fanaticism, sacrifice, love – in a pathological revolt against their suppression. Like romantics, avant-gardists, and even some feminists, von Trier conflates femininity with mental illness into an emblem of creative dissent. Bess, Karen, and Selma wilfully participate in passionate self-immolation, rehearsing the martyr's deliverance of a sinful, pitiable, and wretched Other. Von Trier's abstemious avant-gardism luxuriates in mourning their emotional intemperance, and his signature style of simultaneous alienation and realism reifies their states of mind as visions of avant-gardist individualism.

The excitingly polemical *Dogville* (2003) and *Manderlay* (2005) of his USA: Land of Opportunities trilogy might finally demoralise von Trier's saintly ingénue as her idealistic suffering is dispossessed by Grace. This trilogy shows that von Trier is starting to address in new ways topical political issues like political asylum, morality, and American imperialism. Grace surpasses his preoccupations with madness and disabilities while remaining passionate about problems of ethical and moral agency. Where Bess, Karen and Selma were von Trier's wretched victims, Grace is his avenging angel who, with a casual arc of her manicured hand, threatens to sweep away a decade of obsession with naïvely feminine piety. But not, of course, until she too has been tortured...

References

Benjamin, Walter (1994; 1931): 'Left-Wing Melancholy'. In Kaes, Anton, Martin Jay & Edward Dimendberg (eds): *The Weimar Republic Sourcebook*. Berkeley: University of California Press.

Björkman, Stig (2003): *Trier on von Trier*. Translated from the Swedish by Neil Smith. London: Faber & Faber.

Brown, Wendy (1999): 'Resisting Left-Melancholy', *Boundary 2*, 26:3, 19-27.

Cixous, Hélène & Catherine Clement (1986; 1975): *The Newly Born Woman.*. Minneapolis: University of Minnesota Press.

Cowper, William (1994; 1785): *'The Task' and Selected Poems*. London: Longman.

Faber, Alaya (2003): 'Redeeming Sexual Violence? A Feminist Reading of *Breaking the Waves*'. *Literature and Theology*, 17:1, 59-75.

Irigarary, Luce (1985; 1977): *This Sex Which Is Not One*. Ithaca: Cornell University Press.

Kavenna, Joanna (2004): 'Tiny Little Lars'. *London Review of Books*, 15 April, 34-35.

Lomas, David (2001): 'The Omnipotence of Desire'. In Mundy, Jennifer (ed.): *Surrealism: Desire Unbound*. London: Tate Publishing Ltd.

Lumholdt, Jan (2003): *Lars von Trier: Interviews*. Mississippi: University Press of Mississippi.

Restuccia, Frances (2001): 'Impossible Love in *Breaking the Waves*: Mystifying Hysteria'. *Literature & Psychology*, 47: 1/2, 34-53.

Roberts, John (1999): 'Dogme 95'. *New Left Review* 238, 147.

Schepelern, Peter (2003): 'Kill Your Darlings: Lars von Trier and the Origins of Dogma 95', Hjort, Mette & Scott McKenzie (eds): *Purity and Provocation: Dogma 95*. London: BFI.

Smith, Murray (2003): 'Lars von Trier: Sentimental Surrealist'. In Hjort, Mette & Scott MacKenzie (eds), *Purity and Provocation: Dogma 95*. London: BFI.

Stevenson, Jack (2002): *Lars von Trier*. London: BFI.

von Trier, Lars (2003; 1984) 'Manifesto: *The Element of Crime*'. In Björkman (2003).

von Trier, Lars (1995): *Breaking the Waves*. London: Faber & Faber.

von Trier, Lars & Thomas Vinterberg (1995): Dogme 95 Manifesto. Available at www.dogme95.dk

Zizek, Slavoj (1999): 'Femininity Between Goodness and Act'. *Lacanian Ink* 14, 26-40.

Notes

1. *Breaking the Waves'* original title was *Amor Omnia* – 'love is all' – a reference to the heroine's epitaph in *Gertrud*; *Ordet* similarly features a mentally ill character with Christ-like connotations performing miracles in an everyday world.

2. Zizek (1999) claims that Bess exemplifies Lacan's edict that the 'sexual relation is impossible.' Restuccia (2001) counters that Bess embodies Lacan's masochistic, mystical 'third order love', and uses psychoanalytic terminology to reinterpret her crusade as 'de-subjectivizing *jouissance*' – a loss of self analogous to madness. Both use Bess' supposed hysteria to corroborate Lacan's definition of 'femininity' as a lack of identification that undermines the phallic order.

3. See: Irigarary (1985), and Cixous & Clement (1986).

Politics of the Auteurial Subject: Time, Narrative, and Intertextuality in *Scenes from a Marriage* and *Faithless*

Sharon Lin Tay

The social and political upheavals of the 1970s transformed, if not radicalised, film culture in the United States and Western Europe.[1] Such a context of social change allowed a re-thinking of gender politics in the cinema, in part giving rise to feminist film theory and criticism as the discourse with which to analyse, question, critique, and challenge the cinematic apparatus and the ideological underpinnings leading to mainstream, or Hollywood, representations of women. With reference to American cinema, the near collapse of the studio system in the 1970s gave rise to two phenomena: the rise of the American New Wave (Kolker 2000; Biskind 1998) and the emergence of a liberal feminist sensibility in mainstream films, what Annette Kuhn calls 'the new women's cinema' (Kuhn 1986:125). Examples of these films would include *Kramer vs Kramer* (Richard Benton, 1979), a divorce and custody drama starring Meryl Streep; *Cagney and Lacey* (Ted Post, 1981), a film about two female police officers that could only have been inspired by feminist activism; *Nine to Five* (Colin Higgins, 1980), a comic exploration of workplace sexual harassment; and *Alice Doesn't Live Here Anymore* (Martin Scorsese, 1974), a film that charts a single mother's trajectory after the death of her husband. In addition, Teresa De Lauretis also observes a spate of 'commercial, man-made "woman's films"' in the early 1980s that gave liberal feminism 'its modest allotment of institutional legitimation' (De Lauretis 1987:138). Given the trenchant feminist critiques of Hollywood cinema, such developments cannot be a bad thing, although De Lauretis reminds us that 'the success, however modest, of this liberal feminism has been bought at the price of reducing the contradictory complexity – and the theoretical complexity – of concepts such as sexual difference, the personal is political, and feminism itself to simpler and more acceptable ideas already existing in the dominant culture' (ibid.).

This essay considers the situation that De Lauretis articulates in relation to Ingmar Bergman's *Scener ur ett äktenskap/Scenes from a Marriage* (1973).

The set of factors surrounding *Scenes from a Marriage* makes De Lauretis' critique even more relevant to this film than to the mainstream American cinema she discusses, given the humanist aesthetics that informs art cinema and the fact that *Scenes from a Marriage* strongly suggests the infusion of liberal feminist sensibilities that characterise certain 1970s films: consider its attention to the domestic sphere, the microscopic exploration of a marriage breakdown, the liberal representation of heterosexual relationships, and that it takes for granted the wife's successful career as a lawyer. Indisputably the father of Swedish cinema and a cinematic master within the critical discourse of a high brow *auteur*-led European arthouse cinema, Bergman is often argued to infuse his films with universal and philosophical themes around life and the condition of the soul without much consideration for the distinct gendered perspective that might colour Bergman's films. For instance, Jesse Kalin's recent volume (2003) investigates Bergman's films from such a reverential perspective, while *Cineaste* recently ran an article by Leonard Quart that describes *Scenes from a Marriage* as 'arguably offering the most moving and complex dissection of marriage ever shown on screen' (Quart 2004:30-5). That the positioning of such a discourse denies the significance of the auteur's gendered identity becomes clear when one comparatively analyses *Scenes from a Marriage* with Liv Ullmann's *Trolösa/Faithless* (2000), a film scripted by Bergman and which references both *Scenes from a Marriage* and the extra-filmic discourse around Bergman's well-publicised relationships with his actresses, notably, Ullmann herself. Asserting *Scenes from a Marriage*'s distinct disregard for gendered subject positions, and the associated sexual politics, the comparative analysis with *Faithless* that this paper attempts also involves a consideration of the cinematic rendition of time, narrative, and intertextuality, which are always implicated in discussions of gendered subjectivities.

Cinema, Time and Gender

The aesthetic differences between *Faithless* and *Scenes from a Marriage* speak to the respective films' sexual politics and how they may be analysed. Perhaps influenced by its original televisual format, the episodic form of *Scenes from a Marriage* glosses over many of the minute details of the marriage the film professes to dissect.[2] The domestic and personal subject matter that *Scenes from a Marriage* dwells on give the film some sort of feminist legitimacy, in a reversal of what De Lauretis describes as the legitimisation of women's cinema through Hollywood's adoption of liberal feminist sensibilities in the 1970s. However, the film's temporal quality reveals the limitations of *Scenes from a Marriage*'s association with the notion of a women's cinema, as thrown into sharp relief by the æsthetic qualities of *Faithless*.

In her study of the emergence of cinematic time in the late nineteenth and early twentieth centuries, Mary Ann Doane considers the standardisation and rationalisation of time necessitated by the rise of capitalism in order to regulate labour (Doane 2002:6). This theory of rationalisation, Doane claims, 'does not allow for the vicissitudes of the affective, for the subjective play of desire, anxiety, pleasure, trauma, apprehension' (ibid.:13), so much so that 'time is, in a sense, externalized, a surface phenomenon, which the modern subject must ceaselessly attempt to repossess through its multifarious representations' (ibid.:9). Although *Scenes from a Marriage* professes a liberal feminist sensibility in its privileging of the domestic and the personal, so much a response to the 1970s feminist call for the politicisation of the personal, the film's temporality functions on the continuum of rationalised and standardised time. The film's episodic form, and the introduction of each new scene with an intertitle bearing some profound statement or truism about relationships, gives the episodes a sense of being set pieces. In other words, what happens in between the scenes that give rise to a subsequent episode between Marianne and Johan is elided, ensuring a neat linearity in the film's depiction of this particular marriage it professes to analyse. In comparison to the women's cinema that 1970s feminist film activism advocates, *Scenes from a Marriage* does not engage with the feminine time that characterises the private female experience, famously explored in Chantal Akerman's *Jeanne Dielman, 23 Quai du Commerce, 1080 Bruxelles* (1976). Bergman's camera, as it were, reserves the exclusive right to subjectivity in a way that is reminiscent of how the classic realist cinema is deemed to exert its voyeuristic control over the image of woman. The aesthetic realisation of a domestic subject matter via a cinematic continuum of surface temporality is therefore not convincing in its professed embrace of the personal.

On the other hand, *Faithless* remedies the flaws of *Scenes from a Marriage* through its deliberate imposture on time and, in the process, allows for the play of subjectivities and desires to flow at the expense of the director's mastery over the film's narrative coherence, temporal continuity, and perspectives. Coming back to De Lauretis' consideration of how one may construct the female social subject in the cinema, she lists the themes encapsulated in the phrase 'the personal is political' as: 'the disjunction of image and voice, the reworking of narrative space, the elaboration of strategies of address that alters the forms and balances of traditional representation' (De Lauretis 1987:145). *Faithless* achieves just that through the ways in which it inserts a consideration of the auteur's gendered body into the fray.

Scenes From A Marriage: Episodic Narrative and Liberal Feminist Sensibility

Scenes from a Marriage charts the marriage of a couple, Marianne (Liv Ullmann) and Johan (Erland Josephson), over the period of a decade in episodic form. Intertitles separate the various segments that make up the film, and each is characterised by a particular phase in the relationship between the two characters. The film starts with the couple being interviewed and photographed for a magazine article about their privileged and exemplary marriage. After the dinner party episode where their guests, another couple on the verge of divorce, tear into each other, the film goes on to show the quiet daily negotiations and cracks in Marianne and Johan's marriage. This culminates in the episode where Johan comes home to tell Marianne that he has fallen in love with a younger woman, Paula, and is moving to Paris with her for six months. Marianne is left distraught. Johan returns, six months later, in a separate episode where the couple attempts to rebuild some sort of post-marriage relationship. He initiates intimacy, which she attempts to resist on grounds that she is trying to get on with her life. He spends the night, but leaves in the middle of it. She shows him a reconciliatory letter that Paula has written to her. In the next segment of the film, they meet to sign divorce papers. The evening begins well, they have sex on the office floor, but ends in acrimony when he changes his mind about signing the papers, enrages her, and then hits her. He confesses that he is tired of Paula. Quite inexplicably, the next segment begins with the couple taking off together to their cottage outside of the city. Now unhappily married to other people, they keep up an affair with each other and come to an acceptance of themselves and understanding of each other.

That *Scenes from a Marriage* is a product of a radicalised 1970s film culture becomes evident when one considers the existence of a similar American film from within the same socio-political context. *Same Time, Next Year* (Robert Mulligan, 1978) stars Alan Alda and Ellen Burstyn as two strangers, married to other people, who experienced an accidental one-night stand with each other. They then proceed to meet each year, over the next three decades, in the same hotel room for their annual rendezvous. *Same Time, Next Year* celebrates the relationship as one that sustains the two characters through their respective trials and tribulations, does not touch on the film's more sordid implications of marital infidelity, and is devoid of irony. Like *Scenes from a Marriage*, the film is an episodic chamber piece (each annual rendezvous is somewhat self-contained), and propounds a liberal sensibility in respect of relationships and domestic arrangements.

The simplistic episodic structure and linear narrativity that govern both *Scenes from a Marriage* and *Same Time, Next Year* provide for the objective point of view that foregrounds a stable subjectivity in both films, be it the auteurial or spectatorial subject. As such, despite their liberal feminist sensibilities on the narrative level, the films do not work towards circumventing the mainstream cinematic conventions that posit the director and spectator as male and that which the 1970s feminist film movement critiques and evades, most notably, via a problematic recourse to the cinematic avant-garde.[3] Although *Same Time, Next Year* and *Scenes from a Marriage* focus on one set of relationships, this main relationship is tangential to the other relationships in which the protagonists are involved but which neither film regards. In this sense, the radical politics of the 1970s socio-political upheavals that permeate film culture become diluted, and the feminist politics that informs the radical agenda to transform the domestic, the personal, and sexual relations becomes co-opted into morally relative masculine fantasies of multiple partners and relationships with diminished responsibility.

Scenes from a Marriage works as a critique of the institution of marriage that hinges on the performance of prescribed gender roles. However, the conservatism of *Scenes from a Marriage*'s representation of gender roles is belied by its bourgeois assumptions, derived from a sense of gender equality predicated on Swedish notions of liberalism, welfarism, and conflict avoidance, that to an extent obscure the inherent differences with which men and women experience their lives in social, political, and economic terms (Persson 1990). On the surface, the film is an objective and liberal rendition of a marriage breakdown where the blame is shared and characters revel in the pain of their bourgeois tragedy, although it results in all shades of (male) melodrama. Within a social-political context of feminist activism and assaults on bourgeois values, *Scenes from a Marriage* concedes to female emancipation in exchange for the release from the responsibilities that patriarchal privileges impose on men. The melodrama resides in Johan's acceptance of his own limitations at the end, a conclusion that elides the power dynamics in the film's representation of gender relations. Comparisons of the sequences with which the film begins and ends show this.

Marianne gains the ability to describe herself and articulates her modus operandi at the end of *Scenes from a Marriage*:

'Till skillnad från dig uthärdar jag. Och trivs. Jag litar på mitt förstånd. Och min känsla. De samarbetar. Jag är nöjd med båda två. Nu på äldre dar har jag fått en tredje medarbetare. Det är min erfarenhet.' (Bergman 1973:192)

(Unlike you, I stick it out. And enjoy it. I rely on my common sense. And my feeling. They cooperate. I'm satisfied with both of them. Now that I'm older I have a third co-worker: my experience.) (Bergman 1974:207)[4]

This is in contrast to the difficulties she experiences in trying to describe herself, apart from her connections to her husband and children, to the journalist at the start of the film. Marianne finds an identity for herself while Johan becomes resigned to his own mediocrity, contrasting sharply with the self-satisfaction with which he talks about himself, and in such glowing terms, in the interview sequence at the start of the film. Albeit that *Scenes from a Marriage* develops Marianne's character and identity in line with feminist imperatives at the end of the film, her realisation of her growing power pivots on the fantasy of equal opportunity and equality between the sexes, a premise that the film chooses not to question in favour of a liberal and progressive conclusion. As De Lauretis observes about the liberal feminist sensibilities assimilated into 1970s American cinema, the independence and autonomy granted to Marianne in *Scenes from a Marriage* comes at the expense of attempts to critique and analyse gender politics. The power dynamics governing the representations of gender relations, and the ethics surrounding the extra-marital affair on which Marianne and Johan embark at the end of *Scenes from a Marriage*, are issues that *Faithless* takes on board thirty years later.

Faithless: intertextuality and (inter)subjectivity

The layer upon layer of intertextual references that *Faithless* presents give the film an intricate complexity that *Scenes from a Marriage*, for all the aesthetic pleasures and liberal sensibilities it provides, lacks. Scripted by Bergman and directed by Ullmann, *Faithless* comes already textured by the extra-filmic information provided by the discourses surrounding its writer and director, and is further compounded by the film's inexorable connection to the earlier *Scenes from a Marriage*. For instance, the female protagonists of both films share a name, the lead actor makes appearances in both films as characters that are intrinsically associated with Bergman himself, and both films share similar plotlines and narrative details (the rendezvous in Paris, etc.). Evidence of such deliberate intertextual associations perhaps renders *Faithless* a remake of the earlier film from a politically invested perspective. Geoffrey Macnab, for instance, notes Bergman's tragic adulterous relationship with a journalist named Gun Hagberg in 1949 as the affair that influenced the ways in which Bergman created female characters in many of his films. Hagberg, says Macnab, also becomes the model for the Marianne character in *Faithless* (Macnab 2000:30-2). Erland Josephson, who in a more youthful incarnation was Johan in *Scenes from a Marriage*, plays the old director (coded as Bergman) in *Faithless*. The film's setting on a remote island references Bergman's self-imposed exile and isolation on the island of

Fårö, necessitating a comment on the construction of the male auteur and a particular understanding of his domestic space.[5]

Faithless' narrative set-up, of an elderly director who conjures up a woman in his imagination to re-live the tragedy of an extra-marital affair and betrayal on a massive scale, attempts to explore the issues that *Scenes from a Marriage* glosses over. The imaginary woman character that materialises on screen is named Marianne, a detail that references Ullmann's character in *Scenes from a Marriage* and increases the intertextual associations. She is summoned into existence by either the director's memory or imagination, and narrates for the director the story of the extra-marital affair she has with her husband's good friend, David, a film director, which then spirals out of control. Intrigued by David's request for sex, she plots a rendezvous in Paris behind the back of Markus, her husband. Events then unravel uncontrollably upon their return as the secret meetings continue and David's jealousy increases, culminating in Markus finding them together in bed. An ugly custody battle for Marianne and Markus' daughter, Isabelle, ensues, leading to an attempt by Markus to blackmail Marianne for sex in exchange for custody, which fuels David's jealous cruelty. David then proceeds to have an affair with an actress on his film set and leaves Marianne. Markus commits suicide. Marianne finds out from the hospital that someone has discovered his body and called for help. She looks up this person and discovers that Markus had kept a mistress throughout their marriage.

The cynicism that characterises *Faithless* cannot be further away from the affirmation of human relationships that *Scenes from a Marriage* advocates, which in turn raises questions about the politics behind the latter film. *Scenes from a Marriage* refuses to acknowledge the consequences of relationship breakdowns and extra-marital affairs on children and the other partners involved, while *Faithless* wallows in the destruction that infidelity and betrayals cause. Most notably, *Faithless* focuses the destructive effects of infidelity on the couple's daughter, Isabelle. Presented as an isolated child who plays alone in her attic room, Isabelle is neglected, often left with her grandmother, bears the brunt of her parents' acrimonious divorce, and is invited to participate in a suicide pact by her depressed father. In effect, she is the one character in the film who serves as the contact point for all the estranged characters, including Markus' mistress, Margareta, who appears late into the film and tells Marianne about her acquaintance with Isabelle. In this sense, Isabelle functions according to the description of Gilles Deleuze's 'universal girl' within the film's topography, given that she roams *Faithless'* narrative interstices and inhabits the gaps between the characters before falling victim to their actions. All of this inscribes trauma into her (damaged) history and botches her process of becoming (Deleuze and Guattari

1988:276-7). In contrast to the two children in *Scenes from a Marriage*, who only appear briefly for the photo shoot at the beginning of the film, then are quickly shepherded out of the shot never to be seen again, the Isabelle character serves to indict Bergman's refusal to engage with the sexual politics that *Scenes from a Marriage* depicts. As Ullmann notes in an interview, 'In *Scenes from a Marriage*, which Bergman wrote and directed, the couple has two children but you never see them. They didn't have any importance in the movie, but I wanted to do something different since I know how tough it is for children when people divorce' (Porton 2004:32-4, 37). Where *Scenes from a Marriage* fails to represent the power dynamics within human relationships, *Faithless* provides a stark picture: those unable to cope with a spiralling network of betrayal end their lives while those left behind live on in guilt. In its too hopeful depiction of a petty bourgeois relationship, *Scenes from a Marriage* ignores the expanding cycle of destruction and that each character is equally responsible, complicit, and guilty except for the children, on whom the tragedy is inflicted. By situating a child as that one innocent victim in *Faithless*, Ullmann insists on culpability in an ethically invested gesture that comments on the feel-good domestic melodrama. This contrasts with *Scenes from a Marriage*, in which the male abandonment of responsibilities that patriarchal privileges entail is passed off as progressive liberalism, of which the woman's emancipation is but the by-product.

Auteurial perspective and sexual politics

The call to construct a 'women's cinema' that departs from what was perceived to be oppressive Hollywood representations of women was resounding in the heady days of feminist film activism in the 1970s. This agenda was to inform feminist film scholarship over the next three decades. In her consideration of women's cinema, De Lauretis writes:

> The project of women's cinema, therefore, is no longer that of destroying or disrupting man-centered vision by representing its blind spots, its gaps, or its repressed. The effort and challenge now are how to effect another vision: to construct other objects and subjects of vision, and to formulate the conditions of representability of another social subject. (De Lauretis 1987:135)

Faithless shows how such an ideal might be achieved, especially through its ready comparison to *Scenes from a Marriage*. The myriad intertextual references discussed above already gives *Faithless* a degree of intertextuality by virtue of 'coming after' *Scenes from a Marriage*, and effectively disturbs the primacy of Bergman's auteurial voice. On a pro-filmic level, Bergman and Ullmann's respective voices as scriptwriter and director are in competition, and translate into the multi-vocality of *Faithless*. That *Faithless* is in part intended to be a commentary on the romantic notion of the male directorial genius at the same time that the film pays homage to Bergman is evident in the interviews that Ullmann gives. Speaking of Bergman's well-documented isolation on his island and status as an art-house auteur, Ullmann is reported as saying:

> Maybe to be a genius you have to be completely heartless. Maybe you have to make choices to be a great artist or to live comfortably with what you believe in. For me, I'd rather live comfortably with what I believe in. There are some who are probably greater artists, but it's no good if you have to tread on someone else's soul. (Macnab 2000:32)

Such sentiments may reflect Ullmann's intricate understanding of the connection between gender and cinematic genius, and perhaps translate into *Faithless'* active subversion of the auteurial voice to flag up the gender politics that surround Bergman and comment on *Scenes from a Marriage*.[6] By so doing, Ullmann incorporates in her film practice the feminist imperative to formulate a new social subjectivity that allows the construction of the female auteurial voice. Within the diegesis, the conversations that the old man has with Marianne and David, alongside the flashbacks, introduce an unstable element to the film's narrative that is in contrast to the omniscience of Bergman's camera in *Scenes from a Marriage*. That the Bergman character in the film conjures up her character undermines Marianne's subjectivity in some measure, although such a narrative strategy also allows the introduction of the woman's voice into the film. As she is engaged in conversation with the old man, she materialises as a subject who is just as complicit as the male characters in the situation, given that her foolhardy decision to start an extra-marital affair is that which propels the tragedy.

The privilege the film accords to Marianne's subjective point of view becomes evident in the scene where she faces David's cruel verbal assault after she returns from meeting with Markus about their daughter, during which she was coerced into sex in return for custody. She narrates the conversation she has with David after she comes home from meeting Markus, after which David abruptly appears in the director's study to second her version of the story. His account in fact emphasises the cruelty to which he subjects her more than her version of the story, being accompanied by the constant crosscutting back to the living room where his verbal assault at her is shot subjectively from her perspective. The point where her lover becomes the ultimate bully at Marianne's lowest ebb is that which causes the director to release a wail of anguish, suggesting that the director is an older version of David living in shame of his past actions. This suggestion is strengthened further by the existence of the music box that Marianne gives to David in Paris, which sits in the director's study and provides the film's musical motif. In other words, the intertextuality of *Faithless* extends to material objects, characters and diegetic motifs, and puts paid to attempts at segregating the private and the public, the domestic and the political, the filmic and the pro-filmic, the fictional and the real, one textual system from another. Most importantly, *Faithless* interrogates the illusion of a privileged auteurial perspective that is not textured by the fabric of sexual politics.

Despite a clear disintegration of the marriage, the sequence from *Scenes from a Marriage* presents a somewhat naïve perspective on the situation, wherein Johan appears not able to stop himself going off with a much younger woman to Paris. The naïveté occurs where Johan comes home to confess about the affair, pack his bags, make practical arrangements for the family, and leaves. The cynicism that characterises *Faithless* evades such a version of male melodrama as *Scenes from a Marriage* maintains. Firstly, the pre-meditated affair Marianne and David embark upon gives no notice to the betrayed spouse and makes no practical provision for Isabelle. Instead, they are caught out in bed together and cause the child to become a victim of marital strife. Secondly, *Faithless* insists that extra-marital affairs arise out of a much darker sentiment than mere personal dissatisfaction. The sequence of *Faithless* where David is at his cruellest refers back to two particular sequences from *Scenes from a Marriage* to comment on the latter film's apparent disingenuous representation of a marriage breakdown. David attributes his rage at Marianne to a sense of 'retrospective jealousy', a term Johan uses to describe what he feels about Paula, when he divulges the affair to his wife in *Scenes from a Marriage*. These two sequences pivot on the use of intimate information about a partner's sex life with the third party against them: in the case of *Faithless*, David uses information he connives out of Marianne about her sex life within her marriage. In *Scenes from a Marriage*, Johan tells his wife about Paula's sexual history and the intimacy that they share. While *Scenes from a Marriage* maintains the façade of general goodwill despite what would be a soul destroying situation for Marianne to have her husband express a desire to leave and tell all about his feelings towards his mistress, *Faithless* holds no such illusion by presenting the brutality that mistrust elicits. Instead of being an expression of love, sex is presented in *Faithless* as a bargaining chip as well as ammunition against those one desires to hurt, bringing into comparison the politically unexamined depiction of sexual relations in *Scenes from a Marriage*.

The custodial battle in which Markus and Marianne engage culminates in Markus' demand for sex in return for custody, a demand that leads to the jealous tirade to which David subjects Marianne when she returns home. That

Markus' *quid pro quo* demand for sex underlines a desire to demean, and exert power over, Marianne is clear. Comparing the obvious motivations behind Markus' demand and those disguised in the scene where Johan and Marianne have sex on the office floor before signing their divorce papers in *Scenes from a Marriage* is one more example of how *Faithless* uncovers the power dynamics that *Scenes from a Marriage* hides. Although Johan refuses to sign the papers and hits Marianne, this episode is separate from the unequivocal depiction of affection between the estranged couple. The seduction they engage in before the flare-up retains an aura of innocence that is untainted by the gender politics that govern their marriage.

The different codes of decency governing the representation of explicit sex scenes notwithstanding, given the thirty years that separate the two films, the ways in which *Scenes from a Marriage* and *Faithless* depict sexual relations speak to the implications of the films' respective understanding of sexual politics. The two sex scenes between the couple in *Scenes from a Marriage*, where Johan comes home for the first time after leaving home and when they meet up in Johan's office to sign divorce papers, are remarkable for the extreme close-ups in which they are shot. The close-ups of the couple's faces as they lie on the floor displace the sexual activity and present sex as the physical equivalent of love and emotional intimacy, to somewhat deceptively melodramatic ends. On the other hand, *Faithless* holds no such illusion and acknowledges in full the use of sex as ammunition or for bartering purposes. Sex is not presented as the physical expression of love and does not exist outside the reaches of sexual politics and power relations, but is instead pivotal for the enactment of these networks of relations: had David and Marianne not consummated the affair, the tragedy would not have unravelled. The two pivotal sex scenes in *Faithless*, between Marianne and David in the Parisian hotel and in David's flat where they are caught by Markus, are in large part long establishing shots that remove the onus from the faciality that the close-ups in *Scenes from a Marriage* exploits. The inappropriate twin beds in the hotel room and the clothes scattered around David's bedroom floor serve as commentaries to the relationship between David and Marianne and gesture to the wider world implicated by their actions.

Towards the end of *Faithless*, the old director conjures up David, who speaks with regret about his faithlessness and dismal behaviour that leads Marianne to drown herself. David's occupation as a film director is clearly spelled out, which invites speculation as to whether the old man in the film is conjuring up these characters or re-living the memories of his youth by summoning up his younger self and the woman he had betrayed. This deliberate ambiguity about the narrator's subjectivity invites speculations about *Faithless'* authorship, given the film's unambiguous autobiographical reference to Ingmar Bergman, its setting up of the character of the old director as Bergman, Ullmann's direction of Bergman's script, as well as the extra-filmic discourse about the relationship (both working and personal) between Ullmann and Bergman. In other words, while *Scenes from a Marriage* does not problematise the authorial voice in its unquestioning acceptance of Bergman's camera and perspective, *Faithless* presents at least two competing authorial voices: that of Marianne and the old director's. The difficulty of following *Faithless*' narrative resides in its unusually complex temporality and resistance to linearity. That Marianne's reminiscences, the accompanying flashbacks, and scenes in the house are woven together renders *Faithless*' narrative somewhat confusing, and warrants a retrospective spectatorship that does not so much identify with the action, but work to make sense of the multi-layered narrative and intertextual references. *Faithless*' fragmentation of the stable auteurial voice of *Scenes from a Marriage* is also evident in the initial contact between Marianne and the old director. Marianne's voiceover, which precedes her physical presence, is heard as an echo that the old director strains to hear, almost at the back of his head. That he has to describe, define, and name her in order for Marianne to physically materialise is an acknowledgement of Bergman's authorship, although what he has conjured up will exceed his mastery and control, to the extent that these shadowy figures from the past, or his imagination, as may be, will invade his physical space. This fragmentation of the Bergman character's stable point of view will result in his impotent, and voiceless, cry of anguish after David's visitation, embodying the extent of the emotional destruction that results in Marianne's drowning. In this way, *Faithless* dislodges the romantic notion of a masterful male auteurial voice and opens up a discussion on the significance of a director's gendered subjectivity.

References

Bergman, Ingmar (1973): *Scener ur ett äktenskap*. Stockholm: Norstedts.
Bergman, Ingmar (1974): *Scenes From A Marriage*. Translated from the Swedish by Alan Blair. New York: Bantam Books.
Biskind, Peter (1998): *Easy Riders, Raging Bulls*. New York: Simon & Schuster.
Deleuze, Gilles and Félix Guattari (1988): *A Thousand Plateaus: Capitalism and Schizophrenia*. London: The Athlone Press.
Doane, Mary Ann (2002): *The Emergence of Cinematic Time: Modernity, Contingency, The Archive*. Cambridge & London: Harvard University Press.
Harvey, Sylvia (1980): *May '68 and Film Culture*. London: British Film Institute.
Johnston, Claire (1976): 'Women's Cinema as Counter-cinema'. In Nichols, Bill (ed.): *Movies and Methods. An Anthology*. Berkeley & Los Angeles: University of California Press.

Kalin, Jesse (2003): *The Films of Ingmar Bergman*. Cambridge: Cambridge University Press.

Kolker, Robert (2000): *A Cinema of Loneliness*, 3rd edition. Oxford & New York: Oxford University Press.

Kuhn, Annette (1986): 'Hollywood and New Women's Cinema'. In Brunsdon, Charlotte (ed.): *Films for Women*. London: British Film Institute.

de Lauretis, Teresa (1987): *Technologies of Gender: Theories of Representation and Difference*. Bloomington & Indianapolis: Indiana University Press.

Macnab, Geoffrey (2000): 'Crimes and Misdemeanours'. *Sight and Sound* 10.2.

Macnab, Geoffrey (2005): 'Back from the Cold'. *The Guardian*, 23 September.

Mellencamp, Patricia (1990): *Indiscretions: Avant-garde Film, Video, and Feminism*. Bloomington & Indiana: Indiana University Press.

Persson, Inga (1990): 'The Third Dimension: Equal Status between Swedish Men and Women'. In Persson, Inga (ed.): *Generating Equality in the Welfare State: The Swedish Experience*. Oslo: Norwegian University Press.

Porton, Richard (2004): 'Actress Behind the Camera: An Interview with Liv Ullmann'. *Cineaste*, Fall.

Quart, Leonard (2004): 'Ingmar Bergman: The Maestro of Angst'. *Cineaste*, Fall.

Rich, Ruby B. (1998): *Chickflicks: Theories and Memories of the Feminist Film Movement*. Durham & London: Duke University Press.

Notes

1. See, for instance, Harvey (1980).
2. *Scenes from a Marriage* exists in a longer televisual form, over six episodes, lasting 295 minutes. The film version, just under three hours, is that to which this essay refers.
3. See, among others, Johnston (1976), Mellencamp (1990), and Rich (1998) for discursive accounts of the feminist film movement and scholarship.
4. The Swedish and English text given here are taken from the published screenplay and its English edition (Bergman 1973 and 1974).
5. Of course, these layers of intertextual references are further complicated by the televisual 'sequel' to *Scenes from a Marriage*, *Saraband* (Ingmar Bergman, 2003), released in the UK as this volume goes to press. *Saraband* is the latest instalment of what could now be termed the *Scenes from a Marriage* trilogy and supposedly the last film that Bergman will make. One rather suspects *Saraband* is Bergman's attempt to have the last word by having Liv Ullmann and Erland Josephson re-play their respective characters in *Scenes from a Marriage*, three decades on. In *Saraband*, Johan retires to a remote location, *à la* Bergman on his island. Marianne visits and gets embroiled in the intricacies of Johan's relationship with his beloved granddaughter and estranged son, all of whom are bereaved by the death of Johan's daughter-in-law. In a newspaper interview, Ullmann contributes to this essay's pursuit of intertextual references by making mention of autobiographical details such as Bergman's unresolved differences with a son who has died and that the film has much to do with his late wife, to whose memory it is dedicated. See Macnab (2005).
6. Despite having the narrative told from Marianne's perspective, Bergman's auteurial voice is firmly entrenched in *Saraband*. Arguably, Bergman's insistence on having the 'last word' in the triology disavows *Faithless*' subversion of *Scenes from a Marriage*'s auteurial voice, if these three films are seen as constituting a cinematic trilogy.

Notes on Contributors

Emma Bell is a doctoral candidate at the University of East Anglia, Norwich, where she also teaches philosophy and film studies. Her doctoral thesis examines the representation of mental illness in avant-gardist art. She has published her work in journals and newspapers. Emma's research interests include visual representations of mental illness and disability, the avant-garde, 'Outsider art' and intellectual history. She is currently planning a monograph on schizophrenia and critical theory, and is researching the Danish artist Wilhelm Hammershøi.

Amanda Doxtater completed her Masters degree in Scandinavian Studies, with a focus on Swedish Literature, at the University of Washington. Her contribution to this project reflects research she conducted while on a Fulbright Grant in Sweden. Working in conjunction with Filmvetenskapliga Instutionen at the University of Stockholm, she researched representations of ethnicity and transnationalism in recent Swedish film. She is currently in the second year of her Ph.D. programme in Scandinavian Studies at the University of California at Berkeley. Her current research interests include Plato's notion of Phasmata, Film Theory, Transnational Cinema, early Danish cinema, Carl Dreyer, Swedish Modernist prose, and Seduction Theory.

Mette Hjort is Professor of Visual Studies at Lingnan University in Hong Kong, Professor of Intercultural Studies at Aalborg University in Denmark, and Honorary Associate Professor of Comparative Literature at the University of Hong Kong. She was previously Director of Cultural Studies at McGill University in Canada, and has also taught at the Copenhagen Business School. She has published *The Strategy of Letters* (Harvard University Press, 1993) and *Small Nation, Global Cinema* (University of Minnesota Press, 2005). A third monograph entitled *On Centre Stage* is forthcoming with the Hong Kong University Press. She is the editor or co-editor of *Rules and Conventions* (Johns Hopkins University Press, 1992), *Emotion and the Arts* (Oxford University Press, 1997), *Cinema and Nation* (Routledge, 2000), *Purity and Provocation: Dogma 95* (BFI Publications, 2003), and *The Postnational Self* (University of Minnesota Press, 2002). She has published an interview book with filmmakers entitled *The Danish Directors: Dialogues on a Contemporary National Cinema* (Intellect Press, 2001) and has translated two books by Louis Marin, *Food for Thought* (Johns Hopkins University Press) and *To Destroy Painting* (University of Chicago Press). She is currently co-ordinating a research project on small national cinemas together with Duncan Petrie. She is also one of the Series Editors for a new Nordic Film Classics Series.

Gunnar Iversen is Professor of Film Studies at the Department of Art and Media Studies at the Norwegian University of Science and Technology, Trondheim, Norway, where he teaches European, North American and Asian film history. He has co-authored and co-edited several books, including *Kinoens Mørke Fjernsynets Lys – Levende Bilder i Norge gjennom hundre år* (1996), *Nærbilder – Artikler om norsk filmhistorie* (1997), *'Bedre enn sitt rykte' – En liten norsk filmhistorie* (1997), *Nordic National Cinemas* (1998), *Virkelighetsbilder – norsk dokumentarfilm gjennom hundre år* (2001), *Blikkfang – fjernsyn, form og estetikk* (2003), and *Estetiske Teknologier 1700-2000* (2003).

Britta Timm Knudsen is Associate Professor of Culture and Media in the Scandinavian Institute, University of Aarhus, Denmark. She is author of a range of articles on film, television and popular culture, including most recently in English 'The Eyewitness and the Affected Viewer. September 11 in the Media' (*Nordicom Review* 2, 2003), and 'It's live. Performativity and role-playing' (in *Performative Realism*, ed. Anne Jerslev & Rune Gade. Museum Tusculanum Press, 2005). She is also co-editor of *Virkelighedshunger I: Nyrealisme i visuel optik* (Tiderne skifter, 2002) and of *Metafiktion – selvrefleksionens retorik* (Medusa, 2001).

Anu Koivunen is Assistant Professor in the Department of Cinema Studies at Stockholm University. She is also associated as a Docent with the universities of Helsinki and Tampere. She is the author of *Performative Histories, Foundational Framings. Gender and Sexuality in Niskavuori Films (1938-1984)* (Finnish Historical Society, 2003), of *Isänmaan moninaiset äidinkasvot*, a monograph on wartime Finnish women's cinema (1995), and of numerous essays on Finnish cinema from the 1920s to the 1980s. She is currently completing a monograph on Finnish television theatre and launching a new research project on discourses of affect in contemporary Nordic and European cinema and TV.

Ellen Rees is Assistant Professor of Scandinavian Studies at the University of Oregon. She received her Ph.D. from the University of Washington in 1995 and is the author of *On the Margins: Nordic Women Modernists of the 1930s* (Norvik Press, 2005) as well as a number of articles on twentieth-century Scandinavian prose fiction and contemporary Scandinavian cinema.

Mark Sandberg is Associate Professor of Scandinavian Studies and Film Studies at the University of California at Berkeley. His research and teaching engages with late-nineteenth-century visual culture and silent film as a medium. He has specific film specialities in Scandinavian cinema history, in certain Scandinavian directors (Sjöström, Stiller, Dreyer, Bergman, von Trier), and in the contributions of Scandinavian visual culture (museology) to the paracinematic visual culture around the birth of cinema. He regularly teaches courses on film historiography, on pre-cinema, silent film comedy, Scandinavian film, and other topics in early and silent cinema. Current film-related research includes a project on metaphors of housing in the silent films of Carl Th. Dreyer. He is author of *Living Pictures, Missing Persons: Mannequins, Museums and Modernity* (Princeton University Press, 2003).

Sharon Lin Tay is a Lecturer in Film Studies at Middlesex University, London. She has written on feminist film theory, Deleuze, world cinema, and women filmmakers. Amongst other things, she is currently researching the development of film theory in conjunction with innovations in digital technologies and the emergence of new media.

Bodil Marie Thomsen holds a Ph.D. from Aarhus University (1994), and is Associate Professor of Culture and Media in the Scandinavian Institute at Aarhus University, where she teaches Film Studies (especially Dogme 95, Lars von Trier, Jean-Luc Godard, Gilles Deleuze), visual theory, media archeology, digital media, and the interface. She was head of the research project Reality, Realism, the Real in Visual Art and Media (www.hum.au.dk/nordisk/realisme/; 1999-2002). She was Visiting Fulbright Professor of Scandinavian Studies at the University of Washington in spring 2005. Bodil Marie's current major project concerns interface culture (www.interfacekultur.au.dk; 2004-2007). She is a board member of the Danish Film Institute's museum. She has published widely in Danish and English on film, media and philosophy, and her books include *Filmdivaer. Stjernens figur i Hollywoods melodrama 1920-40* (1987).

Bjarne Thorup Thomsen is Senior Lecturer in Scandinavian Studies in the School of Literatures, Languages and Cultures at the University of Edinburgh. His research interests include nineteenth- and twentieth-century Scandinavian literature, especially Selma Lagerlöf, H.C. Andersen, C.J.L. Almqvist and Knut Hamsun, literary nation-building, as well as film studies. He is author of the forthcoming *Lagerlöfs litterære landvinding: Nils Holgersson og nationen*, and editor of *Centring on the Peripheries: Essays on Scandinavian, Scottish, Gaelic and Greenlandic Literature* (Norvik Press, 2006).

C. Claire Thomson is UCL Mellon Research Fellow at University College London (2004-2006), attached to the programme Identities and Culture in Europe Since 1945; her particular focus on the role of the visual arts and literary genres in shaping and representing nationhood and sovereignty. She was previously Lecturer in Scandinavian Studies at the University of East Anglia, Norwich, where her teaching included Nordic cultural history and literature, European cinema, translation theory and Danish language. Claire holds a Ph.D. from the University of Edinburgh (2003), and has published a range of articles on Danish and Scottish literature, primarily on the literary negotiation of space, history and nationness, as well as on translation theory and the 'posthuman' imagination. She is working on a monograph entitled *Footprints in the Snow: History, the Body and Ecology in the Fiction of Peter Høeg*.

Index

Explanatory note: Films are listed under their Scandinavian and international (English) titles, except where this results in contiguous entries; in such cases, the films are listed under their English title. The director of each film and year of premiere is provided in brackets; key directors have their own entries.

The Scandinavian letters æ/ä, ø/ö, and å are alphabetised after z, according to Scandinavian convention.

BJARNE THORUP THOMSEN (ED.)

Centring on the Peripheries
Studies in Scandinavian, Scottish, Gaelic and Greenlandic Literature

Are the peripheries the new centre? How do the 'debatable lands' of Scandinavia and Scotland write their relations with their national centres, and with each other? Is the story of the margins just a figment of the metropole's imagination? How have postcolonialism and postnationalism made themselves felt in the literature of the cultural patchwork of Northern Europe? In these sixteen essays, Scandinavian and Scottish scholars trace ways to tell the stories of connections, boundaries and localities that might go undetected by historians and artists in the metropolitan centres. The literatures of the islands, borderlands and landscapes of the North and Baltic Seas are set in dialogue with contemporary literary and socio-political approaches to the study of local, national and global cultural constellations, disrupting conventional cartographies that paint the margins as passive victims of geography or economics. The essays demonstrate that relations between 'core' and 'periphery' are in constant flux, and that narratives of community, identity and history on the peripheries often do not aspire to the forms and kudos of core and canon. Centring on the Peripheries opens up unexpected perspectives on cultural roots and on the routes between cultures, revealing surprising literary alliances and historical parallels. It will appeal to scholars of cultural identity, postcolonialism and European literature, and to readers who delight in exploring the borderlands of the literary canon.

Bjarne Thorup Thomsen is Senior Lecturer in Scandinavian Studies in the School of Literatures, Languages and Cultures at the University of Edinburgh.

ISBN 1 870041 66 6

UK £16.95
(2006, paperback)

ELLEN REES

On the Margins
Nordic Women Modernists of the 1930s

This study examines the work of six women prose writers of the 1930s, placing them for the first time within the broader context of European and American literary modernism. These writers – Stina Aronson, Karen Blixen, Karo Espeseth, Hagar Olsson, Cora Sandel and Edith Øberg – have been doubly marginalized. Their work has long been viewed as anomalous within the Scandinavian literary canon, but, apart from Karen Blixen, it also remains marginalized from examinations of women writers produced outside Scandinavia. This is a 'connective study' which examines the literary strategies, preoccupations, and responses to changes in society shared across national boundaries by these writers. They all sought inspiration from foreign literature and culture, and made themselves literal or figurative exiles from their homelands.

Ellen Rees is Assistant Professor of Scandinavian Studies at the University of Oregon. She has published widely on Scandinavian prose fiction and cinema, and is currently researching a monograph on Cora Sandel.

ISBN 1 870041 59 3

UK £14.95
(2005, paperback)

FREDDIE ROKEM

Strindberg's Secret Codes

Strindberg's works are enigmatic, taking the form of riddles that constantly ask readers, directors, actors and spectators to find new and creative solutions. Focusing on the plays, these original and searching essays seek to uncover the hidden secrets of Strindberg's codes as a writer. They include studies of many of his most celebrated works, including *Miss Julie*, *The Father*, *The Dance of Death*, *Creditors*, and the chamber plays, which are subjected both to close textual readings and analysed in performance. Freddie Rokem explores their unconscious processes and compares Strindberg's complex but endlessly fascinating project with the work of Ibsen and Freud in what is one of the most challenging books on his theatre in recent years.

Freddie Rokem is Professor of Theatre Studies at Tel Aviv University. He has published widely on contemporary Scandinavian drama, including *Theatrical Space in Ibsen, Chekhov, and Strindberg* (1986). His book *Performing History: Theatrical Representations of the Past in Contemporary Theatre* received the Athens Prize in 2001.

ISBN 1 870041 55 0

UK £14.95
(2004, paperback)

For further information, or to request a catalogue, please contact:
Norvik Press, University of East Anglia (LLT), Norwich NR4 7TJ, England
or visit our website at www.norvikpress.com